ISLAMIC HUMANITIES

Shahzad Bashir, Series Editor

Publication of this Luminos Open Access Series is made possible by the Islam and the Humanities Project of the Program in Middle East Studies at Brown University.

1. *Forging the Ideal Educated Girl: The Production of Desirable Subjects in Muslim South Asia*, by Shenila Khoja-Moolji
2. *Witness to Marvels: Sufism and Literary Imagination*, by Tony K. Stewart
3. *God's Property: Islam, Charity, and the Modern State*, by Nada Moumtaz
4. *Placing Islam: Geographies of Connection in Twentieth-Century Istanbul*, by Timur Hammond
5. *Pious Labor: Islan, Artisanship, and Technology in Colonial India*, by Amanda Lanzillo

Pious Labor

Pious Labor

Islam, Artisanship, and Technology in Colonial India

Amanda Lanzillo

UNIVERSITY OF CALIFORNIA PRESS

University of California Press
Oakland, California

Suggested citation: Lanzillo, A. *Pious Labor: Islam, Artisanship, and Technology in Colonial India.* Oakland: University of California Press, 2023. DOI: https://doi.org/10.1525/luminos.173

Cataloging-in-Publication Data is on file at the Library of Congress.

ISBN 978–0-520–39857-3 (pbk.)
ISBN 978–0-520–39858-0 (ebook)

32 31 30 29 28 27 26 25 24 23
10 9 8 7 6 5 4 3 2 1

CONTENTS

ACKNOWLEDGMENTS

The process of research and writing this book was collaborative, shaped by conversations over tea and coffee and meandering walks with dear friends. I am especially grateful to the archivists and librarians who preserved and made accessible the histories and treatises at the core of this book, and to artisans and manufacturers who allowed me to visit their workshops.

The research for this book was made possible by a Fulbright-Hays Doctoral Dissertation Research Abroad Fellowship, an American Institute of Indian Studies Junior Fellowship, an American Historical Association Bernadotte E. Schmitt Grant, and a Library of Congress Florence Tan Moeson Fellowship, as well as by Indiana University's Department of History, Dhar India Studies Program, and the Office of the Vice President of International Affairs. Follow-up research was funded by the Princeton University Committee on Research in the Humanities and Social Sciences. Completion of the manuscript was supported by an Association of Asian Studies Publication Support Grant.

Research for the book began as part of my doctoral dissertation at Indiana University. My adviser, Michael Dodson, has remained a dedicated mentor, guiding this work for many years. I was fortunate to have on my committee Paul Losensky, whose literary eye helped me to become a better historian; Ron Sela, whose advice shaped how I pursued my archival research; and Kaya Şahin, who pushed me to think comparatively and read widely.

My research depended on the kindness of friends and colleagues across South Asia. Namratha Rao, Koval Bhatia, and Ginger welcomed me to Delhi and made the city home. Safa Mohsin Khan and the entire Mohsin Khan family provided extensive support and welcomed me on a family visit to Meerut; they also introduced me to Taab Anwer, who provided support in Aligarh. Seema Alavi enabled and encouraged my research. On return visits to Delhi, I was warmly hosted by Ayesha Jhunjhunwala and family. Rana Safvi graciously shared her knowledge of the city. I am also grateful to Sikandar Chingezi.

In Lucknow, Ahtesham Khan and the American Institute of India Studies Urdu program faculty provided extensive support. Anu, Sanjay, Kriti, and Stuti Behari became a second family in Lucknow. I appreciate the help of Shama Mahood at Lucknow University. I thank Apoorva Dixit and family for hosting me in Bhopal.

I appreciate the help of librarians across India, especially at the Raza Library and Saulat Libraries in Rampur, the Aiwan-e Urdu and Salar Jung in Hyderabad, the National Archives, Jamia Millia Islamia and Jamiat Ulama-i Hindi in Delhi, the Allahabad Public Library, the Uttar Pradesh State Archives in Lucknow and Allahabad, the Khuda Bakhsh Library in Patna, the Awami Idara in Bombay, the Maulana Abul Kalam Azad Library in Tonk, and the Maulana Azad and Iqbal Libraries in Bhopal.

In Lahore, I benefited from assistance and advice from Salima Hashmi, Kamran Asdar Ali, Zahid Usman, Nadhra Shahbaz Khan, Tahir Kamran, Doa Sarmad Khan, Kanwal Khalid, Syed Adeel Ijaz and Muhammad Zaid, as well as librarians at the Punjab Public Library, Punjab Archives, and National College of Arts.

My dear friends Mallika Leuzinger and Simon Pickstone hosted me during follow-up research in London, and Mallika also provided significant feedback on this book. My relatives, Ann, John, Emma, and Katie Buckley, provided a warm welcome in London. In D.C., at the Library of Congress, I received assistance from Jonathan Loar and Hirad Dinavari.

I wrote this book during my time with the Princeton University Society of Fellows, where I was encouraged to experiment with new ideas and learn from other disciplines. Michael Gordin, Beate Witzler, and Rhea Dexter made the Society a warm intellectual home. Michael Laffan, Gyan Prakash, Divya Cherian, Daniel Sheffield, and my frequent coconspirator Harini Kumar shaped my growth as a scholar. I benefited from conversations with Muhammad Qasim Zaman and Ben Baer and support from Sam Evans. My fellow Cotsen fellows continue to inspire and challenge me, and I am especially grateful to Célia Abele, Aniruddhan Vasudevan, Maya Kronfeld, Melissa Reynolds, Joshua Freeman, and Nicolás Sánchez-Rodríguez. I appreciate the friendship and skilled librarianship of Deborah Schlein and Ellen Ambrosone.

The book was improved thanks to the close reading and advice of Prasannan Parthasarathi, Megan Robb, SherAli Tareen, Julia Stephens, Michael Laffan, and Gyan Prakash at my 2022 book workshop, supported by the Princeton Society of Fellows. The trajectory of the book was shaped by advice from Projit Mukherji, Anand Yang, J. Barton Scott, and Andrew Amstutz at the 2020 American Institute of Indian Studies dissertation-to-book workshop. I also received helpful advice from Aleksandra Kobiljski, Aparajith Ramnath, Eugenia Lean, and Joseph Alter at the Association for Asian Studies Technology in Asia Workshop in 2022.

Some of the many other scholars and friends who provided support and feedback include Arun Kumar, Adhitya Dhanapal, Karen Leonard, Naveena Naqvi, Thomas Chambers, Mircea Raianu, Nur Sobers Khan, Hasan Hameed, Maya Wahrman, Charlotte Giles, Aparna Kumar, Majed Akhter, Kenny Linden, Jessica Chandras, Rebecca Manring, Peter Guardino, Razak Khan, Yunus Lasania, Shweta Krishnan, Thomas Newbold, Asif Siddiqi, Pranav Prakash, Amita Vemptai, Nicky Bell, Maria-Magdalena Pruß, Aqsa Ijaz, Daniel Morgan, Gianni Sievers, Ali Altaf Mian, Michael Krautkramer, Isabel Alvarez-Echandi, Nicolás Silitti, and Denisa Jashari.

Many individuals have helped me with translations from Urdu and Persian. I am especially grateful for suggestions and help from Ahtesham Khan, Mohammad Asad, Tabrez Ahmad, Safwan Ahmad, Ashutosh Srivastava, Mohsin Khan, and Paul Losensky. Vinit Vyas and Kajaal Joshi provided translations from Gujarati and Hindi respectively. Haidar Ali of Rekhta, Syed Muneeb Iqbal, and Nabila Khadija Ansari provided me with several images. I thank Farima Mostowfi for sparking my love of languages.

I have recently found a new intellectual home with the Brunel University Division of Politics and History, as well as interdisciplinary community in the Brunel South Asia Studies research group. I am grateful to my colleagues at Brunel for their warm welcome, and I look forward to growing new relationships here in London.

I thank the British Library, the Raza Library and Rekhta Digital Library for permission to use images in their collections. My writing has benefited from the skilled editing of Amber Riaz.

Working with the University of California Press has been a delight. I thank Shahzad Bashir, as editor of the Islamic Humanities series, for his enthusiasm and for advice that shaped the trajectory of this project. Eric Schmidt guided this work and helpfully demystified the publishing process. LeKeisha Hughes has provided great assistance in preparing the book for publication. I am grateful to Elisabeth Magnus for her work as copy editor. I am indebted to the anonymous reviewers for their careful reading and helpful suggestions. I feel fortunate that funding from the Islamic Humanities series has enabled the open access publication of this book. I appreciate the indexing work of Alexander Trotter.

This book exists thanks to the boundless patience of my family. My parents, Jo-Ann and Richard Lanzillo, have been constant sources of love and support, embracing my long periods of travel in South Asia. My sister, Eliza Lanzillo, and her partner, Patrick Kellett, kept me in good spirits over many years of researching and writing. My in-laws, Kathy Charlotten, Alberto Ramos, and Benjie Ramos Charlotten, lovingly welcomed me into their family and home. My dog, Fara, took me for long walks. My husband, Alberto Ramos Charlotten, has embraced many roles, as cheerleader, critic, editor, travel agent, and my primary source of emotional support. This book would not exist without him.

NOTE ON TRANSLITERATION

In transliterating Urdu, Persian, and Arabic words, I have followed the American Language Association–Library of Congress (ALA-LC) romanization standards, with adjustments for readability. A few of the Urdu works that I study here had English titles, transliterated into Perso-Arabic script. In these cases, I noted the Urdu spelling and kept it in all notes but used the common English spelling in the main text (*Indian Architect* in the text, *Inḍiyan arkitīkt* in notes). For terms that are frequently used in English, I used the common American English spelling, typically that reflected in Merriam-Webster.

I have written the names of the artisans and authors that I profile in this book without diacritical markers in the text. The names of authors who wrote in Urdu or Persian are given in ALA-LC romanization in the notes, adapted to reflect the pronunciation of names (Karīmullah, rather than Karīm Allāh).

In most cases, I have indicated the plural of Urdu, Persian, and Arabic words by adding an s to the singular, for instance *kārīgar*s. A notable exception is *ashrāf* (sing: *sharīf*). Translations are my own, unless otherwise noted.

Introduction

> The pure Lord gave such power to the blacksmith
> To turn to wax what was iron by nature.
>
> . . . .
>
> You have raised the status of the jeweled blade;
> Now all acknowledge the mettle of your sword.
>
> . . . .
>
> All workshops depend on your wisdom;
> The capitalist keeps his head bowed before you.[1]

These verses, extracted from a longer Urdu *naẓm* or poem, were written by Nazir, a blacksmith and bladesmith based in the North Indian city of Rampur in the mid-twentieth century. I first encountered Nazir and his poetry as part of a collection that the librarians of the renowned Raza Library in Rampur had put together to honor the city's artisanal and material heritage.[2] Nazir's versified account of his trade immediately grabbed my attention, because it evoked several traditions that, in researching this book, I had come to associate closely with earlier generations of Muslim artisans who worked in the late nineteenth and early twentieth centuries.

Nazir emphasized God's revelation of knowledge and skill to blacksmiths, even as he also placed these smiths in a context of industrial labor, in a workshop subject to the whims of a capitalist or *sarmāyahdār*, the possessor of wealth. Through his insistence on the smith's inherent relationship with the divine, and the imagery of the humbled capitalist forced to bow his head to the smith's God-given prowess, Nazir asserted social status for blacksmiths. Nazir evoked a widespread belief that God had revealed knowledge of blacksmithing to the Prophet Dawud (David) by turning iron to wax in his hands, arguing that the practice of blacksmithing was a pious practice of Islam. In a context where ownership or authority was often ceded to members of the middle class and where artisans had limited control over their materials, styles, and technologies of production, Nazir offered an alternative vision of his trade: he claimed an Islamic, God-given status for blacksmiths, highlighting not only the economic importance and social dignity of artisan communities but the distinct forms of Muslim piety embedded in their trades.

When Nazir asserted a Muslim past and future for his trade, he drew on ideas about the relationship between Islam and artisanship that had been rearticulated, reimagined, and circulated among artisan communities across North India over the course of the previous century. In the late nineteenth and early twentieth centuries, many Indian artisans transitioned to new, often industrialized, wage-based sites of work, especially in rapidly expanding cities associated with colonial authority and industry.[3] They also engaged with rapid changes in the materiality and technology of their labor, ranging from new plasters to steam engines, and from lithographic presses to electroplating. Muslim artisans asserted religious traditions for their work to make sense of these changes and claim new knowledge. In doing so, they challenged their marginalization within strengthening North Indian social hierarchies, with many contributing to the consolidation of regional working-class identities through an Islamic idiom.

Pious Labor provides a history of Muslim laboring cultures in North India, tracing the nineteenth- and early twentieth-century experiences and ideas that contributed to Nazir's portrayal of blacksmithing. It tells the stories of urban metalsmiths, stonemasons, tailors, boilermakers, carpenters, and press workers across the North-Western Provinces and Oudh (known as the United Provinces of Agra and Oudh after 1902) and Punjab in the late nineteenth and early twentieth centuries.[4] *Pious Labor* traces histories of Muslim culture making from below through creative readings of an overlooked archive of Urdu artisan technical manuals and community histories and with a specific focus on the intersections of embodied and textual knowledge.

Muslim artisans engaged with religious pasts to make sense of changes wrought by the transition to a colonial economy. Their claims on the piety of their work reflected an effort to reassert authority over technology and material knowledge in a moment when technical authority was increasingly vested in the colonial state and the middle class. From the expansion of European political influence in India in the eighteenth century, colonial administrators had sought to discipline Indian labor to address European economic interests.[5] As a result, over the course of the subsequent decades, Indian artisans were deprived of many historical forms of technical authority and autonomy.[6] But by engaging with new sites of knowledge circulation that expanded from the mid-nineteenth century—especially vernacular print and urban industrial workshops—Muslim artisans sought to challenge their economic, technical, and religious marginalization within Indian class and social hierarchies.

Pious Labor shows that from the mid-nineteenth century, Muslim workers drew on narratives of Muslim pasts and claims to distinctively Muslim identities to imagine new roles for their skills and their trades. In doing so, they reasserted and reimagined traditions and practices that I term *artisan Islam*. I use *artisan Islam* to refer to a broad range of narratives about laboring Islamic pasts, claims on the piety of work or technology, and the development and intersection of Muslim social, religious, and laboring spaces among artisans. In *Pious Labor*, I argue that through artisan Islam, Muslim workers both challenged and negotiated colonial capitalism and the consolidating social hierarchies in North India. Through claims on the piety of their work, Muslim artisans integrated their material and embodied knowledge with religious narratives, asserting social status and technological authority in a colonial economy that often robbed them of both.

DEFINING ARTISANS AND ARTISANSHIP

"Artisan" is a category so broad that its utility can sometimes be questionable. For E. P. Thompson, *artisan* could refer to anyone "from the prosperous master craftsman, employing labor on his own account and independent of any masters, to the sweated garret laborers."[7] Moreover, Indian artisans often did not—and do not—identify with this term. Instead, as Nita Kumar demonstrates, many preferred identities that were expressly associated with their specific trades.[8] The chapters of this book are thus organized by trades and practices in recognition of the fact that individual trades often held greater salience for artisans than the category of artisanship itself.

At the same time, I have chosen to use the term *artisan* because it intersects with categories that the authors of Urdu-language trade manuals and community histories used to describe their communities. The most important of these was *kārīgar*, which I translate both as "artisan" and "laborer," reflecting the fact that in nineteenth- and early twentieth-century Urdu (as well as Hindi and Punjabi) the word was used to reference both the skills associated with craftworkers and the status of a wage earner. The authors of artisan manuals and community histories often relied on the category of *kārīgar* to emphasize their own shared interests with people who read their texts (or heard them read aloud). *Kārīgar* was an especially important identifier for communities in which many artisans were shifting between trades, such as bladesmiths who turned to surgical tool manufacturing, or woodcarvers who turned to furniture making. While "artisan" was often a category applied from above—by the colonial state, middle-class overseers, or Indian patrons—its rough equivalent, *kārīgar*, held widespread relevance in the worlds of Indian labor.

Another factor complicating our definition of *artisan* is that colonial industrial policy in India often enforced distinctions between "artisanal" and "industrial" labor that did not reflect these workers' own understandings of their trades and communities. *Pious Labor* argues that as many artisans transitioned to new fields of industrial work—such as boilermaking, railway carpentry, or print labor—they adapted both their technical skills and their community narratives of the Muslim past. Despite the distinct challenges inherent in colonial industrial capitalism, many artisans moved flexibly between familial workshops and capitalist- or state-run factories, transferring and applying their technical and religious knowledge from one to the other.

Consequently, I have maintained a capacious definition of *artisan*, one that upends colonial depictions of industrial laborers as divorced from artisanship. Simultaneously, my approach to the category of "artisan" seeks to challenge colonial portrayals of "cottage artisans" as uninterested in technological and material change. The category of *kārīgar* may ultimately suggest paths beyond the artisan-industrial worker divide, providing space to consider the flexibility and multiplicity of individual experiences of industrial and artisanal labor.

WHY MUSLIM ARTISANS?

The histories of South Asian labor and artisanship have often assumed Hindu social, religious, and caste identities as a norm among workers, positioning Muslim workers as complications or sources of potential religious conflict. This is due, in part, to what Chitra Joshi characterizes as the dominance of studies of "fragmentation and conflict" among Indian workers.[9] For instance, Dipesh Chakrabarty's study of jute-mill workers in late nineteenth- and early twentieth-century Calcutta remains among the most prominent theorizations of community and religious identities among Indian laborers. Chakrabarty critiques portrayals of religious community and identity that "situate this working class in a web of immutable, unchanging loyalties," arguing, instead, that "the meaning of these [religious] 'ties' changed through colonial-era industrialization."[10]

But what did shifting ties of religion look like for Muslim workers? Were workers' religious identities reflected primarily in the strengthening of oppositional religious communities, of modern "communalism," as suggested by Chakrabarty's exploration of "riots" among Muslim millhands?[11] Were they directed toward shifting socioreligious authority, shaped by the Muslim elite, sparking mass participation in political projects related to both Indian independence and Muslim "separatism," ultimately reflected in the Pakistan movement?[12] This book does not discount the strengthening of these forms of assertion of Muslim identity in the context of urban industrialization, but it also argues that Islam held a far wider range of meanings for Muslim artisans and laborers. Artisan Islam was never siloed, and Muslim workers did engage with elite, middle-class, and nationalist movements, but these were rarely the only ways that Muslim artisans and laborers asserted ties of religion. Instead, Islam was central to how Muslim *kārīgar*s narrated and taught their work, learned new technologies, negotiated shifts to new fields, and contested their marginalization within North Indian social and economic hierarchies.

Pious Labor thus joins recent scholarship that analyzes the religious, social, and laboring worlds of Muslim artisans and workers on their own terms, both historically and in the contemporary context.[13] At the same time, *Pious Labor* not only integrates Muslims and Islam into the study of artisanship and labor but also centers artisans and labor in our study of South Asian Islam. Persistent colonial-era narratives portray laboring-class Muslims as religiously marginal and less orthodox than their elite counterparts. Scholarship about Islam in late nineteenth- and early twentieth-century South Asia may inadvertently reinforce these narratives because of the frequent focus on the Muslim middle class, on the *'ulama*, and on new sites of intellectual production, to the exclusion of laboring-class Muslims.[14]

I therefore integrate workers' experiences of Islam into an understanding of Islamic history beyond the "exclusive" claims of a supposed canon, emphasizing the way in which *kārīgar*s made meaning for Islam in their specific social and economic contexts.[15] I draw, for instance, on Nile Green's study of the promotion of "customary" Islamic practices and forms of authority among millworkers, dockhands, and other laborers in colonial Bombay, which emphasized the role of Islam in working-class life.[16] Green studies workers' participation in Muslim "theolog[ies] of intervention" via "holy men," through the archives of mobile religious leaders.[17] I reorient this analysis by centering Muslim narratives embedded within technical manuals and community histories that were authored by Muslim artisans themselves, drawing on an Urdu-language archive of artisanal production and artisan practices of Islam.

In a few cases, the spaces and practices of worship among North Indian Muslim artisans intersected with those of their Hindu and Sikh counterparts.[18] I have chosen, deliberately, not to characterize these forms of shared space or practice as "syncretic." In its most positive use, *syncretism* highlights shared experiences to argue for a potential world not riven by the contemporary majoritarianism that threatens the lives and livelihoods of religious minorities across South Asia. But as we shall see throughout the book, concepts such as "syncretism" have also been taken up pejoratively by those who hope to "purify" workers' religion, and they frequently fail to account for how practitioners themselves understand their faith practices.

Most significantly, in the nineteenth and early twentieth centuries, colonial administrators were invested in drawing class and caste boundaries within Indian religious communities and identifying orthodox religious practices. Colonial ethnographers frequently described artisan Islam in India as perverted by contact with Hinduism and as not really Islam at all but instead a reflection of laboring-class Muslims' lack of understanding of their supposed faith. One British administrator summed up this perspective succinctly in 1895, describing local Muslim artisans as "followers of the Prophet only in name."[19] Moreover, as SherAli Tareen demonstrates, debates among Muslim reformist scholars likewise often included polemics about the need to "purify" the religious practices of the so-called cattle-like Muslim masses.[20] And colonial and elite Muslim anxieties about the religious practices of laboring-class Muslims were sometimes in conversation with each other, retrenching understandings of artisan Islam as deviant.

In many of the community histories and technical manuals that form the backbone of my archival approach, artisans sought to demonstrate the specifically Muslim pasts of their trades and the specifically Muslim piety reflected in their work and technologies. Their careful insistence on the exclusively "Islamic" nature of their practices likely reflected artisans' own cognizance of elite and colonial framings of their practices as unorthodox. Like many Muslims whose practices have been externally labeled "popular" and "syncretic" rather than "normative" or "formal," they engaged in what Torsten Tschacher termed "a defense of contentious practices" against the ascriptive assumptions of both elite Muslims and the colonial state.[21] Rather than reading syncretism into these archival materials, I follow the lead of the authors of these histories and manuals and, in turn, analyze artisan Islam as reflective of a distinctly Muslim practice. Simultaneously, I consider whether and why artisan manuals might reflect a conscious effort to "defend," reshape, or even elide material and religious practices that were criticized or debated by other Muslims or by the state.

CONFRONTING CASTE THROUGH ARTISAN ISLAM

Taking artisans' engagement with Islam seriously also forces us to contend with the complex and sometimes ambiguous role that caste plays in South Asian Muslim communities. The relative paucity of studies of labor, artisanship, and the working classes within South Asian Islam has contributed to an elision of the role of caste in shaping conflict and contestation within Muslim communities. Caste—and experiences of caste marginalization—are motivating factors in many of the Urdu-language technical manuals and community histories that I analyze in this book. And as several recent works have noted, from the mid-nineteenth century, caste-like social hierarchies often underscored the writing of members of the consolidating Muslim middle class, who sought to advocate for their economic and class position based on *sharīf* (pl. *ashrāf*), genteel, descent.[22] But the very existence of the *ashrāf* and their practices of social distinction necessarily imply a community against which "genteel" Muslims defined themselves.

Sociologists of South Asian Islam often note the category of *ajlāf*, laboring or "common" classes, to identify this "other" against whom *ashrāf* communities defined themselves. The term *ajlāf*, however, was rarely embraced as a social identity by Muslim workers themselves. Instead, Muslim artisans and laborers more often advocated for their own trade or kinship communities beyond the supposed *ashrāf*/*ajlāf* binary.[23] Indeed, whether *ajlāf* as a category held widespread salience beyond efforts to distinguish the non-*ashrāf*—often by *ashrāf* writers—seems unlikely. Laboring-class Muslims more often sought to highlight what made their communities distinctively pious and skilled and to emphasize their histories as sites of potential religious or technological authority.

By arguing that caste-like hierarchies informed the experiences of Indian Muslim artisans and laborers, I am not suggesting that their experiences can be mapped directly onto Hindu artisans' experiences of caste, which themselves were also plural.[24] Studies of Muslim *birādarīs*—kinship networks that are usually endogamous and sometimes tied to specific trades—have emphasized that they are not always direct corollaries of Hindu *jatis* or caste groups.[25] Moreover, like Hindu caste structures, *birādarīs* and other Muslim forms of caste-like association in North India underwent significant change as a result of both urban industrialization and colonial property law and ownership practices. In Punjab especially, mid-nineteenth-century colonial property law and inheritance practices were often implicitly or explicitly tied to *birādarī*, contributing to a reconstruction and reification of genealogical pedigrees as the basis for status and community.[26]

Against this backdrop of reified caste marginalization, laboring-class Muslims wrote and circulated manuals and community histories through which they aimed to improve their social standing and promote their forms of religious and technological authority. In some cases, these efforts conformed to a process of "ashrafization," which Joel Lee, in a study of Dalit Muslims, defines as "the effort to raise one's social status by claiming *ashrāf* status and adopting the social practices of the Muslim elite."[27] I do not argue that "ashrafization" was a universal approach among Muslim artisan communities. Instead, following Lee, I recognize that Muslims excluded from *ashrāf* status employed a variety of religious and social narratives, often simultaneously, to claim dignity and status for their communities. Some of these reflected *ashrāf* aspiration, but they coexisted with narratives that emphasized the piety of labor and the social importance of laboring communities.[28] Caste contestation took place not only along *ashrāf–ajlāf* lines but also within and across laboring communities as Muslim workers sought to define their trades and their communities as possessing specific, sometimes exclusive, Muslim pasts.

TECHNOLOGY, LABOR, AND RELIGION

Pious Labor integrates the study of South Asian Islam with the study of artisanship and labor. It also brings both fields into conversation with histories of technology. Recent scholarship in the expanding field of South Asian history of science, technology, and medicine has emphasized elite Muslim religious engagement with technological and scientific change in the wake of colonial claims on scientific authority.[29] Likewise, the relationship between craft, artisanship, and technology in colonial and postcolonial South Asia has been central to several recent studies.[30] The contributions of Muslim artisans and laborers, however, have remained largely absent from both trends. *Pious Labor* not only addresses this lacuna but also places Muslim artisans at the center of technological change in colonial India, asking how Muslim claims on technology informed class and laboring identities. It disrupts persistent assumptions about the technological marginality of both colonized peoples and laborers, highlighting Muslim artisans' creativity in their use of and meaning making for new technologies.

Muslim artisans did not present their adoption of shifting technologies—even technologies closely associated with the colonial state—as technological "transfer" from Europe to Asia.[31] Instead, as Projit Mukharji has argued in the context of small-scale medical technologies, their narratives "braid[ed] distinctive strands of knowledge and practice."[32] Specific practices—boilermaking, electroplating, and others—became the spindle around which Muslim artisans braided their forms of knowledge.[33] These processes of meaning making for artisan-industrial technologies might also be characterized by what David Arnold has termed "acculturation," in which new machines simultaneously "conform[ed] to" and were "transformative of" cultures that used them.[34]

Pious Labor expands our understanding of how technology was "acculturated," and how knowledge systems were "braided," by highlighting distinctly Muslim claims and imaginations of technical knowledge. Beyond this, however, it also centers the importance of these claims on technical practices within class identities. It argues that artisans sought to assert new places for themselves within the consolidating social and class hierarchies of North Indian Muslims by asserting their distinct physical relationship with the technologies they used. Muslim artisans sometimes argued that the very thing that placed them in "lowly" positions in class or caste hierarchies—the physical labor carried out with their own hands—made them masters of technology in ways that members of the middle classes could not hope to achieve.[35] Because they understood these technologies and skills as Islamic, their command over them implied a Muslim practice that elevated artisans as distinctly, even inherently, pious.

Practices of translation, vernacularization, and linguistic adaptation were central to Indian efforts to assert new, localized uses and meanings for technologies that were introduced through European colonial authority. Adapting scientific and technical knowledge into South Asian languages required the integration of new knowledge with the material and social culture of the vernacular language.[36] Simultaneously, as Charu Singh shows, the authors of Indian scientific and technical treatises worked to establish equivalences "at the level of the word itself."[37] Within artisan manuals, however, practices of vernacularization and translation not only cultivated localized meanings but also established difference from and awareness of elite claims on technical knowledge. Most of the artisan manuals and treatises examined in this book did not describe themselves as translations from other languages. Nonetheless, practices of translation and vernacularization underscored manual composition. Many manual authors compiled materials drawn from contemporary English-language treatises—or earlier translations thereof—that circulated in South Asia.

Efforts to localize technologies and establish linguistic equivalences through artisan manuals reflected artisans' struggles to negotiate shifts associated with the colonial industrial economy. Sometimes this meant rooting new terms in Indian and Islamic artisanal and material pasts. In other instances, it meant promoting adapted, transliterated English terminology as more accessible to artisan and industrial workers than the Urdu neologisms—sometimes created from Arabic roots—preferred by elite Muslim scientists and scholars. In either case, artisan decisions about how to express concepts and practices in Urdu reflected their cultivation of authority over new technical knowledge. Their practices of translation claimed new technologies as relevant to their own physical skills, trades, and histories. Through this process, they distinguished their translated knowledge from the emerging scientific and technical translations that circulated among both middle-class supervisors and Muslim scientific societies.

AN ARCHIVE FOR MUSLIM ARTISANS?

Muslim artisans have often been overlooked as intellectual and technological agents, in part because of the nature of the archive that they produced. Engaging this archive, which is constituted primarily of artisan technical manuals and community histories in Urdu, requires taking seriously the cultural and religious narratives embedded in artisan technical knowledge. In *Pious Labor*, I read vernacular manuals that explained new technologies and material practices not only for their technical descriptions but also for their minor asides and use of metaphor, their introductory poems and marginal notes, their small statements that reveal popular imaginations of technological change.

I locate the core archive of this book in two intersecting genres, the "technical manual" and the "community history." In English, the titles I have assigned to these genres suggest a sharp distinction, but in Urdu their titles often overlapped, and indeed, the interplay between the description of technical practice and that of religious community history is often most suggestive of how artisans negotiated colonial economic and material change. Many of these texts—be they primarily technical manuals or community history—were framed as a *risālah* (treatise), a *kasbnāmah* (book of trade), a *tazkirah* (compendium), or simply a *kitāb* (book) on a particular trade, community, or technology.

In many cases, these artisan manuals and community histories were concise, between six and sixty pages long. They were often printed on cheap paper by local publishers. Their short form and relatively low cost—often between six pies and a few annas—suggest that authors were concerned with making pious knowledge available among communities that had limited money to spend on books. Likewise, sketches and illustrations, when included, were often simple, drawn up by the authors themselves, or copied from other texts, perhaps to keep the costs of the books low.

Regardless of their titles and framing, the texts analyzed here sought to explain to artisans how to practice their trade piously under deepening colonial and middle-class technical authority. Many of the artisans who wrote about their labor (and had access to publishing) in trades such as carpentry, metalworking, and tailoring were *mistrī*s, whom I frame as "master artisans" in this context. This category includes Thompson's "prosperous master craftsman" who led his own workshop and employed other workers, as well as some artisans who secured state patronage and employment.[38] Many were upwardly mobile, or at least more successful than their contemporaries in transitioning their skills to the colonial capitalist market. I also borrow the language of "master artisans" from Tirthankar Roy, who has highlighted their successful negotiation of shifting systems of capital, employment, and supervision. While Roy characterizes these successful transitions as primarily a reflection of the "agency of the innovative individual," I am most interested in how these figures spoke to and for artisan communities.[39] In the artisan manuals and histories that I analyze, master artisans asserted authority and agency in their trade, but they often sought to claim this authority for their communities rather than for individuals.

Although this book positions artisan manuals and histories as an overlooked archive, most technical writing in Urdu in the late nineteenth and early twentieth centuries was not authored by artisans—*mistrī*s or otherwise—and most of it was not aimed at laboring artisan cadres. Artisan technical manuals occupied one corner of a growing corpus of Urdu printed literature about technology. Many of the earliest projects of scientific and technical vernacularization into Urdu were carried out within colonial educational institutions. From approximately the 1830s, some colonial educationalists positioned Urdu as the most suitable Indian vernacular for communicating Western scientific knowledge, leading to the development of Urdu translations of English textbooks and treatises.[40] As noted earlier, beginning in the mid-nineteenth century, Indian scientific societies also engaged in projects of vernacularization that included the adaptation of technical manuals. And as I examine in chapter 2, middle-class Muslim industrialists promoted their own visions of technological authority by publishing technical treatises and compendia that profiled new trades and technologies.

These varied forms of Urdu technical writing intersected with each other, with authors borrowing liberally from other manuals and textbooks. Master artisan authors of technical manuals and community histories frequently engaged with other types of Urdu writing about their trade. In the case of electroplating, for instance, artisan manuals reoriented middle-class claims about the Muslim nature of the technology to center artisan skill and labor. In other cases, such as a woodworking manual profiled in chapter 4, both the author and the intended audience of a manual are ambiguous, and it is possible that the text circulated among both artisans and middle-class industrialists, or even consumers. In this context, I note the multiple potential uses of the text, embracing its ambiguity to trace the ways technical knowledge and material practices circulated among consumers and producers across a range of social classes.

The artisan manuals and histories that form the backbone of this book circulated in a crowded print-knowledge economy. In the long run, it was usually artisan skill that lost out in a contest for technological authority between cadres of artisan workers and the middle-class Indians who often became their supervisors in industrialized contexts. But the manuals and histories that were authored by and circulated among artisans nonetheless reveal that beyond the level of elite knowledge systems, workers creatively integrated new technologies into their bodies of religious and material knowledge and their practices of work.

HOW SHOULD WE READ ARTISAN ARCHIVES?

Reading artisan archives requires abandoning an underlying assumption of much of the scholarship on Indian artisans, namely, that because many artisans were illiterate, their communities did not read, produce, or engage with text. I do not suggest that most *kārīgar*s could in fact read or read well. But forms of community literacy, orality, and the engagement with the text as object all contributed to the circulation of technical manuals and community trade histories from the mid-nineteenth century.

The manuals and community histories central to *Pious Labor* reflect the circulation of artisan knowledge through overlapping practices of literacy and orality in the context of an expanding and increasingly accessible North Indian vernacular print economy. Some manuals and community histories explicitly tell us about their intended use, noting that they were meant for people who read them or heard them read aloud.[41] In other cases, manuals and histories relied heavily on versification, suggesting intended practices of circulation through memorization.[42] Moreover, artisans likely engaged with printed manuals and trade histories not only as collections of knowledge but also as objects that marked their authority over the knowledge contained within. In visits to present-day scissor-making workshops in Meerut, I found that artisans sometimes still display lithographed pages that promise protection for their shop and provide Quranic verses or prayers relevant to their trade. The printed word became a reminder of pious knowledge, perhaps only rarely read but consistently present, sometimes even "sacralized," in Mahmood Kooria's terms, as a marker of religious wisdom.[43]

Muslim artisans thus engaged with and used text. But engaging with and using text do not foreclose the centrality of embodied knowledge of a trade. Artisans nested textual knowledge within other ways of knowing and communicating their skills and trades. Traditional archival methodologies do not necessarily provide ways to account for the interplay between embodied and textual knowledge.[44] To contend with the limitations of the textual archive, I return repeatedly to the question of how artisan manuals and histories were used alongside other forms of training, teaching, and knowing. My readings aim to restore the material function of the texts and to imagine their place within a workshop, factory, or site of training. I analyze the relationship between the materiality of the text and the physicality of labor, and the potential interactions between workers, their work, and their books.[45]

In conceiving the intellectual, religious, and social worlds of Muslim artisans through the printed Urdu manuals and community histories that they used, I also build on recent scholarship on laborers' intellectual and print practices outside of the South Asian context. In his study of the political and literary worlds of Puerto Rican labor, Jorell Meléndez-Badillo examines how cadres of self-identified "enlightened workingmen" sought to speak for workers, "creat[ing] and dominat[ing] their own means of knowledge production."[46] Likewise, in the context of the United States, Tobias Higbie has noted that "the concerns, doubts, and ambitions of workers indelibly stamped the urban public sphere" of the early twentieth century as they circulated political and intellectual debates through both print and oral exchange.[47] *Pious Labor* enters into conversation with this work by asking how we might reconceptualize the "knowledge production" of Muslim artisans and laborers to include the intersections of their religious and laboring identities.

Despite the comparative utility of this scholarship, there are limitations unique to South Asian Urdu writing of artisan knowledge and laboring identities. The most significant of these is that not all Muslim artisans across North India used Urdu or understood it well, even as a spoken language. This book incorporates stories from the North-Western (later United) Provinces, where various registers and dialects of spoken Hindustani, or Hindi-Urdu, were used by Muslim workers.[48] It also draws on examples from Punjab, where many artisans used registers of Punjabi (or Saraiki or other languages) in their daily lives. While the authors of artisan manuals often announced their intentions to write in a popular-register Urdu that was accessible to *kārīgar*s, the fact remains that they often wrote in Urdu instead of Punjabi, even in Punjab. Their choice of language reflects the more widespread, state-supported, nature of publishing in Urdu over languages such as Punjabi.[49] It also reflects the urban contexts of the artisan communities analyzed in this book. Because many of these communities consisted of migrants from elsewhere in North India, Urdu was often used as a shared language. Likewise, while many artisan community histories were local, several of the authors of manuals explicitly aimed for their texts to be read by Muslim workers across India. They chose Urdu as the language most likely to attract readers and listeners across multiple cities, even beyond North India.[50]

IDENTIFYING AND ENGAGING ARTISAN ARCHIVAL COLLECTIONS

To identify artisan manuals and community histories, many of which are uncatalogued, I have relied on the knowledge and kindness of archivists and librarians. I have been especially dependent on the work of often undercompensated librarians in small regional public libraries, including those working in libraries that have experienced flooding or are missing walls that endanger the collections. I note these challenges to make it clear that the records I have collected are glimpses of larger, perhaps missing, histories of Muslim artisans and their material, religious, and textual traditions.

I have also sometimes encountered bemusement at the types of sources I have chosen to investigate, particularly at my focus on technical manuals. Even the most accommodating librarian once exclaimed, "*Another* one?" when I requested to look at the third electroplating manual in his collection, and he wondered aloud whether the texts really differed from each other. Some of my Urdu tutors, without whom this book likewise would have been impossible, expressed concern that I was not more interested in "good" Urdu writing and poetry. I believe that these responses are due to a widespread perception, not only in South Asia but globally, that technical literature lacks cultural and religious content. I aim to offer a convincing counterpoint in this book. Writing about technology not only reflects religious, cultural, and social knowledge; it also demonstrates how workers assert religious and cultural knowledge to negotiate technical change, and how they assert technical knowledge to negotiate religious and cultural contexts.

WHICH TRADES, WHICH ARTISANS, AND WHERE?

Pious Labor examines the religious, social, and laboring lives of scribes and press workers, metalsmiths, tailors, carpenters, boilermakers, and stonemasons. The decision to focus on these trades was in part a practical one—a reflection of the artisan manuals and trade histories available to me. At the same time, it was also based on my desire to suggest new directions in the study of South Asian artisanship by decentering the questions that have traditionally been asked through studies of weavers and textiles. Despite the plurality of industries grouped under the category of "artisan" in contemporary South Asian historiography, studying artisan labor has most often meant studying weavers and textiles manufacturing. Focusing here on trades other than weaving should not diminish the centrality of textiles and textile workers to our understanding of how colonialism remade the Indian economy and Indian labor. After all, weavers and other textile workers were centrally positioned within the changing global trade systems of the eighteenth and nineteenth centuries, and in India their industries were radically remade during the rise of European political and economic influence.[51]

By focusing this book on trades other than weaving, I tell stories that have sometimes been overlooked in studies of artisans and artisanship. Trades such as carpentry, stonemasonry, and blacksmithing also faced upheaval beginning with the rise of European imperial power in India. Unlike weavers, however, many of the workers in these fields did not face the most extreme forms of deindustrialization and displacement to agricultural work by European imports.[52] Like weaving, trades such as carpentry, stonemasonry, and metalsmithing were reoriented to address the demands of the colonial state and its representatives in India, but artisan experiences of this state reorientation differed significantly.

For instance, carpenters and woodworkers were recruited both for railway labor and as joiners and fitters in European-owned factories from the mid-nineteenth century. Other artisans, such as weaponsmiths, were forced out of their trades by a combination of cheaper imports and colonial laws limiting their trade. As I discuss in chapters 2 and 5, these workers usually turned to other trades that used similar skill sets, such as alternative forms of metalsmithing in the case of weaponsmiths. These were major, complex transitions for these individuals and informed how they understood their religious practices and their relationship with technologies of production. But the specific ways that artisans negotiated and experienced these transitions—and asserted religious claims on their new trades—have been overlooked because they do not necessarily match the experiences of textile workers.

I locate these transitions in urban North India. I define *urban* broadly, to include growing metropolises and industrial centers like Lahore and Kanpur (Cawnpore), as well as midsized cities such as Meerut and Sialkot. I also include the capitals of regional, quasi-autonomous princely states located geographically within the North-Western Provinces and Punjab, particularly Rampur and Bahawalpur. My focus on the urban reflects the impact of migration—which I explore most closely in chapter 4—as cities of various sizes served as important sites for the exchange of material and religious knowledge among artisans. Despite the limited nature of colonial investment in the infrastructure of urban India, artisans were drawn to cities around the mid-nineteenth century because of forms of military, railway, and public works expenditure, which were shaped by state responses to the anticolonial Uprising and war of 1857. Likewise, a post-1857 expansion of Indian mercantile and landholding economic interests in North Indian cities meant that artisan labor was in high demand, with both state and Indian capitalists sometimes complaining of their want of labor, spurring recruitment of artisans from smaller towns and villages.[53]

By the late nineteenth century, cities were also the centers from which middle-class Muslim reformist organizations sought to discipline the religious practices of Muslim workers, often drawing together local and transregional ideals of orthodoxy.[54] New intersections of local and transregional Muslim knowledge were engendered through the print economy and new forms of travel, and cities were often the first spaces where these competing religious ideas were contested and spread.[55] Urban artisans responded or adapted to middle-class challenges to their religious practices. Moreover, through urban encounters, they incorporated translocal and transregional ideals into their own assertations of the Muslim past. By locating artisan Islam in urban settings, I build on Michael Dodson's characterization of the city as "always in a state of 'becoming,'" as multiple "pasts and potential futures multiply and jostle for view."[56] The migration and growth of artisan communities in urban India, along with their transitions to new trades and technologies, forced artisans to confront these multiple pasts and potential futures and to assert or claim them for themselves and their communities.

THE GENDER(S) OF PIOUS LABOR

Pious Labor engages with archives that restore the claims of artisans and laborers to both Islamic and technological authority. Overwhelmingly, these voices are male, and in most cases the artisans profiled labored in trades popularly gendered as masculine. Women did, however, work in many of these trades. Particularly in the context of small-scale, family-run workshops, women engaged in forms of labor related to trades such as blacksmithing and carpentry, even if the finished products were often attributed to their male kin.[57] But just as women artisans—as well as third-gender or gender-nonconforming workers—were often erased by colonial record keepers, they were also often absent in the vernacular archive of artisan Islam.

The absence and erasure of artisan women from both the colonial and vernacular archive should not be read as a benign coincidence. Instead, it reflects a purposeful masculinizing of trades. This was a tactic that some male artisans used to advocate for their own religious and technical authority, which was increasingly challenged and usurped by members of the middle class and representatives of the colonial state. Indeed, several of the authors of the manuals and community histories that we will meet in this book explicitly sought to assert the masculinity of their labor as a means of subverting middle-class Indian and European writings about their trades.

In manuals and trade histories, these writers characterized pious knowledge of their labor and technologies as something that was passed through male lineages of *ustād* and *murid*, master/teacher and disciple/student. This is most evident in chapter 3, which discusses the trade of tailoring; this is also the one chapter in which I engage with an artisan manual authored by a woman. In the context of tailoring, I argue that the late nineteenth-century development of educational and charitable programs that sought to teach girls to be seamstresses sparked a backlash among male tailors. In response, some male tailors sought to assert and circulate male authority over their trade, arguing that knowledge of how to sew according to God's revelation could only be passed from father to son or (male) *ustād* to (male) *murīd*.[58] The key site of contestation was between state and middle-class projects that feminized sewing, and working-class male projects that sought to restore the masculinity of the trade through a religious idiom and narratives of the Muslim past. As I argue in the chapter, while an analysis of these competing projects helps us understand how artisan practices became popularly gendered, both narratives exclude the experiences of working-class women, who remain starkly absent from my archive.

These masculinizing processes are less explicit in other texts and other trades. Nonetheless, they often underscore the assumption of manual authors that their intended audience was male. They also intersect with consolidating middle-class debates about gender, labor, and the role of women in the home, sometimes informed by colonial, (post-)Victorian projects and policies.[59] As Samita Sen has shown in the context of Bengal, in the late nineteenth century class was mapped onto women's nondomestic labor in new ways. "Working women"—meaning those who did nondomestic work—were often assumed to reflect familial poverty.[60] Women's labor outside the home was understood as undermining a family's respectability. These norms were sometimes articulated as reflective of religious practice and status by members of both the Hindu and Muslim middle classes.[61] Artisan writers were undoubtedly aware of widespread class and social assumptions that accompanied women's nondomestic labor, and the fact that they chose not to explicitly reference women's artisanal labor is ultimately unsurprising.

The absence of women from much of the historical record that I engage in this book should not be read as an absence of women from the religious or economic worlds of artisanship that I explore. Instead, this absence itself suggests male workers' efforts to project artisanal and religious authority and status against a backdrop of widespread narratives that masculinized trades, labor, and even public urban space more broadly.

ORGANIZATION OF THIS BOOK

The chapters of *Pious Labor* are organized by trade rather than chronology, reflecting the degree to which artisan Islam was often asserted through specific trades and technologies. Most chapters cover the period from roughly 1860 to 1935. They trace the ways that distinct Muslim artisan identities were asserted from the consolidation of the British Raj after 1857 through the global economic depression of the 1930s. While I follow some trades across the entirety of this period, focusing on change over time, in other instances I have chosen to zoom in on moments of contention or debates within the trade. This reflects the often piecemeal nature of my archival materials, in which artisan Islam disappears and reappears from view depending on which materials have been preserved and remain accessible.

Each chapter opens with a short story or description of a text that is especially evocative of its subsequent argument. The chapters are grouped by key forms of contestation and debates over religious, technological, and material authority that shaped Muslim artisan expressions of their religion and their trades. Chapters 1 and 2 examine how artisans negotiated and challenged consolidating middle-class authority over new industrial trades and technologies. Chapter 1, "Lithographic Labor," focuses on the rise of the vernacular print economy from the mid-nineteenth century in North India, examining new religious and social solidarities asserted by scribal workers and other artisans at lithographic printing presses. Chapter 2, "Electroplating as Alchemy," analyzes metalsmiths' engagement with the technology of electroplating to argue that Muslim artisans creatively reoriented middle-class claims on Muslim pasts to support their own forms of technological authority.

Chapters 3 and 4 analyze the circulation of artisan knowledge and training. I argue that artisans engaged with sites of knowledge circulation—the print economy and urban industrial workshops—as a means of contesting their social marginalization within both colonial narratives and elite Muslim conceptions of religious authority. Chapter 3, "Sewing with Idris," examines tailors' pious knowledge of their trade in the context of an expanding print economy. Male Muslim tailors engaged with print to challenge their own marginalized religious positionality, but they did so, in part, by excluding women tailors from their claims of piety. Chapter 4, "Migrant Carpenters, Migrant Muslims," asks how migration to large urban centers such as Lahore and Kanpur contributed to the exchange of both religious and technical knowledge among Muslim carpenters and woodworkers. Shifting ties of religious identity engendered by urban industrialization served not only consolidating middle-class claims on religious cohesion but also carpenters' own claims on the pious practice of their work.

The final two chapters turn to questions of state employment and patronage, interrogating how artisans negotiated recruitment by colonial railway projects and public works departments, as well as patronage from the rulers of regional princely states. Chapter 5, "The Steam Engine as a Muslim Technology," analyzes how Muslim master artisans transitioned to trades such as boilermaking in railway locomotive workshops, and how they contested their marginalization within new technical hierarchies. Chapter 6, "Building the Modern Mosque," likewise emphasizes the emergence of new hierarchies of technical oversight within construction. It does so in the context of the princely patronage of stonemasons, analyzing conflict and contradiction between masons' own understanding of the Islamic relevance of their work and elite Muslim attempts to spur the revival of "Islamic architecture."

The Conclusion draws the chapters together to examine the broader impacts of artisan Islam on labor solidarities in the immediate lead-up to Partition and independence. It reflects on the degree to which practices of Muslim artisan knowledge circulation were disrupted and remade in the wake of Partition. And it argues for a future of Islamic studies in South Asia that centers the lives, work, and ideas of Muslims who have sometimes been excluded or marginalized through an insistence on the primacy of canonical thinkers and texts.

Ultimately, *Pious Labor* joins Nazir in his evocation and celebration of the power that God gave to blacksmiths. The six chapters together emphasize the vitality and plurality of artisan Islam and the creativity of Muslim artisans' engagement with emerging technologies and trades. The creativity and expansiveness of Muslim artisans' religious and material traditions exceed what a single monograph could hope to describe. Nonetheless, in telling the stories of colonial-era social, industrial, and economic change through the eyes of Muslim artisans, *Pious Labor* suggests new approaches to histories of Islam in South Asia, revealing how Muslim workers asserted claims on their own pasts and practices.

PART ONE

Creating New Muslim Trades, Claiming New Muslim Technologies

1

Lithographic Labor

Locating Muslim Artisans in the Print Economy

FROM SCRIBAL TREATISE TO LITHOGRAPHIC STRIKE

In 1885 Karimullah Khan, a court scribe in the small North Indian city of Rampur, compiled a series of directives explaining the role of scribes in print work. For a scribe to describe printing is unsurprising, as print in South Asian Perso-Arabic script languages—Urdu, Persian, and others—had been popularized, not through typographic letterpresses, but through lithography. Publishers relied on scribes to copy texts for lithographic print. But Karimullah Khan did not write out the directions in a printed textbook or with the support of a regional lithographic press. Instead, he compiled them in a vibrantly decorated Persian-language manuscript (figure 1), with patronage from the reigning nawab of Rampur, which, at the time, was a quasi-autonomous princely state under British colonial suzerainty. The text, in most observable ways, conformed to a long-standing Indian Persian tradition of manuscript textual production about scribal work.

Titled *Daftar-i khaṯṯāṯ* or *The Book of Scribes*, the text described the history and practice of *nastaʿlīq*, the style of script commonly used for Persian, Urdu, and several other Perso-Arabic script languages in South Asia. Early chapters described "the drawing of smooth lines" and "the preparing of margins," topics that would not have been out of place in any Persian calligraphy treatise from the preceding centuries.[1] But the final chapter was titled "The Art of Print," marking a significant departure from the earlier scribal treatises.[2]

In this unusual addendum, scribes learned the art of lithography. Karimullah described how to make, hold, and use a lithographic pencil—a grease crayon—to write on paper that would then be transferred to the lithographic stones. He traced

بسم الله الرحمن الرحیم

حمد بیحد خوش قلمی را سزد که رقم اول دفتر ایجادش لوح و قلم است

و ثنای بیعد خوش رقمی را زیبد که بدیوان قضایش از حروف کاف

و نون اختراع عالم خطوط صفحات اشجارش دلیلی است بر خوش نویسی او

و نقوش اوراق گلزارش سبیلی ست برنگ آمیزی او

لو کان البحر مدادا لکلمات ربی لنفد البحر قبل

ان تنفد کلمات ربی ولو جئنا بمثله مددا

و نعت رنگارنگ آن نقش اول چمن کائنات که خود نقاش ازل

FIGURE 1. The intricately decorated first page of the *Daftar-i khaṭṭāṭ* of Karimullah Khan. The script is a good example of *nastaʿlīq* in manuscript form. (1885. Pers., no. 2454, Raza Library, Rampur, Uttar Pradesh).

this process of transference, describing how a scribe could move his text from paper to stone:

> Whenever printing is required, the aforementioned [grease] pencil is taken up and used to write upon the recommended starched paper [*kāghaẕ-i āhārdār*]. After that, the [lithographic] stone is heated to a moderate level over the burning charcoal, and the copy paper is slightly dampened, and then the side upon which words are written is placed onto the printing stone [*sang-i munṭabi'*], until all the letters have reached the stone in reversed form.... The letters on the stone are then covered with an ointment of water and gum Arabic [*ṣamgh-i 'arabī*] and left for one night.[3]

Karimullah Khan then described the process of applying ink and oil to the stones in the morning, to transfer the text from the stones to printing paper, as well as the importance of "mirror-writing"—writing in reverse—directly on lithographic stones. This, he explained, could be used to "correct" texts after they had been transferred to the stones and before printing.[4] The text thus suggested that knowledge of lithography was not so different from the ability to fashion a reed pen or to form smooth lines. Karimullah portrayed lithography as part of the region's scribal tradition, a technology that allowed scribal continuity, important for scribes who hoped to demonstrate their respectability and skill.

Half a century later, in late April 1935, lithographic press workers at several of the most prominent Muslim-owned presses in the city of Lahore walked out on strike. The workers were employed by the city's largest Urdu-language newspaper, *Zamīndār* (The landlord), as well as at two local presses that printed Urdu, Arabic, and Persian books and periodicals: the Mansur Steam Press and the Muslim Printing Press.[5] Many of the striking scribes were employed as independent pieceworkers for the presses, and they demanded more consistent access to work and pay. They were joined by machine-men and other nonscribal lithographic press workers—a broad community of press *kārīgar*s who complained of stagnant wages and delays in payment in the context of the global economic depression.[6]

The press workers' strike attracted attention from all-India and regional unions and leftist parties. As left-leaning organizations across Punjab distributed pamphlets to the strikers and passed resolutions of support, colonial administrators assigned to monitor "dangerous associations" fretted that regional trade unions and communist groups might expand their reach to the so-called Muslim presses of urban Punjab.[7] While the striking workers apparently expressed limited interest in these groups, the strike did spark efforts to organize a union for *kātib*s or copyists or scribes, coordinated by the larger Punjab Press Workers' Association.[8] Attempts to organize a union specifically for *kātib*s are suggestive of scribes' continued relevance to book production, a widespread sentiment that they were taken advantage of by press managers, and social and economic distinctions that separated them from other press workers.

Karimullah Khan's *Daftar-i khaṯṯāṯ* and the strike of lithographic press workers in Lahore seem unrelated at first. After all, they were separated by fifty years and over three hundred miles. The *Daftar-i khaṯṯāṯ* was written in a small provincial city, where manuscript scribes often relied on elite princely patronage. It reflected the fact that print had not fully replaced manuscript production but had developed alongside it, with scribes engaged in both forms of production. The strike took place in a context of urban industrial print capitalism. The strikers walked out from industrialized lithographic presses—factories—that employed scores of workers, not only scribes but also machine-men, ink makers, stone wipers, bookbinders, and others.

But these seemingly distinct moments were, in fact, part of a larger, shared history of lithographic labor. Muslim scribes asserted narratives about technological change in the field of book production that informed their economic and social relationships within the expanding North Indian lithographic print economy. Claiming a distinct Muslim tradition for scribal work, scribes sought to distinguish themselves from growing cadres of nonscribal lithographic workers, even as they sometimes aligned with these nonscribal press laborers during conflicts with press management. The *Daftar-i khaṯṯāṯ* and the Lahore lithographic strike reflect a connected history through which scribes and other lithographic press workers negotiated radical technological and social change within their spaces of labor.

• • •

This book is a history of Muslim artisan communities and their engagement with technological change in colonial India. But in many ways, it is also a history of print. The rapid development of the Urdu print economy in mid-nineteenth-century India meant that religious framings of trades and technologies moved quickly across the Indian subcontinent and sometimes beyond it.[9] Through print, Muslim religious traditions for work were contested and reinterpreted by artisans and laborers. Although many Muslim artisans could not read or were semiliterate, new publications circulated within artisan communities through a combination of literacy and orality by the 1860s. Texts were printed with the assumption that they would be read aloud and circulated within artisans' neighborhoods and workshops, and they ultimately shaped how workers understood both their trades and their religious practices.

Book production itself also underwent radical change in its organization and technologies from the mid-nineteenth to the early twentieth century. The *kārīgar*s who worked at lithographic presses and produced publications about technological change negotiated shifting relationships between social status, religion, and technological knowledge. Although I have begun this book with a study of how scribes and other workers negotiated the emerging and industrializing print economy through Muslim traditions, I do not suggest that their experiences were representative of North Indian artisans more generally. On the contrary, I show that the experiences of lithographic laborers were often exceptional. Scribes saw greater elite Muslim—and even colonial—acceptance of their religious traditions for their trade than the other communities, such as tailors and carpenters, analyzed in this book. The archival sources for print workers' histories are also more extensive than the archives for most of the other communities studied here, given their higher levels of literacy and the centrality of the written word to their understanding of their trade. Still, it seems appropriate to consider how lithographic press workers asserted Muslim pasts in the print economy, because it is through their labor that we have access to many of the traditions analyzed in subsequent chapters.[10]

In the last two decades, a reconsideration of South Asian print history has sparked scholarly interventions that center presses within the political and religious economies of colonial India. These works have analyzed the rise of commercial publishers as intellectual and social representatives of new Indian middle classes, as well as the role that they played in asserting and defining religious communities.[11] Recently, this scholarship has also turned to the question of how publishers understood and engaged with print technology, including through reference to their religious traditions. Megan Robb, for instance, has argued that the proprietors of North Indian Muslim-run presses characterized publication of books and periodicals as a "*farẓ*, or duty understood in religious terms."[12] Outside of the South Asian context, the recent work of Ahmed El Shamsy highlights the role of Arab press editors as intellectual actors, several of whom tied "modern institutions of knowledge" to classical Arab-Islamic thought.[13]

This chapter builds on this recent scholarship, while also positioning presses as sites of labor, asking how press laborers themselves made sense of shifting technologies of production and whether press workers developed distinct intellectual traditions surrounding their work. This is important because lithographic presses relied on the persistence of long-standing scribal communities, while also precipitating new forms of scribal training and the consolidation of nonscribal lithographic laboring cadres. My use of "artisan Islam" in this chapter centers Muslim pasts that scribes asserted as they negotiated lithographic technologies and models of training.

Lithographic press workers developed their own narratives about the relationship between religious identities and lithographic work, which were often distinct from those asserted by press owners and managers. But Muslim lithographic laborers' engagement with a Muslim tradition for printing was stratified. It reflected social and economic differences between scribes who could claim to be rooted in manuscript traditions, scribes who trained within the presses, and other lithographic laborers, including ink rollers, machine-men, and stone wipers, some of whom were illiterate. Muslim traditions for scribal work and print labor ultimately served to connect manuscript scribes of 1880s Rampur to lithographic strikers of 1930s Lahore.

SCRIBES, BOOK WORKERS, AND THE RISE OF LITHOGRAPHY

Prior to the popularization of lithography in India after 1824, scribes and calligraphers were typically employed in three types of overlapping positions. First, scribes were employed in courtly settings, as state and personal secretaries. Second, scribes and calligraphers were employed producing manuscripts in workshops sponsored by wealthy or royal families.[14] In the most elite of these workshops, there were high levels of scribal differentiation, with those from the most prestigious educational lineages working as *khūshnavīses*, calligraphers producing calligraphic art and highly prized manuscripts, and larger numbers working as *kātibs* (scribes), producing most texts. In the manuscript workshops of smaller courts or noble families, however, these categories were sometimes collapsed.[15] Finally, scribes could find employment by offering their services to copy books, letters, and other texts for the public, usually paid by the piece. Organized into small independent workshops, these scribes were often trained by their fathers or apprenticed to another member of the trade community.

In both courtly workshops and independent operations, scribes were joined in book production by other workers, such as bookbinders, ink makers, and illustrators.[16] Just as independent bookbinding workshops often cluster around printing houses in India today, these aligned artisan communities historically clustered together in Indian bazaars. Scribes' traditions about scribal labor and book production—those referenced in Karimullah Khan's work—were recorded frequently in manuscript form.

In many regions of the world and in linguistic traditions in which the transition to print relied on movable type, print threatened the structures of scribal employment. But in South Asian lithographic traditions the demand for scribes expanded, and scribes learned new forms of book production. From the 1780s, European employees of the British East India Company at Fort William in Calcutta promoted typographic printing for Persian, Urdu, and other languages that used the Perso-Arabic script, as did missionaries, who hoped to use print to spread the Bible and Christianity. Representatives of the colonial state promoted typographic printing because they believed that it would lessen the Company's dependence on Indian munshis, or secretarial scribes, who acted as writers and often also as translators, communicating between the Company and Indian elites.[17] Indeed, much of the previous scholarship on colonial-era scribal transitions has focused on secretarial scribes and their navigation of changing modes of employment in what Bhavani Raman frames as the "colonial bureaucratic order."[18] But even as secretarial scribes asserted a new clerical middle-class-ness centered on the bureaucratic office, other communities of scribes retained artisanal modes of production. While some secured the patronage of local elites within large manuscript workshops, most maintained small family workshops from which they were commissioned. It was primarily these "artisanal" scribes and calligraphers—rather than secretarial scribes, who occupied a distinct social and class status by the mid-nineteenth century—for whom lithographic labor offered a pathway to sustain their trade and skills.

The movable-type print used at Fort William never attracted large-scale readership. Instead, it was primarily used for printing language textbooks and readers to educate new Company employees. Nineteenth-century experiments in Perso-Arabic movable type overcame many of the technical challenges experienced by earlier attempts to render the script legible in type, including problems rendering letter compounds and dots.[19] Despite increased legibility, typography was not embraced by many Indian readers or producers of Perso-Arabic script books. On the production side, this was partially due to the high cost of obtaining and running a movable-type press in comparison to a lithographic press. It also stemmed from aesthetics, because *nastʿalīq* features sloping lines and curves that early movable type was unable to reproduce.[20]

The spread of Perso-Arabic script print in India began in earnest after the introduction of lithography in 1824, when the British East India Company acquired lithographic presses for each of its presidencies. The trade was rapidly popularized over the subsequent two decades by cadres of private Indian publishers, who required the labor of an expanding number of scribes.[21] Over the following decades, Indian-owned lithographic printing houses flourished across the subcontinent.[22] Lithography dominated Perso-Arabic script printing to the near exclusion of typography. It was also frequently used for other Indian languages and scripts that were more easily rendered in movable type, in part because the economic barriers to entry were lower for lithographic than typographic publishers.

By the late 1860s, Indian-run lithographic printing houses not only dominated local markets but also exported books abroad to Indian diasporas and other communities who read Perso-Arabic script languages.[23] From its inception, lithographic printing in India was a significant site of employment for scribes, and Indian printed books mirrored their manuscript predecessors. They often included extensive colophons that identified the scribe, as well as versified chronograms to indicate the date of publication. Though this practice diminished slowly through the 1880s and 1890s, even early twentieth-century printed texts sometimes identified the scribe or scribes responsible for their composition.[24]

CLAIMING PERSIANATE SCRIBAL PASTS FOR LITHOGRAPHY

Karimullah Khan composed his scribal history in Persian, reflecting the North Indian and transregional pasts that he sought to claim for scribes as they transitioned into the print economy. The pace of the decline of Persian in nineteenth-century India is sometimes overstated, but by the mid-1880s, when Karimullah Khan wrote his treatise, printing in Urdu in North India dwarfed that in Persian.[25]

The British East India Company had discarded Persian as an official language in the 1830s, but the language had persisted in an official capacity for several decades in many princely states like Rampur. However, even Rampur changed its official language to Urdu in the 1870s.[26] Karimullah Khan asserted scribal rootedness in a specific set of traditions associated with Persian linguistic and literary practice by selecting Persian as his language of composition, rather than choosing the "vernacular" Urdu, as many other late nineteenth-century scribal treatises had done.

The scribal traditions referenced in the *Daftar-i khaṯṯāṯ* emerged through a long period of Persian-language literary and administrative dominance in several regions of South Asia.[27] In North India, Persian was patronized by the Ghaznavids from the eleventh century but became the primary literary and political language of North Indian dynasties over the course of the thirteenth to eighteenth centuries.[28] The scribal practices associated with this linguistic space were rooted in a transregional calligraphic tradition that had developed out of Arabic but had consolidated specifically for writing Persian. Several of these practices, and specifically *nasta ʿlīq* script, emerged in the fifteenth century in Khorasan, the region that is today eastern Iran and western Afghanistan.[29]

Earlier scribal treatises on *nasta ʿlīq* carefully traced the evolution of the script back to Khorasan, while also emphasizing the polycentric nature of expertise in calligraphy across North India, the Deccan, Central Asia, Iran, and the Ottoman Empire.[30] Tracing one's educational lineage to earlier greats from Iran or Central Asia, or even being able to produce a convincing imitation of their work, remained a mark of scribal prestige well into the twentieth century in India. Karimullah Khan sought to link the emerging lithographic work to these historical worlds of *nasta ʿlīq* and manuscript production. Citing his own *ustād*, famed manuscript scribe ʿEwwaz ʿAli Malihabadi, as the inspiration for the text, he emphasized the importance of learning "the rules of writing" from teachers "possessed of grace" in contexts "free of temptation and sin."[31] In doing so, he argued for scribal social and educational exclusivity. For Karimullah Khan, a scribe could not be effective or respectable without a connection to the models of training and education associated with the transregional spheres of Perso-Arabic scribal production, regardless of whether he worked in lithographic or manuscript production.

BROADENING SCRIBAL CLASSES

Karimullah Khan's *Daftar-i khaṯṯāṯ* was far from the only late nineteenth-century text that addressed potential lithographic scribes. Other texts operated from a very different set of assumptions about the social positionality, training, and backgrounds of scribes. They reflected the increased demand for scribal skill that accompanied the rise of large-scale lithographic workshops, and the expansion of the trade to include scribal workers without the hereditary and educational backgrounds that Karimullah Khan valorized. For instance, in Kanpur (Cawnpore) in 1874, a scribe named Muhammad ʿAbdul Rahman had compiled his own treatise. Titled *Raīl khushnavīsī* (Rail calligraphy), the text was written in Urdu, rather than Persian, and it was printed through lithography, rather than copied in a manuscript by a scribe. Most significantly, rather than addressing scribes who had learned manuscript production in princely workshops, ʿAbdul Rahman wrote for "boys" who had learned to "write, but in poor hand."[32]

ʿAbdul Rahman proposed a new, "easier" model of learning *nastaʿlīq* for scribal work. He centered this model on an extended metaphor of the railways, in which the "ink is the engine" and "every letter is as clear and cleanly made as a railway line."[33] He suggested that this model of learning scribal work could be picked up easily by boys who hoped to find *rozgār* or employment, including in the rapidly expanding lithographic presses of Kanpur. Indeed, the book was printed by Kanpur's largest Indian-owned press, the Nizami Press, in part to improve the skill set of its potential workers.[34] ʿAbdul Rahman noted that the text also had the support of the British director of public education for the region, who saw it as teaching employable skills.[35]

Karimullah Khan wrote with the assumption that his treatise would supplement, not supplant, educational lineages that provided training for manuscript scribes. Conversely, while ʿAbdul Rahman noted his own connections to a prominent regional scribal lineage, he assumed that his readers would not have access to this model of training and that they would learn their skills primarily for press labor. He provided these boys with a basic command of scribal work that would allow them to earn "a few rupees" by producing piecework or taking up apprenticeships through the presses.[36] He thus contributed to the creation of a new cadre of scribes, cultivated specifically for the lithographic print economy.

Moreover, where Karimullah Khan described the mechanical processes of lithography for scribes, ʿAbdul Rahman assumed that new scribes would learn the mechanical skills of lithography within the presses. Thus he did not provide a detailed description of the technical processes of printing. He focused instead on the work that a student would do on his *waṣlī*, a practice pasteboard, emphasizing that repeated exercises there would lead to sufficient improvements to find work and additional training.[37] This reflected not only his assumption that scribes would continue to learn the trade within the presses but also the fact that within large presses like the Nizami Press, workers were increasingly specialized. While a scribe in a small press in Rampur might realistically need to know how to apply gum Arabic to lithographic stones before printing, in larger urban presses this work was done by emerging cadres of nonscribal laborers who were often trained in specific, differentiated technical practices. Even as ʿAbdul Rahman sought to expand the potential scribal labor force to boys without the prestigious training preferred by Karimullah Khan, he also suggested a more circumscribed role for them within the presses.

SCRIBAL KNOWLEDGE AS MUSLIM KNOWLEDGE

Despite significant differences in the assumed class and social positionalities of their audiences, both *Daftar-i khaṯṯāṯ* and *Raīl khushnavīsī* are notable because they tied scribal work to a Muslim religious identity and practice. It is important to note here that scribes working in Persian, Urdu, and other languages that used Perso-Arabic script had historically been drawn from multiple religious communities. The Mughal court, its successor states, and regional elites regularly patronized Hindu caste and community groups that were seen as "scribal" in nature, most notably *kayasthas*, including for Persian and Urdu manuscripts. Members of these communities continued to secure employment as producers of *nastaʿlīq* and other Perso-Arabic scripts through the mid-nineteenth century.[38] Until the early nineteenth century, non-Muslim scribes were often featured in Persian scribal treatises as potential models of scribal work.

Among the most prominent North Indian, Persian-language scribal treatises authored in the period immediately preceding the rise of lithographic print was the *Taẕkirah-yi khūshnavīsān* (Compendium of calligraphers). It was composed in 1824 by Ghulam Muhammad Dehlvi, a scribe based in Lucknow, and it provided advice on how to undertake scribal work and detailed biographies of prominent scribes.[39] Dehlvi's 1824 treatise profiled several *kayastha* scribes and calligraphers, portraying them as rooted in the same educational milieu as prominent Muslim scribes. It portrayed a world of scribal production and training that, while having a Muslim-majority, was religiously plural.[40] At the same time, Dehlvi's work—like many scribal treatises that preceded it—asserted that the history of Perso-Arabic scribal work was essentially an Islamic one and that the precepts of writing had been first revealed by God to the first prophet, Adam.[41]

In the late nineteenth century, there was an increased erasure of non-Muslim scribes from scribal treatises, accompanied by a renewed and expanded assertion of Islam as a source of a shared scribal past. This shift suggests that the importance of Muslim religious identity among scribes increased in the age of print. As earlier forms of training and patronage ruptured, scribes emphasized Islam as a factor that distinguished their trade, drawing on new articulations of artisan Islam that made space for multiple spaces of training. This shift was especially pronounced in texts such as the *Raīl khushnavīsī*, which did not assume that scribes had access to prestigious educational lineages and prominent *ustāds* but instead assumed that they learned scribal work from texts and in the presses.

By articulating a shared Muslim past for scribal work, authors like ʿAbdul Rahman sought to tie together lithographic scribes from multiple social and economic backgrounds. Invoking the Quran to claim a Muslim nature for scribal work,

ʿAbdul Rahman's introduction explained that the work of men is in the hands of God. He cited, for instance, God's protection of the ark of the Prophet Nuh (Noah), quoting the thirty-sixth surah (*ya-sin*), "We carried their seed in the loaded Ark, and we have made similar things for them to ride in."[42] Further emphasizing God's influence over the "hands of men," he suggested that the ways in which scribes piously carried out their work reflected the will of God. And he reminded his readers of sayings associated with prominent figures in Islamic history. Citing a saying attributed to ʿAli—the Prophet Muhammad's son-in-law—he noted that "what cannot be completely attained, should not be completely let go," suggesting that while scribes might not be able to perfect their knowledge, they must nonetheless pursue it.[43] In centering figures like ʿAli as sources of inspiration for potential scribes, he suggested that the correct practice of scribal work was dependent on one's knowledge of Islam and a shared Muslim past.

Perhaps most importantly, late nineteenth- and early twentieth-century scribal manuals like the *Raīl khushnavīsī*—those aimed at expanded scribal communities—reoriented the extant scribal tradition of the revelation of script and writing to the Prophet Adam. Earlier scribal treatises like the *Taẕkirah-yi khūshnavīsān* claimed that God's revelation of writing to Adam had been passed down from *ustād* to *murīd* through long, unbroken chains of scribal education.[44] But this narrative was less resonant among scribes trained in, or for, lithographic presses who lacked access to prestigious scribal lineages.

In the *Raīl khushnavīsī*, ʿAbdul Rahman celebrated God's revelation of printing to Adam but claimed that boys could learn to write in a pious way that reflected the divine and prophetic nature of writing without access to a scribal lineage.[45] Scribal skills learned through textbooks, and improved through presswork, he suggested, were just as likely to be pious and reflective of God's intentions for the written word. As I show in chapters 3 and 4, this narrative reflected a renewed celebration of the prophetic revelation of artisan trades in the late nineteenth century, which often emphasized the importance of learning to practice the trade in the manner revealed to a prophet, whether through an unbroken lineage of training or not.

The broadening of the social and educational backgrounds of scribal workers—spurred by the demand for scribal labor at lithographic presses—thus contributed to an increased emphasis on scribal work as rooted in an explicitly, and exclusively, Muslim tradition. Lithographic presses in the late nineteenth century recruited scribes from the prestigious educational lineages that were highlighted by Karimullah Khan, and these scribes with prestigious training were the most likely to be named in the colophons of late nineteenth-century lithographs. But by the mid-1870s, the larger presses in cities such as Lucknow, Lahore, and Kanpur relied on scores of scribes, many of whom were drawn from the families of nonscribal Muslim artisan communities and learned scribal work in the context of the presses.

These large presses released dizzying arrays of daily and weekly periodicals, pamphlets, poetry collections, religious literature, political treatises, histories, technical manuals, textbooks, and popular fiction. Their demand for scribal labor was not fully met by regional scribal lineages, and as suggested by the Nizami Press's commissioning of *Raīl khushnavīsī*, they increasingly sought to train potential lithographic scribes themselves. The creation of these new cadres of lithographic scribes spurred the search for new sources of authority and social distinction. Given that many could no longer claim connection to prestigious scribal lineages, scribes instead argued that the Muslim traditions of scribal labor distinguished them from other types of workers, and they emphasized the Muslim piety of their work as a source of social identity and trade cohesion.

LITHOGRAPHIC LABOR BEYOND SCRIBAL WORK

Within the presses, however, scribes were also joined by nonscribal laborers. By the turn of the twentieth century, the largest lithographic presses on the subcontinent employed several hundred workers. Ulrike Stark estimates that by 1890 the Naval Kishore Press employed over nine hundred people at its Lucknow press alone, in addition to several hundred others at its branch operations in Lahore, Kanpur, and the princely state of Kapurthala.[46] This number decreased significantly after 1895 because the press became one of the earliest in North India to adopt steam-powered printing, decreasing its manual labor demands (figure 2).[47] Nonetheless, this number shows that presses in urban North India were among the cities' most significant private industrial employers and had the largest factories.

The Naval Kishore Press maintained both typographic and lithographic units for various scripts, although most of their book and periodical production—and almost all print production in Urdu, Persian, and Arabic—was lithographic.[48] In the lithographic department, print workers included generalized machine-men, as well as stone wipers, ink rollers, and even lithographic ink makers. The lithographic department of the Naval Kishore Press also employed some in-house scribes and calligraphers, but many other independent scribes did piecework for the press.[49] Piecework was often more well renumerated than directly employed wage labor, and it allowed the most prominent scribes to maintain independent workshops, continuing their role in the manuscript economy. But it was also often inconsistent and financially unstable, particularly for the new cadres of scribes who worked and trained primarily in the presses and lacked rootedness in prestigious workshops.

Most lithographic presses in North India, however, never reached anywhere near the scale of the Naval Kishore Press or its large-scale, urban competitors. Many presses were small, family- or individual-run enterprises, based in towns, small cities, and *qaṣbah*s.[50] In Rampur, for instance, the most prominent private press of the late nineteenth and early twentieth centuries was the Ḥusanī Press, which released the state's only weekly periodical. The Ḥusanī Press was founded in 1866 and was likely Karimullah Khan's point of reference for lithographic

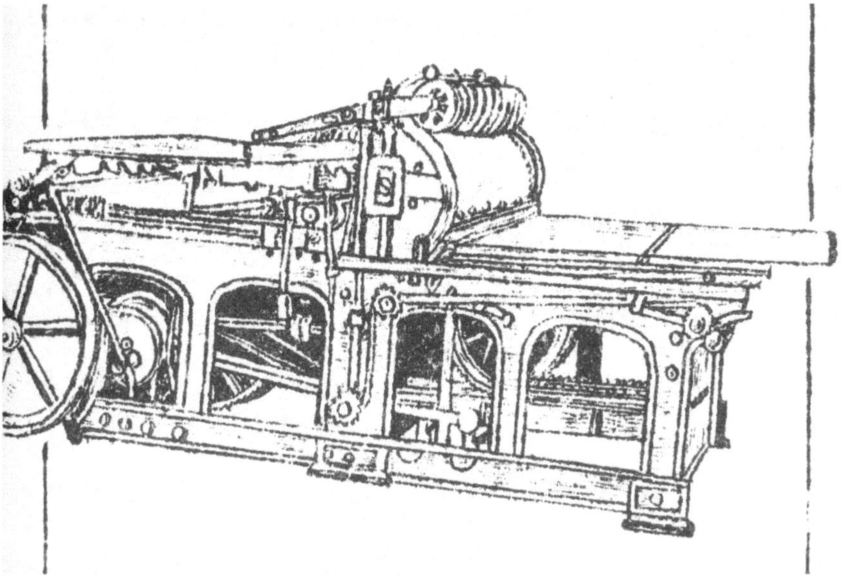

FIGURE 2. Sketch of a steam-powered lithographic press from a 1909 compendium of technologies and trades. Muḥammad Rafīʿ Riẓvī, *Makhzan al-fawāyid* (Moradabad: Maṭbaʿ al-ʿulūm, 1909). (© British Library Board, Urdu.D.570, p. 122)

technologies and practices along with the state lithographic press. By 1911 the Ḥusanī Press was owned and managed by four brothers—the sons of its founder—and employed four permanent laborers. These laborers were described in a colonial report as "illiterate and employed for mechanical work only."[51] The press's scribal labor demands were met entirely by pieceworkers, suggesting that the precarity of scribal employment that sometimes characterized large presses in major cities extended to their smaller, more provincial counterparts.[52]

In both cases, scribes usually earned higher pay than other lithographic workers. Although wage reports lack detail, reports on the administration of factory regulations in the United Provinces—which included notes on presses that employed more than fifty people—suggest that between 1900 and 1910, skilled machine-men—often blacksmiths by training—usually earned eight to twelve rupees per month in the presses, and "unskilled" press laborers, including stone wipers and paper carriers, likely earned about two to four rupees per month.[53] Scribes employed directly by the presses earned about fourteen to sixteen rupees per month, though the fact that most were employed as pieceworkers means that these wages tell us little.[54] The most prestigious scribes—those with access to the lineages praised by Karimullah Khan—could earn up to a rupee per day, though most earned about half that, and many struggled to secure consistent work throughout the month.[55]

As in the case of scribes, nonscribal lithographic laborers were not uniformly Muslim. At North Indian private presses, whether managed by Muslims, Hindus, Sikhs, or Christians, the labor force was always religiously heterogeneous. Nonetheless, by the late nineteenth century, press labor was often popularly associated with Muslims. At both lithographic and typographic presses in major North Indian cities including Lahore, Lucknow, Allahabad, and Kanpur, press laborers were majority Muslim. At the United Provinces Government Press, which undertook primarily typographic but also some lithographic work, Muslims made up nearly 70 percent of the over one thousand press laborers.[56] Detailed records about the employees of privately run presses, even the large-scale presses, are rare, but references to "Muhammadan" press workers at both state and private presses abound in the colonial archive and English press.[57] They paint a picture of a growing industrial field that was never exclusively the domain of Muslims but was widely viewed as an appropriate and appealing trade for Muslim boys. Print work, both scribal and otherwise, was framed as an attractive and relatively well-paid form of labor for the sons of Muslim artisans, especially blacksmiths and others perceived to have mechanical skill, who pursued work as press-based machine-men.[58]

THE BOOKBINDERS' STORY

The records of colonial-era lithographic presses suggest that the primary distinction in book production was between scribes—with their long-standing claims on a tradition for their trade—and new cadres of "mechanical" workers who lacked such traditions and accompanying status. However, several other communities of book workers also sustained traditions for their trades that referenced manuscript production while adapting to the economic and industrial realities of the emerging print economy. Prior to the rise of print, writing on other types of book labor was more limited, though textual evidence suggests the religious, cultural, and technical traditions that circulated among workers such as bookbinders and ink makers. For instance, the *Risālah-yi jild sāzī* (Treatise on bookbinding), a Persian-language manuscript composed in India around the early nineteenth century by Sayyid Yusuf Hussain, was a versified treatise advising bookbinders on the moral and practical dictates of their trade. In an opening section titled "The Reason for the Existence of Binding," the manual tied the trade to the production and protection of the Quran. It narrated the story of the Prophet Muhammad's companion and the third caliph, Usman bin Affan, and his compilation of a written Quran after he noted differences in its oral circulation, and then explained that to leave the Quran unbound would show a lack of reverence and a failure to protect its words.[59]

As with scribes, bookbinders' knowledge was rooted in the transregional exchange of technical practices. Manuscript copies of the *Risālah-yi jild sāzī* were produced and circulated not only across North and South India but also in Iran. Indeed, most of the recent academic attention to the text has come from Iran and scholars of the wider Persianate world.[60] Unlike scribes, bookbinders do not seem to have maintained extensive written records of their educational lineages and claims on transregional educational descent. The *Risālah-yi jild sāzī* noted the role of Sufi *pīr*s, guides/saints, in protecting and passing on the knowledge of the trade and praised *ustād*s who taught the trade to apprentices. But unlike contemporary scribal treatises, it did not blend a telling of lineages with its descriptions of work, focusing instead on explaining techniques in a versified manual format. This likely reflected the nature of bookbinding, in which apprentices learned the trade through practice under the guidance of master binders, but one's status in the trade was less dependent on the ability to claim illustrious lineages of training.

At the same time, aside from the fact that they possessed a preprint written tradition for their trade, bookbinders shared at least one other important characteristic with scribes: they often performed piecework for the presses, rather than securing wage-based employment within them. William Hoey, the tax commissioner in Lucknow who compiled an 1880 compendium on trades and manufactures in that city, characterized bookbinders primarily as independent artisans, many of whom maintained their own workshops from which they were commissioned by presses or individuals. According to Hoey, given the cost of materials—pasteboard, sheepskin, marble paper, thread, and paste—and the amount of time required for work, an independent Lucknavi bookbinder could usually earn a profit of nine annas over two days.[61] Indeed, while government agencies and presses usually employed bookbinders directly, they too occasionally had books bound through independent workshops, and they often recruited bookbinders as pieceworkers rather than wage employees.[62] Moreover, in the case of the largest presses, which doubled as stationers, bookbinders were sometimes required to purchase the materials and tools of their trade from the presses. The Naval Kishore Press, for instance, sold the cloth for bookbinding.[63] Bookbinders' dependence on presses for piecework, combined with their need to purchase materials up front, suggests that it is possible they went into debt to their employers, highlighting the economic precarity of their trade in the print economy.

PRESSES AS SITES OF LABOR

The industrialization of presses, the dangers inherent in the work, and the sense that the wages offered by press managers were insufficient for the cost of urban living meant that by the early twentieth century, printing was a trade known for management-labor conflicts and strikes. The earliest efforts by press workers to agitate for improved wages and working conditions took place in government presses. Government presses relied on typography for most of their production in English, but they primarily used lithography for Urdu from the 1850s through the 1940s. The government press strikes of the early twentieth century were characterized by demands—especially among pieceworkers, a group that often included both lithographic scribes and bookbinders—for improved pay, forms of leave, and limitations on the fluctuations in the amount of work offered or assigned.[64] These strikes also pushed the administrators of government presses to investigate alternative sources of press labor.

For instance, following a large-scale strike at the government presses in Calcutta in 1905, colonial administrators sought to curtail the influence of press workers while also mitigating the effects of potential strikes on their government printing. To do so, they developed lithographic and typographic training schemes and programs in regional jails, not only in Bengal, but across the subcontinent.[65] Indeed, jail administrators had sought to secure income by developing printing as a jail industry as early as the 1840s, and jail printing had previously been heralded as a more affordable source of printing by the state. In Lahore, the city's courts moved all their vernacular lithographic printing to the Lahore Central Jail in 1895.[66] Reflecting the fact that both lithography and typography were physically demanding processes for workers, within Indian prisons they were categorized as "hard labor," alongside assignments such as "pounding bricks," "stone quarrying," and "road making," for able-bodied convicts.[67]

Likewise, for many nonscribal "mechanical" laborers outside of prisons, press work was dangerous, sometimes even deadly. For instance, at the Public Printing Press of Lahore in 1924, a "boy, while helping a machine-man repair a belt, was wrapped around the main shaft, with the result that his left arm and both legs were fractured." Transported to the hospital, he died later the same day.[68] The colonial notice of the boy's death in the annual factory report from Punjab was reflective of the widespread use of child labor in industrialized presses. The physical dangers presented by press work were cited as a complaint against management by some striking press laborers throughout the first three decades of the twentieth century, though they were usually portrayed as secondary to disputes over wages.[69]

PRESS PROPRIETORS AND NARRATIVES OF MUSLIM LITHOGRAPHIC LABOR

In response to rising agitation among press workers for improved wages and conditions from the early twentieth century, press proprietors increasingly sought to intervene in workers' narratives about the relationship between Islam and press work. Muslim press owners especially sought to engender forms of religious solidarity between their workers and management, sometimes even by co-opting and reorienting the language used by scribal communities and asserting a connection between Muslim piety and press labor for their workers.

Some proprietors—including Munshi Mahbub ʿAlam, who was the owner of one of the most prominent presses of turn-of-the-century Lahore—turned toward transregional models of Muslim piety in press labor, which they attempted to inculcate into their workers. Mahbub ʿAlam owned and managed the Khādim al-Ṭaʿlīm (Servant of Education) Press, which published several artisan and industrial manuals. The Khādim al-Ṭaʿlīm Press and Mahbub ʿAlam were also well known throughout Punjab for the publication of a popular weekly and daily newspaper titled *Paisah Akhbār* (Penny paper). Born into a landholding family in Gujranwala District, Mahbub ʿAlam began publishing from there around 1886, before moving himself and his press to Lahore in 1889. As its name suggested, the *Paisah Akhbār* was known for its low price. At its peak, just before the First World War, it had a daily circulation of approximately three thousand copies, with its weekly edition printing more than nine thousand copies.[70] These numbers made it among the most widely circulated vernacular weekly papers in Punjab in the period before the First World War.

Mahbub ʿAlam, like many other prominent publishers of North India, sought to develop a workforce that was well educated in lithographic work. He imagined this workforce as formed of pious, diligent, modern Muslims, and his publications reflect his efforts to find models for this ideal Muslim workforce beyond those in India. In 1908, he published a 970-page Urdu-language travelogue—portions of which had previously been serialized in his newspaper—chronicling his journey to the Paris Exposition Universelle of 1900, and his subsequent travels across Europe, Egypt, and elsewhere in the Ottoman Empire.[71] Throughout the travelogue, Mahbub ʿAlam expressed interest in the state of the press in the cities that he visited—from Vienna to Damascus—but he devoted the most energy to this topic during his stays in Istanbul and Cairo. This showed that those cities, and especially Cairo, were centers of consolidating transregional print industries, from which books and knowledge circulated through Muslim scholarly worlds, as well as broader political networks of Arabic readers.[72] Mahbub ʿAlam found a flourishing print culture, reliant upon engaged editors and what he saw as a well-trained, Muslim print labor force.[73]

Most impressed by Cairo, he wrote, "In comparison to India, there is a more developed tradition of printing and selling books." He observed that several presses, particularly those dedicated to religious texts, produced books that "exceeded the quality of those found in Europe." And he emphasized the high level of education among the proprietors of the city's newspapers, and the quality of the laborers that they employed, though he noted that lithography had fallen out of favor in the city, typography replacing it.[74] The more rapid transition to movable type in Istanbul and Cairo was due in part to state support and patronage for typographic presses, as well as limitations on private presses that may have chosen to use lithography for financial reasons.[75] At the same time, aesthetic considerations were different than in India, as producers of Arabic books and newspapers—and sometimes those in Ottoman Turkish—often used the *naskh* style of the script, rather than *nastaʿlīq*. *Naskh* is straighter and more angular than *nastaʿlīq* and does not feature the same sloping lines.[76] While early attempts at producing typographic *naskh* faced similar technical challenges as seen with *nastaʿlīq*, by the early twentieth century, improvements in the aesthetics of the typographic *naskh* script meant that many readers of Arabic embraced typed text.

Despite the differences in form and style of book production, Mahbub ʿAlam took away several lessons from the Cairo presses, including the importance of "good education" for "Muslim youths," who might seek employment in the presses. Describing a conversation with the editor of *al-Muʾayyid* (The restorer)—which, he mused, "might be the largest newspaper by Muslims in the world"—he noted that elementary education was widespread among young Egyptian Muslims and that "most are hardworking." He was cautioned by his interlocuters, however, that when "Muslim boys worked for the British or the French" before joining the presses, they were liable to develop bad habits, including "drinking and laziness."[77] Nonetheless, Mahbub ʿAlam left both Cairo and Istanbul with the impression that "the presses here are of higher quality than in India," as reflected by their large numbers of educated and industrious Muslim employees.[78]

Muslim educationalists also engaged with efforts of press proprietors such as Mahbub ʿAlam to develop a modern and pious Muslim workforce modeled on an idealized understanding of the industrial training of Muslim boys in places like Cairo and Istanbul. A 1914 report of the All-India Muslim Education Conference in Aligarh included scribal work and lithography in its discussion of "industrial" education for Muslims. A resolution passed at the conference that year encouraged "every Muslim workshop owner" to open up a "training class" to spur industrial education and employment opportunities, especially among working-class urban Muslims.[79] Presses were among the workshops and factories expected to undertake this endeavor.[80] For Mahbub ʿAlam and the educationalists of the Aligarh-based conference, training productive press workers would reflect a wider success of wealthy Muslims in conditioning poorer boys to be simultaneously pious and knowledgeable about modern industrial technologies and practices.

LITHOGRAPHIC LABOR AND EARLY TWENTIETH-CENTURY PRESS STRIKES

The efforts of Mahbub ʿAlam and other press proprietors to educate modern, moral, Muslim press workers does not seem to have engendered the hoped-for religious or social solidarity between management and labor in the context of Muslim-run presses. On the contrary, while Muslim industrialists sought to make use of press workers' religious traditions to undercut the emergence of class-based social identities, artisan and worker traditions remained distinct from those promulgated by the middle class. These traditions may have ultimately informed the emergence of organization and agitation for improved working conditions and pay among lithographic laborers.

Press strikes remained a major concern for both government and private presses throughout the 1910s and 1920s. For the most part, strikes at private, Indian-run presses were short-term agitations, usually organized without the formal backing of a union, often around a specific demand such as a wage increase. They often went largely unremarked in the colonial record, noted only in broad lists of strikes that had occurred within a given year.[81] In other cases, agitations among press workers, especially at smaller presses, were not categorized by the state as strikes at all. Instead, they were characterized as localized conflicts between workers' efforts to earn wages that matched the increasing costliness of life in North Indian cities and publishers' efforts to earn profits in a challenging economic environment. Nonetheless, the records of the 1910s and 1920s suggest a period in which private presses, like their government counterparts, were periodically shut down by conflicts over wages and treatment of workers.

By 1920, local Indian-run presses were engaged in tense showdowns with their "calligraphists" (scribes), machine-men, and printers over wages, and some reports portrayed the strikes as successful in improving the economic conditions of the workers.[82] In March of that year, for instance, the Indian director of Intelligence reported:

> The vernacular presses in Lahore, which had to face a strike of calligraphists, and a threatened strike of machine-men and printers, have given in to the calligraphists and machine-men. The wages of the latter have been increased by 25 percent, and of the former by 30 percent. The calligraphists are, however, still dissatisfied, for they wanted a raise of 100 percent. It is generally believed that they will get what they want. They only have to improve and consolidate their organization, and the owners of the vernacular papers will find it difficult to resist their demands.[83]

This report suggests a degree of shared struggles between scribes and other lithographic laborers, such as machine-men, while also revealing the widening economic and social distinctions between the groups. The higher level of organization among scribes reflects the fact that they continued to assert that they were a distinct category of press workers with a Muslim religious tradition, past, and piety that set them apart from other book producers. To an extent, this was not unique. Many other press workers were drawn from extant Muslim artisan communities. Even when members of these communities participated in wage labor in industrialized factories—including the presses—they often maintained both social and professional ties to familial or community workshops. Colonial industrial reports, such as a report on iron and steel work authored by the Anglo-Irish Indian Civil Service officer W. E. J. Dobbs in 1907, portrayed a marked divide between modern industrial laborers and the "traditional" independent artisan.[84] But as chapter 2 shows, artisans moved flexibly between different sites of labor, and their religious traditions for their work circulated with them.

As a result, many of the Muslim artisans who engaged in lithographic labor likely participated in the circulation of Muslim traditions for familial trades such as metalsmithing and carpentry. These included a religious tradition for blacksmiths that tied their labor to the Prophet Dawud and claimed that the ability to work with iron had been revealed to him by God, based on a reference to the thirty-fourth surah of the Quran: "We [God] softened iron for him [Dawud]."[85] Just as scribes relied on an Islamic idiom to assert a continuity for their trade after its incorporation into increasingly industrialized presses, it is likely that metalsmiths and other artisans also turned to the religious traditions of their familial or community trades to make sense of their role in the presses. These traditions are explored in chapters 2 and 5; it is important to note here that they circulated not only within workshops maintained by metalsmiths or other artisans themselves but also in a wide range of factories, including the various presses.

Assertions of community and social distinction based on religious traditions for their trades did not necessarily prevent scribal and nonscribal press workers from creating forms of solidarity within the presses. For many lithographic workers, the rising urban cost of living of the 1920s, followed by the economic depression of the 1930s and the accompanying stagnation in wages, meant that new forms of solidarity within the presses became vital to securing their livelihoods. To understand the contours and limitations of these solidarities, I return now to the Lahore lithographic strike of 1935. I explore the ways in which the social context of the lithographic presses in the city shaped press workers' efforts to improve their wages and working conditions.

LITHOGRAPHIC LABOR AND THE LAHORE PRESS STRIKES OF 1935

The Khādim al-Ṭaʿlīm Press and its *Paisah Akhbār* had receded in prominence in Lahore in the years following the First World War. They were replaced by new Urdu-language daily newspapers and large-scale presses. Among the most prominent of these was the *Zamīndār*, a popular daily newspaper that had a daily circulation of approximately 7,500 copies in 1935.[86] To a greater degree than the *Paisah Akhbār* before it, the *Zamīndār* aroused the frequent consternation of Lahore's colonial administration. In intelligence reports, it was characterized as a "troublesome pan-Islamic paper" with an "attitude of antagonism" toward the government, and administrators expressed regular concern about its high level of popularity among Muslim readers. Zafar ʿAli Khan, the proprietor of the paper, was repeatedly arrested throughout the 1920s. He was accused of "inciting feelings of enmity" between Hindus and Muslims. He was also routinely surveilled for his promotion of Khilafat movement (1919–24) agitations, which advocated for the authority of the Ottoman caliph in the wake of the First World War and allied with the Indian National Congress in its calls for independence.[87]

The contributions of Zafar ʿAli Khan and the *Zamīndār* to the development of the Urdu press in Punjab have received significant scholarly attention, especially among historians of Pakistan.[88] Usually unremarked, however, is the fact that throughout the 1920s and 1930s, the *Zamīndār* was also rocked by a series of strikes among its press workers. In his publications, Zafar ʿAli Khan sometimes broadly aligned himself with the causes of Indian labor, even delivering lectures in support of striking workers during the large-scale Lahore railway strike of 1920.[89] However, as Ahmad Azhar points out, Zafar ʿAli Khan's relationship with labor agitation was always complicated. He aligned with striking workers when he thought they might contribute to the weakening of the local colonial political regime, but also occasionally expressed disdain for workers' demands for higher wages. In one significant speech, he cautioned Muslim workers that seeking "bread, at the cost of forsaking God, could only be a source of shame and ill-fortune."[90]

Unlike the *Paisah Akhbār*, which had been printed at the associated Khādim al-Ṭaʿlīm Press throughout its run, the *Zamīndār* rolled off various presses throughout the city, in part because, beginning in 1913, Zafar ʿAli Khan's own presses were repeatedly confiscated.[91] For much of the 1920s, the newspaper was printed at the Muslim Printing Press, and in the 1930s, at the Mansur Steam Press.[92] A cadre of scribes employed as pieceworkers moved between the presses that produced the newspaper, while other laborers, both scribal and nonscribal, were brought on by the presses themselves. In April-May 1935, scribes associated with the *Zamīndār* paper, as well as scribes and other laborers employed by both the Muslim Printing Press and the Mansur Steam Press, all engaged in strikes, suggesting the mobility of workers between the two presses and the paper.

Colonial reports did not note the outcome of the April-May 1935 lithographic strike. Indeed, colonial administrators seemed largely unconcerned about the frequent strikes among the workers at private, Indian-owned lithographic presses, except insofar as these strikes provided an opportunity for the expansion of regional and all-Indian trade unions. While these administrators saw labor as a potential threat and Muslim political and social identity as existing threats, they also posed a false dichotomy between laboring and Muslim identities. The so-called Muslim press was treated as synonymous with the interests of middle-class proprietors such as Zafar ʿAli Khan. It was seen as a threat because of its potential to spur forms of transregional political association and attachment to alternative authorities that undermined the British Empire.

Muslim press workers were subsumed within this state discourse of the threat posed by (often elite) Muslim political action. Their distinct economic and political interests and forms of labor agitation were ignored, except in the rare cases—like the Lahore press strike—when prominent leftist groups asserted solidarity with them. State reports in the wake of the Khilafat movement suggested that Muslim workers' primary allegiances were to their coreligionists, including their managers, and that any "threat" they posed to the state or status quo was rooted in their

Muslim-ness, not their laboring identities. In doing so, these reports overlooked the potential for workers' Muslim traditions to contribute to class-based solidarities and agitations against management.

Still, in the 1930s, lithographic labor strikes were occasionally the subjects of colonial correspondence when they attracted support from leftist political organizations and unions. M. G. Hallett, then secretary for the Home Department, was concerned about the spread of communist ideology within regional unions. He compiled extensive police reports on the activities of the Punjab Press Workers' Association, which held a meeting that year in Amritsar. They expressed concern that this union, founded in 1928, was influenced by the regional leaders of the Naujawan Bharat Sabha (Youth Society of India), a leftist organization founded by the prominent revolutionary Bhagat Singh before his execution in 1931.[93] During the 1935 union meeting in Amritsar, members passed resolutions in support of the striking workers. Police reports fretted, moreover, that Punjab press strikes might be influenced by an aspiring all-India union, the Lal Bavta (Red Flag) Press Union. Founded in Bombay in 1934, the union was accused of "bring[ing] about lightning strikes in printing presses without any justification," though the same police reports admitted that its influence seemed to be geographically limited.[94]

Despite efforts from the Punjab Press Workers' Association to engage the striking lithographic laborers, colonial administrative concern about the spread of well-organized trade unionism in the lithographic presses was usually misplaced. Labor agitation among the workers at Urdu-language presses was characterized by short-term small-scale agitations in the 1920s and 1930s rather than popular participation in large, all-India, or regional unions. The lithographic workers' lack of enthusiasm for all-India and regional unions reflected what Dipesh Chakrabarty has framed as a central "paradox" of labor organization and agitation in colonial India. Despite high levels of worker militancy and frequent strikes, most workers did not join unions, and the unions they did join were often "unstable," meaning they formed and collapsed from year to year.[95]

However, at least one new union did emerge from the Lahore lithographic strikes, suggesting the continued hierarchies of labor within the presses. The *kātibs*' union, specifically for scribes, was formed under the auspices of the Punjab Press Workers' Association. Though small, its presence suggested a wider recognition of scribes' claims to social and laboring distinctiveness. Indeed, scribal strikes and labor organization remained a feature of the Urdu print economy even after the gradual popular shift to typography beginning in the mid-twentieth century. In 1989, the *New York Times* featured a short article on the lithographic scribes of Delhi, titled "Calling Strike, Urdu Scribes Sheathe Pens."[96] Over fifty years after the Lahore lithographic strike, and more than a century after Karimullah Khan composed the *Daftar-i khaṭṭāṭ*, the small number of remaining Indian Urdu scribes continued to argue for their community's social distinctiveness and to agitate for improved wages and conditions.

• • •

Did the shifting assertions about the Muslim nature of scribal work matter for the striking lithographic workers of Lahore? The broader form of this question—the degree to which artisan Islam informed trade-based, and even class-based identities—underscores several of the subsequent chapters in this book. In the case of lithographic workers, and especially scribes, artisan Islam mattered but not necessarily in the ways we might expect. Contrary to the hopes of press proprietors like Zafar ʿAli Khan and Mahbub ʿAlam, shared Muslim identity did not seem to create a significant level of solidarity between Muslim press proprietors and their primarily Muslim labor force. Instead, narratives of a Muslim tradition for scribes expanded the potential social and educational backgrounds from which scribes were drawn, even as they also drew boundaries around the traditions of their work, excluding nonscribal lithographic laborers. Though lithographic scribes agitated against press management in conjunction with nonscribal labor cadres, they also argued that their skill and its rootedness in a Muslim tradition of textual production set them apart from other press workers. In an increasingly industrialized lithographic context, where a diminishing percentage of scribes could claim prestigious lineages of training, a shared connection to a distinctly scribal Muslim tradition created a new space for scribes to assert the bonds and boundaries of their trade.

Unlike many of the other Muslim traditions of work that are analyzed in this book, scribal claims on a Muslim tradition were often acknowledged and accepted by other Muslims in the region. When the 1824 *Taẕkirah-yi khūshnavīsān* was published in 1910—unusually, through movable type—by the Asiatic Society in Calcutta, it included an extensive introduction by Muhammad Hidayat Husain, a Persian professor at Calcutta's Presidency College. Hidayat Husain embraced the text's claims on an Islamic prophetic tradition for scribes. Arabic script, he reiterated, was created and perfected through prophetic intervention, beginning with Adam and Idris.[97] Likewise, he claimed that proper knowledge of the script was circulated by early Muslims in the generations following the Prophet Muhammad's death.[98]

In a similar way, trade union organizers in Lahore seem to have recognized scribes' claims on distinctiveness within the presses. In calling for a union for *kātib*s, the leaders of the Punjab Press Workers' Association characterized scribes as a distinct class of workers. This could be interpreted as recognition of their economic distinctiveness, given that many—though not all—lithographic scribes were pieceworkers. But other lithographic press workers were sometimes also employed or paid by the piece. Even if the organizers of the Punjab Press Workers'

Association had limited interest in the Muslim traditions of scribes, they recognized the boundaries of the trade, which scribes had asserted for themselves through Islam.

Ultimately, then, scribes' claims on the Muslim nature of their work shaped their social identities and forms of solidarity and collaboration within the emerging hierarchies of labor in lithographic presses. Hierarchies between scribes who could claim prestigious educational lineages and those who had trained primarily within the presses persisted well into the twentieth century. But the artisan Islam of scribes offered a narrative of connection and a social bond between lithographic scribes, creating a trade-based identity through which forms of agitation for improved pay and working conditions were eventually organized. In the subsequent chapter, we will examine a narrative of connection and social bonds centered on a specific technology—electroplating—to ask how Muslim artisan communities subverted middle-class and elite claims, not only on the economy, but on scientific and technical knowledge.

2

Electroplating as Alchemy

Labor and Technology among Muslim Metalsmiths

THE PUZZLES OF LATE NINETEENTH-CENTURY ELECTROPLATING MANUALS

> Plating [metals] is the best of all crafts.
> The goldsmith is confounded by it, the alchemist astonished.
> Tin, copper, and iron, quicksilver, lead, and bronze,
> Zinc and silver . . . in a flash, it made them all like gold.
> Oh scholars! The transformative ion, which changes shapes and forms
> Is beyond philosophical intellect![1]

These verses concluded an 1872 Urdu-language manual on the technology of electroplating, published in the North Indian city of Meerut by the Hāshmī Press, a small regional press. The text, titled *Tuḥfah-yi talmī*ʿ *bah-kharbāyī* (The gift of plating through electricity), explained how to create a thin metal coating over another material—usually another metal—through electrolysis, or the use of an electric current generated using a water-based solution.

Authored by Hafiz Anwar ʿAli, who described himself as a retired court inspector in the North-Western Provinces and a "master in the industrial arts," the *Tuḥfah-yi talmī*ʿ informed its readers that electroplating was "common knowledge" among metalworkers in Europe.[2] Through sixty pages of description, it explained how to prepare an aqua regia (nitrohydrocloric acid) solution to dissolve metals for gilding and plating, and how to clean and scrape the metal that one intended to plate. It described the properties of metals ranging from platinum to copper and from tin to gold. And although the text was not extensively illustrated, it featured a few small sketches of how to create and use a battery and how to transfer electric current to transfer the metal-plating.[3]

The *Tuḥfah-yi talmī*ʿ is among the earliest works in a small surge in Urdu-language publishing about electroplating. This took place roughly between 1870 and 1910 but was most concentrated between 1870 and 1900, when at least seven Urdu publications wholly or partially on electroplating were released in the North-Western Provinces and Punjab alone.[4] The existence of these late nineteenth-century Urdu electroplating manuals, many published from relatively provincial cities—Meerut city was home to about eighty thousand people as of 1872—presents a puzzle. Contrary to what might be suggested by the flurry of publishing on the topic, electroplating was not widely used as an industrial technology before the turn of the century. Colonial reports suggest that in Meerut there were no major electroplating firms before 1890, despite the fact that the city was known for its manufacture of scissors, the handles of which were often plated with gold, brass, and later nickel.[5] Instead, a few metalsmiths—likely about five to ten in Meerut—used electroplating to meet European demand for electroplated cutlery and dinnerware, and may have occasionally been employed by scissor makers as well.[6] And even in more industrialized cities such as Amritsar and Kanpur, colonial reports suggest that approximately fifteen to twenty workers per city regularly practiced electroplating before 1890.[7]

Why, then, did presses across the North-Western Provinces and Punjab print hundreds of copies of electroplating manuals and periodicals? Who were the audiences for these materials, and why, if there was not an especially large-scale electroplating industry, were they so interested in learning about electroplating? A second mystery presented by these electroplating publications may help us solve the first. One of the most notable aspects of the materials, regardless of where they were published, is that many speak to an explicitly Muslim audience. The framing of the texts, with occasional references to Quran or hadith and frequent references to the revelation of knowledge for Muslims by God, suggests that the authors expected their audiences to be Muslim and to understand the practice of electroplating through a lens of Islam. Several, like the *Tuḥfah-yi talmī*ʿ, also claimed that electroplaters had taken up or improved on the work of *kīmiyāgar*s—alchemists in the Islamic tradition. In the context of nineteenth-century North India, where Urdu publications attracted readers from a wide array of religious backgrounds, why did the authors of most electroplating manuals assume a relationship between Muslims and electroplating?

The answers to these questions offer insight into the class and social dynamics of Muslim artisan workers and a consolidating class of Indian Muslim capitalists in colonial-era India. They suggest that these communities used references to Islam and the Muslim past to explain and make sense of technological change in their industries. But equally, and perhaps more importantly, they suggest that knowledge of new industrial and artisanal technologies became a mark of social status, a way of asserting one's positionality within the class and social hierarchies among North Indian Muslims. As these social hierarchies were reinscribed and reified through both colonial policy and the consolidation of a Muslim middle class, metalsmithing communities asserted engagement with technologies like electroplating for themselves to contest their social and economic marginalization.

In the case of the *Tuḥfah-yi talmī'*, a careful reading suggests that it was not, in fact, intended for use among artisan metalsmithing communities. Instead, it reflected the efforts of members of the Muslim middle class, such as Anwar 'Ali himself, to assert their command over technology, science, and industry, and the ability of Urdu to communicate scientific knowledge representative of colonial modernity.[8] But within fifteen years of the publication of the earliest Urdu electroplating manuals such as the *Tuḥfah-yi talmī'*, artisan metalworkers began to claim the technology for themselves through electroplating manuals aimed at laboring audiences.[9] They engaged with some of the same language, imagining themselves as the *kīmiyāgar*s of industrial modernity. They played on the fact that *kīmiyā*, in Urdu, references both classical alchemy and modern chemistry to assert their simultaneous command over colonial-era technologies and regional Muslim pasts. At the same time, they also subverted the middle-class norms of earlier manuals and instead asserted the Muslim piety inherent in the physical skill of artisan communities.

• • •

Most of the chapters in *Pious Labor* trace how artisans asserted Islamic narratives about their trades from within their own communities. They frame middle-class engagement with artisan narratives as secondary to artisans' own understandings of their Muslim pasts. In this chapter, however, I tell a more complicated story of the interpenetration of middle-class and artisan understandings of Islam and technology. Dhruv Raina and S. Irfan Habib have argued that in the nineteenth century, middle-class Indian practitioners of science "subvert[ed], contaminate[d] and reorganize[d] the ideology of science as introduced by Europe."[10] Through a study of electroplating manuals, I argue that processes of "ideological subversion" took place not only at the level of global scientific transfer but in a context of religious- and class-based claims on technologies.

In its earliest use in South Asia, electroplating was not limited to industrial applications. It was also pursued as a hobby by members of the emerging Indian middle class, who used it as evidence of their command over technological modernity. When a small number of Indian Muslim artisan metalsmiths were commissioned to electroplate beginning in the 1860s and 1870s, it is unlikely that they initially framed their work using the narratives of electroplating promulgated in publications such as the *Tuḥfah-yi talmī'*. Instead, they more likely engaged with Muslim oral traditions for metalsmithing and manual plating that circulated within their hereditary and trade communities.[11] However, between the 1880s and 1910s, the practice of electroplating in India slowly expanded, moving from niche art to an important if still limited part of the industrial economy in many North Indian cities. In this context, both the audience and contents of electroplating manuals changed. Increasingly these manuals addressed metalworkers. To do so, they connected electroplating to artisan religious and material worlds, rearticulating middle-class narratives as a form of artisan Islam.

The Muslim artisan metalsmiths who engaged with electroplating reimagined middle-class Muslim narratives about electroplating for themselves and positioned Muslim artisans and laborers as the natural inheritors of new material and technical practices. Texts aimed at artisan metalworking communities framed these workers as the alchemists of industrial modernity, in command of the alchemy of the past and the chemistry of the future. At the same time, they integrated electroplating with extant community histories, embodied skills, and Muslim traditions. This chapter thus focuses on the capaciousness of artisan Islam and its ability to reorient middle-class narratives about technological change.

As we explore throughout this book, middle-class Muslims sometimes viewed artisan Islam as a threat to their understanding of a normative or orthodox religious practice. But Muslim artisans demonstrated a flexibility and an ability to reimagine middle-class narratives for emerging industrial technologies in conversation with their own, extant traditions for their trades. Whereas the earliest electroplating publications, including the *Tuḥfah-yi talmī*ʿ, appear to have addressed primarily members of an emerging industrial-capitalist class, beginning in the 1880s electroplating manuals explicitly addressed artisan metalworkers. One of the most significant shifts in this period was the use of verse to communicate knowledge about electroplating and the rise of texts that were written to be read aloud, circulating through overlapping practices of literacy and orality within workshops and factories. These shifts suggest new intended audiences and an adaptation of electroplating publications to speak to the social and class interests of Muslim artisan communities.

Following an analysis of electroplating manuals, their contents, and their intended audiences, the chapter turns to the experiences of one specific community of urban artisans and laborers who engaged with electroplating. It focuses on manufacturers of surgical tools in Sialkot, a city in Punjab near the border with the princely state of Jammu and Kashmir. Like Meerut, Sialkot was a midsized city with regional renown in specific forms of metalsmithing. But in Sialkot, the electroplating industry grew far more rapidly than elsewhere in Punjab or the North-Western Provinces. While exploring why this was the case, I ask how local Muslim traditions surrounding metalwork intersected with new claims on electroplating in Sialkot. I demonstrate that electroplating manuals became part of the movement of workers and ideas between industrialized and home-based workshops. Through this culture of mobility and flexibility, Muslim metalsmiths circulated intersecting religious narratives, community identities, and forms of technological expertise.

HISTORIES OF (ELECTRO)PLATING IN SOUTH ASIA

To understand the history of electroplating in South Asia, including its circulation and use among Muslim artisans and laborers, we must weave together two stories. The first is that of the technological experimentation that enabled the use of an electric current for metal-plating and the emergence of electroplating as a commercial trade globally. The second is a far longer history of metal-plating and gilding in South Asia. Electroplating texts aimed at members of the Indian middle class—rather than artisans and laborers—often portrayed electroplating as an abrupt break with earlier practices of plating. They connected electroplating not to an extant artisan tradition but to the experiments of either Europeans or precolonial scientists and alchemists with connections to Muslim courts. Conversely, those manuals that spoke to artisan metalworkers explained electroplating and electrometallurgy as part of a continuum of plating practices, suggesting that workshops and workers might choose from a variety of methods that included—but were not limited to—electroplating.

The earliest attempts to plate metals using an electric current took place in Italy using the recently invented voltaic pile battery around the turn of the nineteenth century. Experiments throughout the 1820s and 1830s focused on improving the consistency of the voltaic battery's currents and the solutions in which plating took place, to make electroplating commercially viable.[12] The first patents on the technology of electroplating were granted in Birmingham in 1840 to artisan-inventors who plated and gilded toys and trinkets. Iwan Rhys Morus has shown that in the wake of these patents, electricity became "an agent of mass production" in Britain.[13] The technology was embraced by producers and consumers globally beginning in the 1850s and 1860s, with articles in *Scientific American* highlighting its widespread adoption in North America.[14] Reflecting middle-class aspiration, electroplating became popular because it allowed increased access to household consumer goods such as cutlery that appeared similar to those used by the wealthy. The ability to rapidly create thin coatings of gold and silver meant that popular, relatively inexpensive goods were now more difficult to distinguish from their costly counterparts made entirely of precious metals.[15]

The earliest reference to electroplating that I have found in the British Indian colonial archive is a mention of a European-run electroplating workshop in Calcutta in 1856.[16] Indian-made electroplated items were displayed at regional arts and industrial exhibitions from at least 1864.[17] As was the case in Bengal, the earliest commercial electroplating enterprises in the North-Western Provinces and Punjab were managed by Europeans, though reliant on Indian workers. Among the most notable was a workshop in Sialkot, run by a European medical officer identified as Mr. W. Spence who recruited local workers skilled in inlay and manual gilding to electroplate surgical instruments. These surgical instruments were displayed at the Punjab Exhibition of Arts and Industries, held in Lahore in 1864, where they won several awards and were praised as reflective of the potential of Indian workmen to embrace electroplating.[18]

As suggested by the fact that Spence recruited workers from local gilding and inlay workshops to his new electroplating enterprise, it is of course possible to plate and gild metals without battery power or an electric current. Indeed, several South Asian metalsmithing communities were, by the mid-nineteenth century, well known for their skill in manual plating and gilding. These included Kashmiri metalworkers, many of whom migrated to Punjabi cities such as Sialkot, Lahore,

Amritsar, and Gujranwala in the nineteenth century, establishing Kashmiri neighborhoods across the region.[19] Other metalworkers who were praised in colonial writing for their abilities in plating included *koftgar*s, artisans who damascened or inlaid steel with gold. While metal-plating and *koftgarī* are different processes, artisans skilled in *koftgarī* were often also commissioned to plate metal wares, as many of the skills overlapped. *Koftgar*s sometimes turned to plating in periods of decreased demand for *koftgarī* or practiced the two skills alongside each other. The processes that these manual platers and gilders used varied based on the metals used. But the common methods included scratching a surface of copper or iron with checked lines, washing it with an acidic solution made from dried, unripe apricots, heating it or applying mercury, and then applying a layer of gold, silver, or other metal "leaf" as plating.[20]

A third, and perhaps the most numerous, community of artisans who engaged in manual plating were *qal'īgar*s, or tinners. Unlike *koftgar*s and Kashmiri gilders and platers, *qal'īgar*s were not characterized as especially skilled or worthy of artisanal prestige in colonial reports. On the contrary, they were depicted as particularly tradition bound and resistant to technological and material change. Nonetheless, they played an important role in the Indian economy because copper and brass cups, plates, and pots are often not safe for use unless plated with tin, a process that was usually carried out monthly by a *qal'īgar*.[21] In cities and towns, *qal'īgar*s often maintained mobile workshops. Their process of tin plating involved cleaning utensils with hydrochloric acid, heating and coating them with ammonium chloride, and finally melting tin over the surface and polishing it.[22]

MUSLIM TRADITIONS FOR METALWORK

Across India, metalwork—including plating—was rarely associated exclusively with a single religious community. Muslims, Hindus, Sikhs, and Christians all worked in some of the largest metalworking trades, including blacksmithing, copper work, and brass work. While most *koftgar*s, *qal'īgar*s, and others known for plating in Punjab and the North-Western Provinces identified as Muslim, they participated in a wider economy of metalsmithing that accommodated many religious practices and beliefs.[23]

Colonial records also portrayed metalworking trades as especially flexible in terms of caste identity. They argued that although *lohār* served as a caste term for Hindu, Sikh, and Muslim blacksmiths, people from other artisan and agricultural caste backgrounds often took up metalwork, especially as they migrated into urban areas. Likewise, they noted that *lohār* as a term was often used as a caste category by smiths who worked with a wide range of metals in addition to iron. As in the case of tailors discussed in chapter 3, the flexible engagement with this marker of caste and social identity, especially among Muslims but also among some

Hindu-identified artisans, sparked occasional colonial consternation. It upset what Joel Lee has referred to as the "state regime of recognition," projects meant to enumerate stable religious, caste, and social categories.[24]

The variety of religious identities within metalworking trades, combined with the relative flexibility of the caste category of *lohār*, also informed colonial ethnographic depictions of metalworkers as religiously unorthodox and marginal members of their traditions. In the case of Muslim metalworkers, one report from Sialkot—where nearly all metalworkers identified as Muslim—characterized metalsmiths and other urban artisans as "followers of the Prophet only in name. They circumcise their children and repeat the creed [*kalima*], but they continue to pay respect to local deities, and employ a Brahmin priest in their social ceremonies."[25]

But the Muslim metalworkers of urban North India did not portray themselves as marginal, unorthodox, or corrupted Muslims. Their traditions for their trade reflected an explicit self-identification with Islam. Among these, the only one regularly recognized in colonial ethnographic writing was an association between blacksmithing and the Prophet Dawud, referenced in the introduction to this book. Most ethnographic writing attributed this to the thirty-fourth surah of the Quran (*Saba'*), which asserts that God "soften[ed] iron" for Dawud and compelled him to take up the art of making "coats of chain mail."[26]

Despite the primacy given to this narrative in the colonial archive, it was not the only way in which Muslim metalsmiths—including manual platers—asserted Muslim religious and social identities and a connection between their trade and Islam. In many cases, their traditions for their trade were tied to local Sufi shrines or saints and were asserted for specific practices within metalwork. As Hussain Ahmad Khan has shown in the case of Punjab, from at least the twelfth century, "Sufis became part of artisan communities, and used a particular vocabulary related to their professional practices to attract colleagues and followers, who popularized Sufis' ideas in their respective communities."[27] For instance, in Lahore, a mid-sixteenth-century tomb honors Sheikh Musa "Ahangar," ("blacksmith" in Persian) a blacksmith-saint who died early in the reign of the Mughal emperor Akbar.[28] Many Sufi lineages in Punjab and the North-Western Provinces underwent financial transformations between the sixteenth and eighteenth centuries by cultivating patronage and support from large landlords or expanding their own landholdings. This meant that by the nineteenth century few lineages remained engaged in the practice of artisanship, though, as Khan has shown, they retained ties to artisan communities through systems of patronage and as the hosts of fairs.[29] In turn, artisan communities often asserted localized traditions about the connections between specific shrines or saints and their trades.

These localized traditions often circulated orally, and they are not well attested in either the colonial or Urdu-language archives. However, many persist—perhaps in an adapted form—through the present day. In a 1999 study, anthropologist Alain

Lefebvre noted oral histories among blacksmiths and carpenters in modern Pakistani Punjab, in the region that includes Sialkot and Gujranwala, two cities that became important centers of electroplating by the turn of the twentieth century.[30] These oral histories center on a Sufi *pīr* called Shura Sharif and attribute the spread and settlement of Muslim blacksmiths throughout the province to his influence. They assert, via the community's connection with the *pīr*, an association with the Mughal state and its patronage. Moreover, they position metalworkers and carpenters as responsible for the conversion of other Punjabi communities to Islam through their association with the *pīr*.[31] These oral traditions reflect a practice of artisan community self-assertion and self-definition through the claiming of Muslim pasts. Their persistence in regional oral histories illustrates that claims on the past circulated orally within artisan communities, both before and after the rise of print.

ELECTROPLATING AND THE MUSLIM MIDDLE CLASS

As noted in the introduction to this chapter, the *Tuḥfah-yi talmīʿ*, among the earliest electroplating manuals in North India, was not intended primarily for audiences of artisans. To that end, it made no reference to the religious traditions and Muslim pasts asserted by metalsmiths. Likewise, it made limited reference to the skills or practices of manual platers, portraying electroplating as innovative and as a break with past practices of plating. To the degree that it did consider pasts for electroplating, it focused on the European inventors of the technology, not regional artisan practices.[32] In contrast, later electroplating manuals explicitly rooted electroplating within a longer tradition and practice of plating, seeking to build on and reference workers' extant metal-plating skills to explain the process of plating through electrolysis.

A treatise published two years before the *Tuḥfah-yi talmīʿ*, titled *Risālah-yi fan-i talmīʿ* (Treatise on the art of plating), printed in Gujranwala in central Punjab in 1870, similarly highlighted the interest of middle-class hobbyists and aspiring capitalists in electroplating. Published by the Gyan Press, a local press, the ten-page publication was framed as a special issue of a local Urdu periodical on the arts and sciences. In an introduction, its authors described themselves as two local "captains of capital" named Ramzan ʿAli and Qamaruddin Khan.[33] They spoke to the interests of an emerging class of Punjabi Muslim capitalists who aimed to use their knowledge of new technologies to employ artisan laborers, not necessarily to engage in artisan work themselves.

The periodical introduced the technology of electroplating before shifting to a question-answer format that allowed the authors to highlight their technical expertise. Questions such as "How does one prepare sulfuric acid and what are its uses?" focused on the types of materials a workshop would need to provide to employ workers in electroplating.[34] The questions chosen suggest that the authors saw knowledge of electroplating as a marker of engagement with models of industrial capitalism but that they did not necessarily expect most of their readers to individually practice the trade beyond the level of a hobbyist's experimentation.

Around the mid-nineteenth century a "new middle class" of Indian Muslims asserted their social distinction from both the working class and courtly elites.[35] In portraying themselves as "captains of capital," Ramzan ʿAli and Qamaruddin Khan situated themselves as representatives of this emerging Muslim middle class of what Margrit Pernau termed "upwardly mobile traders and merchants," who expressed pride in their professions and their claims on "self-improvement."[36] And the authors positioned electroplating as one of many new scientific, technological, or industrial breakthroughs in which an educated Muslim capitalist should be proficient by publishing their work as a special issue of a magazine that targeted Urdu readers with a general interest in "the sciences and the arts."[37]

In this context, references to Islam and Muslim piety in the *Risālah-yi fan-i talmīʿ* read not only as a framing device but also as an assertion of social positionality. The authors explained, in their introductory comments, that they had "turned to God the granter of success, placing trust in him alone," in their attempt to "understand the great and small work of electroplating." In doing so, they connected their piety as Muslims to their dedication to industrial and technological knowledge. They framed their work as bettering the Muslim community, not only materially but also spiritually, explaining that they had "taken up the pen of truth" to enlighten "anyone who searched for knowledge."[38]

Similarly, in the Meeruti *Tuḥfah-yi talmīʿ*, the author, Hafiz Anwar ʿAli, described himself as a retired court inspector for the North-Western Provinces who had developed an interest in the industrial development of his city and region. He wrote for the consolidating middle class who increasingly asserted ownership and authority over urban artisan workshops and factories. The work may also have been aimed at his own class of Indian government workers who sought, not necessarily to own a workshop, but rather to demonstrate an interest in what the state termed "industrial arts" as a marker of their own technological modernity. The *Tuḥfah-yi talmīʿ*—like its contemporary the *Risālah-yi fan-i talmīʿ*—is thus suggestive of Projit Mukharji's argument that "members of the colonial middle class were engaged in class-identity formation by consuming small technologies."[39] They reflect the fact that not only consumption of technologies but also consumption of knowledge about technology became central to class identity for many middle-class Indians.

These texts aimed to adapt what their authors consciously framed as "European" knowledge not only into the Urdu language but also into the religious and social idiom of the Muslim middle class. They sought to demonstrate that members of this class were simultaneously the inheritors of Muslim tradition and promoters of an Indian Muslim future. Reflecting his claims to an Indian adaptation or reimagination of a European modernity, Anwar ʿAli explained in his introduction that his goal was to bring "knowledge that is common in Europe" to India.[40] Written in a high register of Urdu, Anwar ʿAli's text aimed to explain the scientific properties of electroplating to hobbyists, aspiring industrialists, and other interested members of his own class. A careful reader may have been able to use his text to practice electroplating, but like the *Risālah-yi fan-i talmī*ʿ, it featured only a small number of visual aids and was aimed primarily at communicating principles, not practices.[41]

NEW CONTENT AND FORM IN ELECTROPLATING MANUALS

Not all electroplating manuals and treatises spoke to this same middle-class audience. Within about a decade—by the early 1880s—the authors of electroplating manuals increasingly addressed the artisan metalworkers who would be responsible for plating metals in a workshop. These new manuals focused on the physical practice of the work, with particular attention to explaining how to set up and use a homemade battery to create an electric current and comparing solutions used to plate different metals. In addition, many of these manuals referenced practices of plating and gilding that were common in India and did not rely on an electric current, portraying electroplating as part of a continuum of regional metalworking practices. Rather than asserting the trade as a technological breakthrough—engagement with which demonstrated the social and class distinction of middle-class Muslim capitalists—the manuals increasingly claimed a technological prowess for metalworkers by highlighting fluidity between different practices of plating and gilding. In doing so, they suggested that it would be possible for artisan workers to integrate electroplating into their extant religious traditions and material practices.

Shifts in the content of electroplating manuals were accompanied by shifts in the form of the books. Manuals increasingly incorporated detailed drawings illustrating the work of an electroplater, as well as versified descriptions of the practice. Versification in electroplating manuals likely contributed to the circulation of the texts beyond the realm of the written word, allowing platers in regional workshops and factories to communicate knowledge about the trade to each other despite limited literacy. Versified content was not limited to praise of the trade or to efforts to root it in a cultural context, as was the case in the concluding verses of the *Tuḥfah-yi talmī*ʿ that spoke of the "confounded goldsmith" and the "astonished alchemist."[42] Instead, versification was used to explain technical and material practices. The *Jāmaʿ-yi tarākīb-i talmī*ʿ (Collection of types of plating), an 1880 manual on electroplating published in Lucknow, was written entirely in

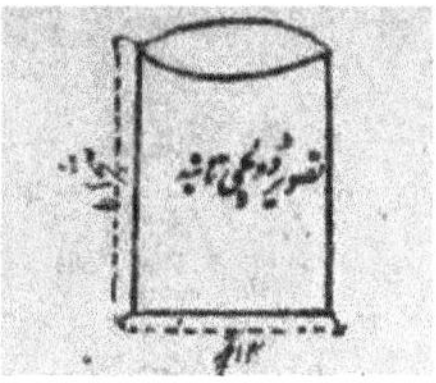

FIGURE 3. A small sketch showing the height and width of a small copper container for electroplating, from Jawaharlal Shaida's *Jāma ʿ-yi tarākīb-i talmī ʿ* (Lucknow: Naval Kishore Press, 1880). (Rekhta)

FIGURE 4. A sketch of an electroplater from Jawaharlal Shaida's *Jāma ʿ-yi tarākīb-i talmī ʿ* (Lucknow: Naval Kishore Press, 1880), with labels on the battery and tools for the plating process. (Rekhta)

verse and featured detailed sketches and diagrams. In an early section titled "On How to Make Batteries," it described how to prepare the copper rods needed to make a copper-zinc battery, framing the verses around a small sketch of the copper vessel (figure 3):

> Make this small container from copper
> Form it just like the shape below:
> The diameter should be at least four inches
> And its height should be nine inches, oh dignified one,
> Then make a single flower stem of copper
> But such that each part of this stem is flattened
> And as for its length, oh trustworthy one,
> It must be four inches . . .[43]

The verses proceed in this manner, offering electroplaters exact dimensions for their batteries, as well as descriptions of how to connect the wires to both the battery and the material to be plated (figure 4).[44] When the manual was published, a large-scale electroplating industry in Lucknow had yet to be established. According to colonial reports, a small number of workmen regularly used electroplating in the region, primarily to plate cutlery for European demand.[45] But the publication suggests that despite this lack of a large-scale regional electroplating industry, electroplating manuals increasingly addressed artisans who engaged more directly in metalwork and plating.

SOCIALLY AND RELIGIOUSLY PLURAL AUDIENCES FOR ELECTROPLATING MANUALS

In addition to its versification, the *Jāma ʿ-yi tarākīb-i talmī ʿ* is notable as the only Urdu electroplating manual of the late nineteenth century—that I have identified so far—that was authored by a non-Muslim. The text was attributed to an author named Jawaharlal, who used the *takhalluṣ* (pen name) Shaida, meaning "lover," for his poetry and identified himself as a member of the "community of Bhatnagar Kayasthas."[46] Like Anwar ʿAli, Shaida was a government employee, though instead of serving the British Raj he worked for the princely state of Udaipur. And whereas Anwar ʿAli was a court inspector who had developed an interest in industry and technology as a hobby and marker of social status, Shaida was an employee of the Engineering Department of Udaipur. He notes in his introduction that he "saw a need" for expanded knowledge of electroplating because of his supervision of government technical projects in Udaipur.[47] Published by the Naval Kishore Press, a prominent Lucknavi press discussed in chapter 1, Shaida's text was likely intended for a religiously, socially, and economically mixed audience.

Reflecting the social and economic plurality of its intended audience, the text spoke to and for both members of the emerging middle class and metalworkers themselves. The versification of the text suggests that Shaida may have sought to demonstrate a courtly ideal of the poet/state employee, a model of which has been explored extensively in the Mughal context in Rajiv Kinra's scholarship.[48] To this end, Shaida sought to demonstrate his command of both industrial knowledge and poetic forms to his own class of state employees and industrial or technical overseers. At the same time, versification reflects the potential for oral circulation of the text among laboring communities. The text's rhyming verses suggest an effort to make the information easy to memorize and to repeat. Indeed, in his introduction, Shaida claimed that his text provided more details, in a more beautiful and accessible form, than other electroplating texts.[49]

Shaida's engagement with references to God likewise suggests a broad intended audience, made up not only of people from differing social and class backgrounds but also of readers—or listeners—of different religious identities. The manual opened with "Bismillah hir raḥman nir raḥim," but this was common practice in texts printed at the Naval Kishore Press in the late nineteenth century that addressed a mixed religious audience. To the extent that its contents referenced God at all, Shaida limited those references to *khudāvand* (the Lord), recognizable terminology across multiple religious communities in South Asia.[50] This language may have allowed readers of multiple religious communities to read or listen to the text through their own religious imagination. While electroplating was a popular technology through which middle-class Muslim men demonstrated their claims on industrial modernity, efforts to claim modernity and social status through electroplating were not limited to Muslims.

Indeed, although they do not appear to have been as widespread as manuals in Urdu, electroplating manuals in other languages also addressed religiously mixed communities. For instance, a Gujarati manual published in Surat in 1899 titled *Gilīṭ nī Copḍī* (Gilding book) made no reference to an intended religious readership, nor did it reference God to explain the revelation or circulation of artisanal skill. Instead, it noted that the text was intended to prevent "injuries." The author, Nagindas Dayaldas, noted that, as the practice of electroplating had expanded, so too had incorrect practices—particularly in the preparation of the battery—that could physically harm the electroplater.[51] Like Shaida's text, *Gilīṭ nī Copḍī* seems to address a socially and religiously plural audience, but religious language was largely absent from the text. It provided extensive detail on how to manufacture and use batteries for electroplating and on how to "gild and plate" using not only silver and gold but also more common materials such as copper. These detailed descriptions may have been of interest to middle-class hobbyists or aspiring industrialists, but they assumed a high level of physical practice and skill. As such, it is likely that they were written with the intention that they would be read or circulated among artisan metalsmiths in workshops.[52]

METALWORKING SKILL AND THE EXPANDING AUDIENCES OF ELECTROPLATING MANUALS

Whether we consider Shaida's *Jāma ʿ-yi tarākīb-i talmī ʿ*, the Gujarati *Gilīṭ nī Copḍī*, or post-1880 Urdu electroplating manuals that addressed specifically Muslim audiences, it is apparent that as the audiences of manuals expanded, so too did the skills and practices referenced in the texts. Where texts aimed at an exclusively or primarily middle-class audience in the 1870s celebrated electroplating as a technological breakthrough, manuals from the 1880s portrayed it as a logical extension of work already done by manual platers in India. Increasingly, these texts assumed that platers would build on embodied skill in manual plating when they took up electroplating.

The *Iksīr-i malm ʿah* (The elixir of plating), printed in Delhi in 1893, was written by Mirza Ibrahim, a practicing artisan electroplater, and primarily addressed metalworkers rather than middle-class hobbyists or aspiring industrialists. It is also notable that it assumed that electroplaters would build on extant skills as manual platers. Many other texts opened with descriptions of how to manufacture a battery for electroplating, but the *Iksīr-i malm ʿah* began with descriptions of "water plating" and "warm plating, meaning leaf plating."[53] The aim of these brief descriptions was not to teach platers how to carry out these practices—given that were likely already quite familiar to most artisan platers—but to present them as part of a continuum of plating practices.

Following these references to manual plating, the *Iksīr-i malm ʿah* described electroplating and the manufacture of a battery. Its author praised the skill and knowledge of the "masters of plating" and noted that "we now know that a battery can also become a master of plating. If [the battery] is made correctly, then the work will be done well."[54] And, while earlier texts aimed at members of the middle class focused primarily on plating in precious metals, especially gold and silver, the *Iksīr-i malmʿah* addressed audiences who worked in a wider range of materials. The *Iksīr-i malmʿah* described copper and iron electroplating, emphasizing their importance for artisans who manufactured boxes and trunks, a prominent industry in the cities and towns of North India.[55] Likewise, it emphasized not only the production of plating but also its repair, a topic that was rarely included in electroplating manuals aimed at middle-class hobbyists but was of central importance for laborers employed in the trade.[56] For instance, in a section titled "The Deterioration of Plating," the text advised electroplaters on how to identify mistakes in silver plating that required repair:

> Sometimes [the silver plating] will become yellowish, in other cases oily and grease-covered, and sometimes it will become blackish. This is all the result of too much potash, though the blackish color may also be from the battery charge. And if the silver has been plated but its dust comes off the item, this is also a fault. Repair it by placing it in a flame or in acid. You must pay attention to each defect that could cause the work to deteriorate.[57]

The *Iksīr-i malmʿah* assumed that its primary audience—metalworkers with experience in other forms of plating—were sufficiently knowledgeable to evaluate whether to use acid or flame to repair "defects" in their electroplating. In the assumptions that it made about artisans' technical knowledge as well as its efforts to claim electroplating skill for laboring communities, it is representative of the types of texts that spoke directly to artisan metalworkers, rather than middle-class hobbyists or industrialists. Though written primarily in prose, it used accessible language and extensive diagrams, suggesting it may have been intended to be read aloud, with its images circulated within a workshop.[58] Its diagrams highlighted multiple potential processes of plating, suggesting that the author expected readers to be familiar with some of the technologies but not all, and to incorporate new knowledge of electroplating into their existing embodied knowledge.

The cover page of the text noted that the author, Mirza Ibrahim, compiled it on the basis of "his own experience" with the trade, emphasizing physical practice rather than command over capital.[59] Indeed, Mirza Ibrahim decried the fact that most authors of electroplating manuals were not, themselves, working practitioners of metal-plating. He accused these authors of other manuals of simply "writing down what they read in other books," without practicing the trade. Conversely, he asserted that he had "been working in a shop in the bazaar for ten years and had done all kinds of work by hand."[60] And, he explained, "no other author" of an electroplating manual had this type of physical experience, making their texts potentially even "dangerous" for users, because they did not contain sufficient practical content.[61]

On the basis of this explanation of his experience, Mirza Ibrahim identified as a metalworker, though likely a particularly successful, upwardly mobile, and economically prosperous one, a "master artisan" who possessed some capital and may have employed others. He was among a small number of metalsmiths who negotiated the increased industrialization of the urban colonial economy in cities like Delhi, successfully maintaining ownership of a workshop in the bazaar in a context where many metalsmiths had shifted to wage labor. From this position, he spoke explicitly to the "craftsmen of the bazaar," as well as "the merchants of the age," asserting authority through—not despite—his status as successful *kārīgar*.[62]

Despite Mirza Ibrahim's authorship, the *Iksīr-i malmʿah* did reflect continued middle-class intervention into the production of manuals, even when they were aimed at artisans. Mirza Ibrahim noted that his publication had received support—presumably funding—from an industrialist and printer named Bulaqi Das. Bulaqi Das owned the Mayūr Press, where the text was printed; he also published a local newspaper.[63] Like many of the publishers profiled in chapter 1, Bulaqi Das was invested in educating potential artisan workers for his own lithographic publishing house and may have also owned other industrial workshops in the city. But despite Bulaqi Das's involvement, the contents of the text make it clear that Mirza Ibrahim intended his text to be read and used by members of regional metalworking communities, not members of the industrial middle class. Indeed, his intended audience was reflected not only through the technical skills that he referenced but also in his cultural and religious framing of the trade, and especially the claiming of "alchemical" pasts for electroplating.

ELECTROPLATING AS ALCHEMY

As I noted in the introduction to this chapter, references to alchemists or *kīmiyāgar*s proliferated in electroplating manuals, including the earliest manuals, such as the *Tuḥfah-yi talmīʿ*, aimed at middle-class hobbyists and aspiring industrialists. The verses that conclude the *Tuḥfah-yi talmīʿ*—referencing the "astonished" alchemists—were printed in 1872 and are the earliest mention of a relationship between *kīmiyā* and electroplating that I have identified. They reflect a trend that expanded in the 1880s and 1890s and was increasingly aimed at artisan metalsmiths, rather than members of the middle class.[64]

The comparison between electroplating and *kīmiyā* is, in several ways, a logical one. Both *kīmiyā* and electroplating suggest the potential transformation of one metal into another and the possibility of turning a base metal into something precious, like gold. However, the use of a language of alchemy for and about artisan metalsmiths is, in the context of Muslim South Asia, unusual. In the western European context, Bruce Moran has shown that from at least the sixteenth century, some writers and scholars attributed alchemy to artisans and craftsmen, characterizing the work of glassmakers and metalsmiths as alchemy.[65] Although he notes that the "definition of alchemy was greatly disputed" in late Renaissance Europe, Moran argues that many writers saw "workshop creations" as alchemical projects.[66]

In the South Asian, Indo-Islamic context, scholars and court authors occasionally recognized the relationships between craft and *kīmiyā*. For instance, seventeenth- and eighteenth-century Persian-language descriptions of crafts that circulated in the courts of regional dynasties sometimes characterized glass and metal crafts as *kīmiyā*. One such collection, the *Majmū ʿ al-Ṣanāi ʿ* (Compendium of trades) was first written around 1620 but was copied repeatedly at the Mughal and regional courts throughout the eighteenth century. It included long segments on the transformative practices of metalwork, such as how to "transform iron into copper," as well as sections on the use of acids to dissolve and plate silver.[67] It integrated discussions of the "alchemical" properties of metal with a focus on a wide range of crafts such as blade-smithing, enameling, masonry, and even paper-making. An edition of the *Majmū ʿat al-ṣanāi ʿ* was published in 1847 by an early Persian typographic press supported by the colonial state-run Calcutta Madrassa, founded in 1770. The cover page of this published edition framed it as a treatise on the "branches of alchemy and magic" (*kīmiyā-o-hīmiyā*) highlighting the ways that categories of craft were subsumed within an understanding of alchemy.[68] This was especially true in the nineteenth century, when there was a resurgence of South Asian Muslim scholarly interest in the history of Islamic alchemy and its influence on European sciences.

Moreover, sections of craft compendia and collections that focused on trades and practices most closely associated with alchemy—including the transformation of metals—were sometimes extracted into shorter manuscripts, which were circulated among wider potential audiences, including merchants, as small manuals. For instance, a short ten-page Persian-language treatise on quicksilver (mercury), copied in Mysore in the mid-eighteenth century, explained the process of tinning and the use of mercury to tin other metals effectively.[69] However, while crafts may have sometimes been understood as alchemical, craftworkers usually were not recognized as alchemists. Text such as the *Majmu ʿat al-sanai ʿ* are notable in part because there is a distinct absence of craftworkers from the discussions of craft. They functioned as guides to the work done within royal workshops but largely omitted discussions of the workers themselves.

Texts such as the *Iksīr-i malm ʿah* thus marked a departure from earlier writing on both metalwork and alchemy, and not just because they targeted a new, laboring audience. They were also distinctive in content, connecting *kīmiyā* to the physical skill and labor of metalworkers rather than to a generalized courtly or intellectual knowledge of craft. This was not true of the earliest references to alchemy in electroplating manuals, such as the verses that concluded the *Tuḥfah-yi talmīʿ* in 1872. These references instead reflected a middle-class rediscovery or reassertion of Muslim traditions of alchemy in colonial India. The middle-class rediscovery of alchemy was informed by the interest of prominent Muslim scholars in what they saw as a Muslim scientific golden age and Muslim influence on European scientific ingenuity.[70] This Muslim middle-class project also connected the two popular meanings of *kīmiyā*—classical alchemy and modern chemistry—by highlighting the degree to which modern European chemistry traditions were indebted to the Islamic alchemical past.[71] But by the time the *Iksīr-i malmʿah* was published in Delhi in 1893, *kīmiyā* had become an important part of how manuals asserted social status for metalworkers themselves rather than for middle-class hobbyists or industrialists.

The *Iksīr-i malmʿah* integrated references to the electroplater-as-alchemist not only through its evocative titular reference to an "elixir" for plating but throughout its contents. It repeatedly referred to batteries as the "modern elixir" that allowed the electroplater to carry out his work. In its extensive chapter on how to make homemade batteries, the text suggested that what set electroplaters apart from those who were "admirers of the work" was their ability to make and repair batteries to carry out their labor. The modern elixir was thus dependent on the electroplater's physical skill and labor.[72]

Moreover, throughout the text, Mirza Ibrahim valorized the physical work of platers and metalsmiths. Writing of the process to plate a small iron box, he claimed that "in the first instance, you may fail and have to repair the work, but you will learn as if at the foot of an *ustād*."[73] By writing of metalsmiths' engagement with electroplating as complementary to their education in a workshop or apprenticeship, he framed the alchemy of electroplating as the distinct purview of craftsmen or *kārīgars*. Likewise, by highlighting physical skill and repeated practice as the source of the electroplaters' skill in a kind of alchemy, Mirza Ibrahim suggested that metalsmiths were worthy of social status by virtue of their labor itself. The metalsmith, he argued, should be respected not only for the traits that he might share with the middle class but for his practice of physical labor, the very thing that distinguished him from the middle class.

MOBILITY AND TECHNICAL FLEXIBILITY IN THE WORLD OF THE MUSLIM ELECTROPLATER

The *Iksīr-i malmʿah*'s language of alchemy suggests the role that the manuals may have played in the social worlds of Muslim metalworkers by the end of the nineteenth century. Engagement with electroplating through manuals like the *Iksīr-i malmʿah* allowed metalsmiths to assert technological and material skill as well as social positionality as Muslims. Simultaneously, they reflected the movement of ideas, people, and practices between industrialized factories and small artisan-led "cottage" workshops, spaces of labor that were usually portrayed as fully distinct and divorced from each other in colonial ethnographies.[74]

These ethnographies also sometimes attempted to distinguish between Hindu and Muslim metalworkers, even if they doubted the piety and orthodoxy of both groups. Muslim metalsmiths were depicted as more likely to be urban than their Hindu (or occasionally Sikh) counterparts. As such, colonial industrial reports and ethnographies suggest that Muslims were more likely to work within emerging centers of industrial labor, including both private and state-run factories and the railways. Colonial writing also posed a strict social and technological divide between Muslim metalworkers who labored for wages in industrialized factories and the "traditional, independent artisan" engaged in "cottage labor" in a city or town. G. Worsley, who wrote a monograph on iron and steelwork for government of Punjab in 1908, argued that there were no similarities between a smith "working in his own house, surrounded by his family . . . working [on] made to order" items, and a smith employed in the "modern factory system."[75] As Abigail McGowan notes, whether colonial administrators assigned positive or negative attributes to each system differed, with some asserting the "essential opposition between the aesthetic and social glories of Indian craftsmanship and the horrors of Western industry."[76] But whether they saw Indian *kārīgars* as inflexible and inert or a source of "aesthetic glory," they broadly agreed that cottage labor was fully distinct from industrialized manufacturing.

Contrary to this presumed sharp divide, texts such as the *Iksīr-i malmʿah* reflected the movement of new ideas and practices between the wage laborer of the modern factory or workshop, and the independent or traditional urban metalworker. Unlike Mirza Ibrahim's self-run, bazaar-based workshop, many of the electroplating workshops in nineteenth-century Delhi were sites of wage labor that until the twentieth century were usually under European oversight. The movement of ideas between these spaces reflected, the persistence of "decentralized" forms of artisanal labor in a period associated globally with proletarianization, and exchange between multiple forms of production.[77] Indeed, in the introduction of the *Iksīr-i malmʿah*, Mirza Ibrahim expressed a hope that electroplating would "spread through the shops of the city," moving beyond the European-run spaces of wage labor to the realm of the independent metalsmith.[78]

Likewise, the *Iksīr-i malmʿah* contested the common colonial portrayal of the independent artisan as obsessed with guarding irrelevant trade secrets. By portraying the electroplater as "possessing secrets beyond the *kīmiyāgar*," Mirza Ibrahim suggested that while trade-specific practices—secrets—marked a skilled metalworker, such practices were neither inflexible nor uncirculated.[79] On the contrary, knowledge of new ideas—"secrets" that circulated textually—seems to have allowed for improved social standing among some Indian Muslim metalsmiths, whether they worked as wage laborers or independent artisans.

ELECTROPLATING AND THE MUSLIM METALSMITHS OF SIALKOT

To understand how the social and religious narratives embedded in electroplating manuals circulated between independent workshops and spaces of wage labor, I analyze the experiences of one specific Muslim metalworking community. Sialkot, in Punjab and a major center for the growth of the electroplating trade in the late nineteenth century, provides an opportunity to read electroplating manuals in context and to consider how workers might have materially engaged with the texts. Sialkot was home to one of the most successful early electroplating factories in the region, a workshop founded in the early 1860s and run by W. Spence. It made surgical tools and other electroplated items. Sialkot remains a prominent center of surgical tools production—and a prominent center of the accompanying electroplating work—producing over 25 percent of the global surgical tool supply.[80]

However, Sialkot is not representative of the growth of electroplating in other cities across India. On the contrary, the practice likely grew more quickly and to a greater level there than in any other city of its size. Home to an urban population of 45,762 in 1881, Sialkot was a midsized provincial city, and as in the case of Meerut, it is somewhat surprising to find a high level of interest in electroplating from the mid-nineteenth century there, rather than in the larger cities of Punjab such as Lahore and Amritsar.[81] At the same time, Sialkot is an especially instructive example because it was home to several well-established and regionally renowned Muslim metalsmithing communities, including groups of *koftgar*s, Kashmiri gilders and platers, and *qal'īgar*s. It is therefore an ideal site to analyze how artisans took up the work of electroplating in the context of both wage labor and family or community-based workshops.

Sialkot's distinct history of metalwork, especially but not limited to weaponsmithing and *koftgari*, allows us to analyze a story of artisan flexibility and mobility. I argue that the reason for the success of early electroplating firms in Sialkot, such as Spence's, was the existence of highly skilled manual platers in the city and its surroundings. More specifically, early electroplating firms in the city relied on the fact that communities of manual platers and other skilled metalworkers had seen their traditional, family trades threatened, entering a period of economic decline or deindustrialization over the past few decades.

THE HISTORIES OF MANUAL PLATING AND DECORATIVE METALWORK IN SIALKOT

Before the rise of the surgical tools industry, the most renowned metalworkers of Sialkot were *koftgar*s, those who practiced decorative inlay work or damascening. The *koftgari* industry grew in conjunction with a regional weaponsmithing industry, with *koftgar*s often commissioned to damascene swords, daggers, knives, shields, and other weaponry. Starting from at least the late eighteenth century, Sialkot and the surrounding towns were also known for the manufacture of arms, some of which were commissioned for the military forces of Ranjit Singh, and eventually also for the British East India Company.

Koftgari workers in Sialkot district were often associated with two neighboring villages located about ten kilometers outside of Sialkot city, known as Kotli Loharan East and Kotli Loharan West. According to regional histories, the villages were settled around the time of the region's conquest by Mughal emperor Babur in 1525, and some local metalworkers asserted that their ancestors were weaponsmiths for the Mughal military forces. The origins of the names are unclear, but with the inclusion of the term *lohār*, the villages were clearly evocative of metalwork. An 1877 Urdu-language history and geographical guide to Punjab explained that "in Kotli Loharan there are numerous shops of *lohārāṇ* [blacksmiths], in which the craftsmanship is greatly respected and quite famous . . . [and] they forge the most wondrous items from *lohā* [iron]."[82]

The decline of Sialkot's weaponsmithing and *koftgari* industries and the rise of its surgical tools industry were broadly inverse processes and were intricately connected. In 1849, with the end of the second Anglo-Sikh war and the British annexation of Punjab, British officials pursued a policy of disarmament, restricting the sale and carrying of weapons.[83] This policy was further strengthened in 1878, when the Government of India imposed the Indian Arms Act. The act created a licensing system for both the ownership and the manufacture of weapons, although there were several exemptions in Punjab, including one that allowed Sikhs to buy *kirpān*s, daggers worn as an article of faith.[84] Combined with competition from European-made weapons, the act marked a moment of crisis for many independent North Indian weaponsmiths, including those in Sialkot and Kotli Loharan.

*Koftgar*s, of course, were able to damascene items other than blades, swords, guns, and shields, and they did so, inlaying plates and cups, pandans, inkwells, locks, hookahs, and jugs, among a wide variety of other objects, some of which were sold abroad. But throughout the second half of the nineteenth century, they faced uneven and unstable demand and struggled to make inroads into rapidly evolving local and foreign consumer markets. Nita Kumar describes the uneven consumer market in colonial India as one that upended economic security for artisans, even among those whose industries did not experience an overall decline in output or demand.[85] Instead, artisans struggled to predict the radically shifting patterns of both local and foreign demand on a month-to-month or year-to-year basis. In the case of Sialkot, the decline of the local arms market drove down demand for the more intricate and expensive forms of *koftgarī*, and *koftgar*s found that they could not consistently make a living from unpredictable foreign demand for *koftgarī* trinkets. This drove debt and pushed some *koftgar*s out of the trade.

THE TRANSITION TO SURGICAL TOOLS MANUFACTURE AND ELECTROPLATING

Spence and the other early founders of surgical tools workshops in Sialkot depended on the labor of artisans who were already skilled in other forms of metalwork, including manual metal-plating, and could easily transition to surgical tools manufacture and electroplating. Sialkoti surgical tools were known for their high quality of work from the industry's inception. Sialkoti-manufactured surgical tools won all three of the prizes offered for surgical instruments during the 1864 Punjab Exhibition of Arts and Industries. The instruments from Sialkot included "bleeding lancets," "lithotomy instruments," "midwifery instruments," and "instruments for extracting teeth," all of which were praised by the exhibition judges.[86] Surgical tools manufacture meant a rise in demand for laborers skilled in silver, copper, tin, and eventually nickel plating—which prevented rust on iron instruments.

*Koftgar*s who had been displaced from their familial trade—or who found it impossible to sustain livelihoods solely through *koftgari*—were in high demand at surgical tools workshops. So too were Kashmiri gilders, platers, and other metalsmiths. This was especially true after 1878–79, when an India-wide famine hit the Kashmiri capital of Srinagar particularly hard, increasing Kashmiri artisan migration to the cities of Punjab.[87] Sialkot was the closest sizable Punjabi city to the border with the princely state of Jammu and Kashmir, and had a well-established Kashmiri Mohalla, which attracted migrant Kashmiris throughout the late nineteenth century. While the largest artisan group of migrant Kashmiris in Sialkot were carpet weavers and textile workers, metalsmithing and papermaking were also prominent professions among the migrants. As noted in the discussion of manual platers in the "Histories of (Electro)-Plating" section, Kashmiri metalsmiths in Punjab cultivated a reputation for high-quality silver plating and gilding, as well as jewelry making.[88] The owners and managers of surgical instruments factories were eager to recruit skilled Kashmiri platers and gilders throughout the last decades of the nineteenth century. Surgical tools factories competed with the railway workshops of the city, as well as some of the city's sporting goods factories, both of which also sought to recruit skilled Kashmiri metalworkers as blacksmiths, boilermakers, and mechanics.[89]

While the earliest surgical instruments workshops that employed artisan metalsmiths as wage laborers were European run, Punjabi capitalists—whether Hindu, Muslim, or Sikh—entered the trade from the 1880s. By the 1910s two of the most prominent surgical tools factories in the city were those owned by S. S. Uberoi and A. F. Ahmad, two local capitalists who also employed workmen to make scissors and cutlery.[90] The company of the latter remains a manufacturer in Sialkot, while the family of the former, who also owned sporting goods factories, migrated to India after Partition and re-formed their company in Jalandhar.[91] Though both were founded before the First World War, these firms expanded exponentially during the conflict, in part because of restrictions placed on imports from Germany that had previously supplied many of the surgical tools used in India.[92]

KĀRĪGAR MOBILITIES

Colonial industrial monographs repeatedly asserted that there was no relationship between modern industrialized factories, like those that manufactured surgical instruments, and "traditional" workshops, such as those of Kotli Loharan's *koftgar*s or the metal-platers of the Kashmiri Mohalla. The two spaces of production were, in this understanding, completely distinct sectors of the economy, and the skills used by *kārīgar*s within them likewise differed markedly. But reading electroplating manuals alongside records of metalworking and metal-plating production in Sialkot shows that this difference was overstated. It hid the mobility of artisans between small family-owned workshops and capitalist-run forms of wage labor. Equally, it obscured the degree to which artisan understandings of the Muslim past—as represented in texts such as the electroplating manuals—circulated across both spaces of work.

The *koftgar*s of Kotli Loharan and the metal-platers and gilders of Sialkot's Kashmiri Mohalla saw their familial trades threatened by European imports and regulations on production, including limitations on weapons manufacture. But despite British prognostications of imminent decline and displacement in the late nineteenth century, some members of these trades maintained and even expanded their workshops. For instance, Kotli Loharan developed a reputation for artisanal wealth in the wake of the First World War, as many of the *koftgar*s and other metalsmiths had been recruited to work as "armorers and shoeing-smiths during the War" and returned home with the funds necessary to expand their workshops.[93] Even before the First World War, smiths in Kotli Loharan sometimes took on temporary, seasonal wage labor and piecework for surgical tools and other factories to buttress their earnings and support the maintenance or expansion of their workshops. Likewise, members of a single family may have had members who chose to maintain a home-based workshop while others left to work on the factories and larger workshops of the city. Reports of child labor in the surgical instruments industry—an issue that plagues the trade today and has led to international condemnation—appeared as early as 1919, suggesting that some smiths may have sent their sons to work for wages, rather than apprenticing them.[94]

Accepting colonial administrators' insistence that "modern" factories that relied on wage labor and "traditional" urban workshops were technologically and materially worlds apart would mean accepting that artisans never incorporated practices from one workspace into another. It would mean accepting that members of the same family, skilled in ostensibly the same trade, never discussed or compared their work among themselves and that they did not learn from or model their skills for each other. This seems unlikely. Moreover, the administrators' writing contradicted the way that the circulation of knowledge among metalworkers was portrayed in vernacular texts such as the *Iksīr-i malmʿah.*

ELECTROPLATING MANUALS AND ARTISAN FLEXIBILITY IN SIALKOT

Electroplating manuals such as the *Iksīr-i malmʿah* spoke to audiences of metalworkers who were familiar with, and may have moved between, different sites of production. Mirza Ibrahim, with his emphasis on physical practice and the growth of electroplating within the "shops of the bazaar," clearly assumed that electroplating was just as relevant for a small, artisan-run workshop as for a larger factory or capitalist-owned firm. Texts such as the *Iksīr-i malmʿah* were written with the assumption that they would be relevant for artisans whether they led their own small workshop, worked for wages in a larger factory, or labored in some combination of those two. They assumed—and promoted—the circulation of narratives about artisans' religious identities and claims on social status across multiple different sites and forms of production.

While the *Iksīr-i malmʿah* itself may or may not have circulated within Sialkot in the late nineteenth century, other manuals on electroplating almost certainly did. How might these manuals have been used to support artisans' claims on social status and Muslim pasts for their trades? As scholars including Khalid Nadvi have noted, one way that metalworkers in Sialkot and the surrounding region sought social mobility was by asserting a *sharīf,* "Mughal" lineage. This referred to descent from the Central Asians who had accompanied the early Mughal emperors into India in the sixteenth and seventeenth centuries or had migrated later to seek service with the Mughal court.[95] This was an important and popular strategy in the context of Kotli Loharan, because regional histories held that the town was founded under the Mughal emperor Babur and that its residents had been weaponsmiths for the court.[96] Asserting a connection to alchemy, with its courtly histories and connotations, may have buttressed this claim, supporting metalsmiths' access to social privileges usually associated with elite or genteel classes of Muslims, the *ashrāf.*

The potential use of electroplating manuals to support social identities rooted in the Muslim past extended beyond efforts to claim a *sharīf* familial lineage and modes of behavior associated with the Muslim elite. Beyond circulating knowledge about new technologies between different sites of labor and production, electroplating manuals contributed to a shared sense of community identification with specific technical skills. The manuals provided artisan metalworkers with access to shared narratives that centered their physical skill and material flexibility, while also asserting their social status and prestige as Muslims through claims on an Islamic tradition of alchemy.

Electroplating manuals and their narratives of technological flexibility and alchemical artisanship did not displace other forms of artisan engagement with Islam within communities such as the metalsmiths of Sialkot and Kotli Loharan. Unlike the earliest electroplating manuals aimed at members of the middle class, which positioned electroplating as a radical break from earlier practices of metalwork, manuals like the *Iksīr-i malmʿah* positioned it as part of a continuum that included traditions of manual plating. The assertion of electroplating as part of a longer tradition of artisan physical practices may have allowed metalworkers to position it within their own, often localized, religious traditions, practices, and community engagement with Islam.

The dramatic increase in the publication of electroplating manuals declined after the first decade of the twentieth century. As the practice became more widespread, demand for manuals that explained it decreased. In both small-scale, artisan-led workshops and in centers of industrial wage labor, artisans likely incorporated electroplating into their embodied skills and their modes of oral education.[97] This incorporation of electroplating into a wider body of skills may have drawn on knowledge that had previously circulated in both oral and written form through electroplating manuals. As electroplating became part of day-to-day practice in several centers of metalwork, artisan engagement with printed texts that positioned electroplating as a mark of social distinction declined. In Sialkot and Kotli Loharan knowledge of electroplating and its relationship with an alchemical past were likely subsumed within other narratives that circulated among artisan metalworkers.

. . .

The puzzle of the popular publication of electroplating manuals in colonial North India suggests that to understand how technologies of industrial production circulated and were interpreted, we must consider the class and social hierarchies within which they were embedded. Urdu texts on electroplating were important not just because they explained a new technology in a context of industrial change. They were also used to assert social status. For members of the Muslim middle class, electroplating manuals demonstrated their values of industriousness and command over capital. But as the manuals became more accessible and addressed—and were written by—artisan metalsmiths, they challenged the artisans' social marginalization. Manuals increasingly emphasized artisans' adaptability and relationship with new technologies and valorized their physical skills.

Even if large numbers of Indian metalsmiths did not practice electroplating until at least the early twentieth century, this imaginary extended beyond the realm of a single technical practice. Electroplating manuals became popular because they offered workers a model of social standing within the hierarchies of North Indian Muslim society. They allowed artisans to assert community identities that commanded prestige within colonial North India but that also reached beyond the adoption of middle-class norms and narratives. These manuals positioned electroplating as an extension of regional traditions related to both metal-plating and the Muslim identities of metal-platers. In valorizing the physical skill and practice of metalwork, they argued that what made artisans distinct from the middle classes—their physical labor—also made them deserving of prestige within Muslim communities.

Ultimately, the story of the electroplating manuals of the late nineteenth and early twentieth centuries is a story of the "subversion, contamination, and reorganization" of a technological practice.[98] But unlike other stories of reinterpretation and meaning making for science and technology in the colonized world, it is not just one in which members of a local elite subverted colonial claims on scientific knowledge. Instead, it is a story of how Muslim artisans subverted elite and middle-class Muslim claims on a new technology. Through electroplating manuals, Muslim artisans asserted new claims on the Muslim past that challenged their economic or social marginalization while simultaneously integrating a new technology into long-standing traditions about their work. In chapters 3 and 4, I retain this focus on how Muslim artisans claimed their trades and technologies as pious and Islamic. I turn to the circulation of these narratives, first through the printing of community histories, and second through artisan migration to growing regional metropolises.

PART TWO

The Circulation of Artisan Knowledge and Traditions

3

Sewing with Idris

Artisan Knowledge and Community History

WRITING THE MUSLIM ART OF SEWING

In 1909, Sheikh Khwaja Muhammad, an "expert in the art of sewing" and a tailor in the city of Allahabad, published a short, seven-page history of his trade through a small local press. Titled the *Risālah-yi Idrīsiyah* (The treatise of Idris), the community history articulated a Muslim past for tailors, known in Urdu as *darzīs* or *khayāṭs*. Tracing the precepts of sewing to the Prophet Idris (Enoch), the third Prophet in Muslim tradition, Khwaja Muhammad sought to provide a religious lineage for Muslim tailors in North India. In doing so, he spoke to and for members of an artisan community that sought new forms of social status in the context of stratified North Indian Muslim society.[1]

Framing the work of tailors as a divinely inspired art with a prophetic genealogy, Khwaja Muhammad claimed that it was Idris who first sewed a garment to clothe himself and that tailoring skills were revealed to him by God.[2] He maintained that sewing was "perfect and complete" upon its revelation to Idris and that the responsibility of contemporary tailors was to pass on this knowledge. He went on to position tailors as fundamental to Muslim belief and practice. He referenced, for instance, the "holy tunic" (*pīrāhan-i sharīf*) that the Prophet Muhammad wore on the night of his ascension to heaven (*mi'raj*), noting that the garment was made following the principles revealed to Idris.[3]

In addition to providing a Muslim past for sewing, Khwaja Muhammad articulated a set of moral and social precepts for tailors. The *Risālah-yi Idrīsiyah* taught Muslim tailors not only how to be good Muslims but also how to demonstrate their religious piety through their trade. For a young or apprenticed tailor to fail to adhere to these precepts and morals would, in Khwaja Muhammad's terms, "bring shame to the teacher and unemployment to the student."[4] "These are the rules that the eternal tailor [*khayāṭ-i azal*], the pure God, taught the Prophet Idris," he wrote, describing first how a tailor must stay outwardly and inwardly pure and say *bismillah* and other prayers over his needle and other tools.[5] For instance, in his fourth rule—for cutting fabric—he declared: "When you take scissors in your hand, recite this prayer: 'God is truly most strong and mighty.' And when you begin to cut, recite 'Children of Adam, did I not command you not to serve Satan, for he was your sworn enemy.'"[6] Khwaja Muhammad's valorization of the piety and religious genealogy of tailors was published and circulated in a competitive North Indian artisanal knowledge economy. By the time of its publication, other writers and educators also sought to explain the work of sewing in print.

For instance, just two years earlier, in 1907, another, notably different text about sewing was printed in Lucknow, 220 kilometers to the northwest. Written by a woman named Shabihunnisa, this alternative narrative of how to sew was titled *Muft kā darzī* (The free tailor).[7] The sixty-page, heavily illustrated manual sought to train young women to be seamstresses, as well as the basics of weaving and embroidery. It was written, according to Shabihunnisa, to "provide full aid" to the "teachers at girls' schools when they teach how to cut patterns and sew clothes."[8] Shabihunnisa's manual focused on the styles of hats, vests, tunics, and coats popular in the region, providing a series of patterns for her students to use, her text emphasizing technological flexibility. Shabihunnisa—a teacher at a state-aided Muslim-led girls' school in the town of Belahra (also spelt Bilehra), located sixty kilometers from Lucknow—emphasized the use of the hand-powered sewing machines alongside scissors, thimbles, and needles (figure 5), and provided patterns for clothes ranging from North Indian kurta pajamas to a European-style waistcoat and a "Turkish hat."[9]

For Shabihunnisa, sewing was a form of practical knowledge that could ensure the economic stability and social respectability of her students. It was, moreover, a skill that was appropriate for Muslim women, and a trade that could be executed from the home. Sewing, she claimed, could enable women to secure economic standing without necessarily entering male-dominated social spaces, thus protecting what she saw as a Muslim, feminine morality.[10]

A member of a prominent landholding family, Shabihunnisa dedicated herself to the moral and economic uplift of Muslim women of her region. She sought to initiate poorer girls—those who did not have access to the sort of home education in which she was trained—into *ashrāf* (genteel) understandings of feminine social respectability. But unlike Khwaja Muhammad, the author of the *Risālah-yi Idrīsiyah*, she did not tie the practice of sewing and creating garments to the Muslim social and religious identities of the makers. To her, sewing was a skill that served a purpose and promised economic uplift, rather than an intimate part of a tailor's religious practice and moral development.

This distinction—between the intrinsic piety of specific labor practices and the possibility of a pious life through economic uplift—set community trade histories, such as the *Risālah-yi Idrīsiyah*, apart from textbooks or treatises written by elite

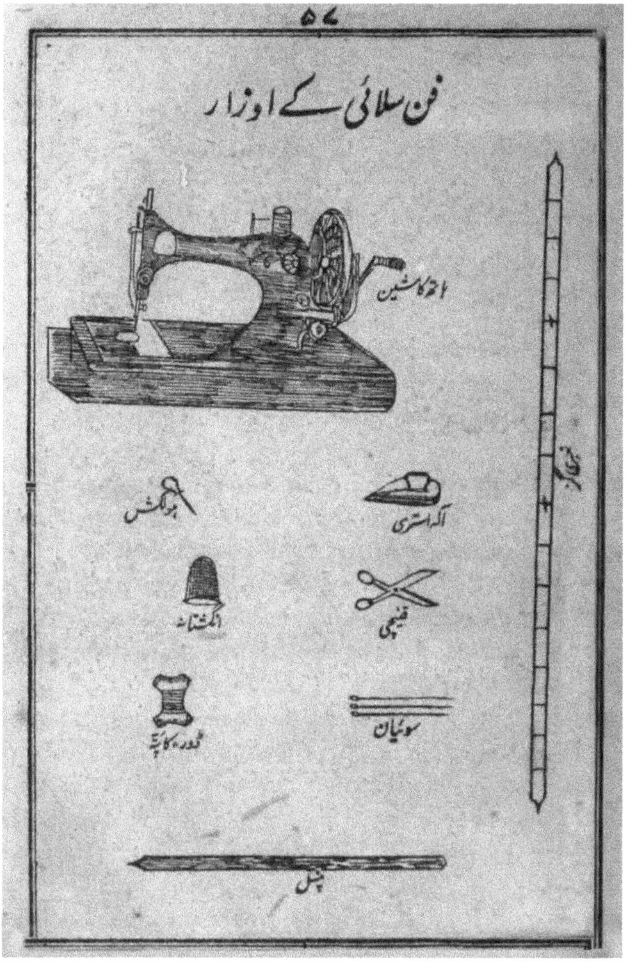

FIGURE 5. Shabihunnisa's *Muft kā darzī* (Lucknow: Isnā ʿAsharī Press, 1907) concludes with sketches of key sewing tools described in the text, including but not limited to a hand-powered sewing machine. (Rekhta)

Muslims. Reading the two texts together reveals conflicts over the definition and practice of pious labor between workers and the Muslim middle class, as well as a contestation of the popular gendering of a trade. Reading the *Risālah-yi Idrīsiyah* alongside the *Muft kā darzī* emphasizes that Sheikh Khwaja Muhammad sought to masculinize his trade in a context where sewing was increasingly framed as an appropriate practice for women.

Women artisans likely maintained their own forms of piety and their own understandings of their labor, but these narratives are largely absent from both texts. Masculinizing treatises such as the *Risālah-yi Idrīsiyah* elided the presence of women tailors and seamstresses from the *darzī*'s workshop. But even technical manuals such as *Muft kā darzī*—which valorized women's participation in the trade as a social good—presented working women largely as receptacles for middle-class knowledge and colonial technologies, rather than masters of the trade themselves. Even in a debate that centered the popular gendering of a trade, conflict over technical knowledge and authority remained the purview of male artisans and the middle class, providing limited space for women laborers to assert their own claims on technical knowledge.

. . .

Together, the *Risālah-yi Idrīsiyah* and *Muft kā darzī* suggest the circulation of competing and contested narratives of what it meant to be a tailor and the relationships between Muslim tailors, their trade, and their religion. These texts show that people who sewed—or taught sewing—debated the origins, social positionality, and gendered nature of their trade. They also debated the degree to which sewing should be taught in formal institutions, how tailors should demonstrate technological and material flexibility, and how to appeal to customers. Reading the *Risālah-yi Idrīsiyah* and *Muft kā darzī* together provides an opportunity to excavate tensions and conflicts between the Muslim middle class—as well as their educational institutions—and the traditions claimed by members of artisan communities.

By the turn of the twentieth century, members of North Indian artisan communities, including tailors, increasingly published and circulated trade histories as means of articulating social identity and community tradition.[11] In the same period, both the colonial state and a wide range of charitable and religious organizations sought to train artisans in skills, technologies, and trades. Muslim artisans were in conversation with elite Muslim and colonial efforts to define and claim tailoring. Through their engagement with an increasingly accessible popular press, Muslim artisans contested the exclusion of their communities from popular understandings of what it meant to be an upstanding or respectable Indian Muslim. Simultaneously, however, they posed alternative exclusions, with texts such as the *Risālah-yi Idrīsiyah* writing women tailors out of their religious and material traditions.

To understand the evolving social positionalities of tailors in turn-of-the-century North India, I first analyze how tailors were characterized in colonial ethnographic projects and the degree to which these projects informed elite Muslim discourse about the trade. I examine how the manual *Muft kā darzī* positioned itself within broader trends in elite Muslim charitable efforts, particularly those aimed at teaching girls to sew. I subsequently return to the *Risālah-yi Idrīsiyah*, reading tailors' community histories in conversation with new forms of education represented by *Muft kā darzī*. I trace contestation between three understandings of what it meant to be a Muslim tailor in North India: those articulated by colonial ethnographies, those promoted by middle-class Muslim institutions, and those asserted by tailors' community histories. Artisan Islam was asserted through religious lineages, prayers, and models of comportment in community histories such as the *Risālah-yi Idrīsiyah*. Elite Muslim narratives of how Muslim artisans should work—as represented by *Muft kā darzī*—both informed and competed with artisan histories. I show, however, that women's experiences of artisan Islam were elided from both types of texts.

MUSLIM *DARZĪ*S IN COLONIAL ETHNOGRAPHIC PROJECTS

Colonial efforts to ethnographically inscribe information about tailors mattered for tailors themselves because colonial policy makers used ethnographic categories to limit artisans' social mobility. Portraying tailors as technologically inept and committed to guarding outdated trade secrets, colonial ethnographic projects asserted that tailors were at best irrelevant and at worst an impediment to the growth of the Indian economy. Ethnographic projects also contributed to the social marginalization of Muslim tailors within Muslim communities because reports characterized Muslim *darzī*s as insufficiently orthodox, as low-caste Hindus in another guise, and as practitioners of a trade most appropriate for women. Texts such as the *Risālah-yi Idrīsiyah* must be read at least partially as a response to the colonial representation of tailors, as an effort to reassert economic, social, and religious status in a context of colonial marginalization.

British ethnographers in India inscribed the category of the Muslim tailor in their writing as part of an effort to build administrative understandings that distinguished laboring Indians from their elite and middle-class counterparts. The developing field of ethnography was an official project, designed to develop scientific knowledge of colonized peoples and improve British capacity to rule them.[12] From the mid-nineteenth century, ethnographic projects were increasingly interested in how caste-like hierarchies functioned among Indian Muslims. Elite Muslims were typically characterized as more orthodox than their laboring counterparts. As in the case of the caste categorization among Hindu and other communities, this reflected the reliance of British ethnographers on elite Indian intermediaries.[13] Ultimately, the ethnographic reporting of caste categories among Muslims informed the way the state responded to their petitions and requests, particularly when those petitions were made on religious grounds.

Colonial ethnographic reports consistently held that Muslim *darzī*s were not "orthodox" Muslims but instead participants in "syncretic" practices rooted in the community's "Hindu" past. And indeed, tailors' religious practices and places of worship did often cut across normative Hindu-Muslim divides. As Shahid Amin notes, both Hindu and Muslim tailors were "ardent worshippers" at the tomb of the Muslim "warrior saint" Ghazi Miyan in Bahraich, and practices of worship there were not divided on a Hindu-Muslim binary.[14] But by emphasizing this as the defining component of artisan religious identity, colonial ethnographies portrayed members of laboring groups like *darzīs* as lesser, unorthodox Muslims, whose practices and beliefs were external to the Muslim past.

A prominent 1896 British ethnographic report on the "castes and tribes" of the North-Western Provinces summarized the colonial perspective on the social standing of tailors. "The occupation is a poor one, and held rather in contempt," wrote William Crooke, the Anglo-Irish colonial administrator charged with reporting on regional caste groups for the Ethnographic Survey of India.[15] Crooke understood caste—and the caste-like hierarchies practiced by many South Asian Muslims—as defined by occupation, and he described *darzīs* as a composite caste group that incorporated both Hindus and Muslims. In his description of *darzīs* as an "occupational caste" that included people from multiple religious traditions, Crooke claimed that Muslim tailors were improperly or insufficiently Muslim and contrasted their practices with those of Muslims whom he perceived to be "orthodox." He wrote that the majority of *darzīs* in the North-Western Provinces "profess to be Sunni Muslims" but "still cling to many Hindu usages.[16] For Crooke, the participation of Muslim *darzīs* in spaces of worship shared with Hindus negated their claims to Muslim religious identity, marking them as separate and lesser-than in local Muslim social hierarchies.

Crooke's views of the construction of caste as rooted primarily in occupation were not universally shared among British ethnographers and administrators. For others, who understood caste as what Bernard Cohn has termed a "concrete and measurable entity" rooted in endogamy and descent, *darzīs* were perplexing.[17] In the prominent *Glossary of the Tribes and Castes of the Punjab*, compiled by ethnographers who saw caste in "concrete" terms, *darzīs* were described as "not a caste in the proper acceptation of the word."[18] Noting that *darzīs* in Punjab comprised both Hindu and Muslim communities, these colonial ethnographers proposed that tailors were drawn from other "proper" caste groups and became known as *darzīs* when they took up the work of sewing. Complicating this picture, however, they noted that "there is a *darzī* guild in every town" in Punjab, responsible for regulating the trade and its membership, acting in a similar fashion to caste associations.[19]

British ethnographers in India thus never shared a uniform, uncontested understanding of the forms of association that tied *darzīs*, both Muslim and Hindu, together as caste or social groups. But from a practical standpoint, Muslim tailors were usually categorized as a "menial or lower occupational class," or sometimes as a "degraded class of Muhammadans," with the Punjab census specifically using the term *arzāl* (degraded).[20] This was a derogatory framing for Muslim communities that were believed to be descended from the lowest-caste Hindu and Dalit converts, below the general laboring (*ajlāf*) Muslim masses.[21] On the basis of this classification, regional administrators sought to exclude *darzīs* from social contexts in which they might have authority over members of the *ashrāf*.

For instance, as part of a 1900–1901 inquiry into the military recruitment of Muslims from the North-Western Provinces, Captain A. H. Bingley lamented that *darzī*s and other "lower occupational classes . . . have found their way into the ranks, and eventually risen to commissioned and non-commissioned grades." Bingley, who had also compiled several prominent ethnographic reports, saw the recruitment of *darzī*s and other Muslim laborers as a problem not just because it threatened to upend *ashrāf* distinction. He also worried that potential social mobility among *darzī*s and other so-called menial Muslims threatened state theories that some Indian communities were "martial races" and therefore better suited to military service.[22] "No self-respecting Pathan or Musalman Rajput can be expected to serve contentedly under native officers of low extraction, whose grandfathers may have been Hindu menial servants," he wrote.[23]

British administrators across North India were invested in forms of *ashrāf* social distinction, which often mirrored Pierre Bourdieu's understanding of a "class habitus," relying on social norms to communicate elite positionality.[24] While South Asian Muslim social distinction had long preceded the colonial state, British administrators sought to compile information on the social norms that characterized Indian Muslim elites and to use them to police social and class boundaries. Colonial administrators in the region specifically sought to limit the access of Muslim laboring communities like *darzī*s to the social category of "Sheikh." Within systems of ethnic and social categorization of Muslims in North India, "Sheikh" was one of the four most significant titles or markers reflecting a *sharīf* identity, the others being "Sayyid," "Pathan," and "Mughal." Those who claimed the title "Sheikh" claimed to be descended from Arab migrants to India, though not, as Sayyids did, to be descended from the family of the Prophet Muhammad.[25]

The category "Sheikh" thus carried with it forms of *ashrāf* privilege and an assumption of Arab descent. But as many late nineteenth- and early twentieth-century colonial ethnographic reports noted, it was also relatively capacious. Referring to oneself as "Sheikh" sometimes allowed *kārīgar*s, especially those who had amassed some wealth, access to social privileges associated with the *ashrāf*. Ethnographic reports regularly quoted a proverb that they claimed was popular across North India: "Last year I was a *jūlāhā* [weaver], this year I am a Sheikh, next year, if prices rise, I shall become a Sayyid."[26] The contents of the saying changed slightly depending on the report, with "butcher" or another artisan category sometimes substituted for *jūlāhā* or "weaver." Regardless, it concisely expressed the idea that members of Muslim artisan classes aspired to, and claimed, *ashrāf* status.[27]

By the turn of the twentieth century, colonial administrators expressed concerns that claims on Sheikh status by upwardly mobile laboring-class Muslims would disrupt state efforts to ensure that only "well-bred" Indians were accepted into military and state service ranks. Thus they increasingly sought to distinguish true Sheikhs from those who, like *darzī*s, were perceived to be from lower-caste, Hindu-convert backgrounds. This became especially important in 1909, when the

Morley-Minto Indian Councils Act slightly increased the number of opportunities for Indians to hold elected legislative council positions and created separate electorates for Muslims.

Following the Morley-Minto Reforms, British administrators repeatedly fretted that "low-born" Muslims might claim Sheikh status when running for councils.[28] *Darzīs* were among the candidates labeled "unsuitable" for council service, and those who attempted to stand for election were decried as "ridiculous" in colonial reports. On multiple occasions, Muslim *darzīs* who registered themselves as candidates were prevented from participating in elections through the intervention of colonial administrators.[29] Ultimately, then, efforts to categorize Muslim tailors as less orthodox Muslims, as descendants of caste marginalized Hindu converts, and as intrinsically lacking in social prestige led to limitations on their social mobility and political engagement, and these limitations were enforced through colonial policies.

MUSLIM *DARZĪS* AND THEIR TECHNOLOGIES AS COLONIAL CATEGORIES

When Khwaja Muhammad published his *Risālah-yi Idrīsiyah* in 1907, colonial ethnographers consistently portrayed tailors as unorthodox and marginal Muslims and fretted that tailors falsified descent as Sheikhs. But this was not the only colonial narrative about *darzīs* that the trade history contested. A second, equally prominent trend in colonial writing was a lamentation that *darzīs* were unable to adapt to the challenges of technological and economic change. This narrative gained prominence after the popularization of the handheld sewing machine in the mid-nineteenth century and was especially powerful after the invention of the electric sewing machine in 1889. However, its roots lay in an earlier colonial imagination of the Indian *darzī* as incapable of adapting to changing European fashions and norms of dress, an imagination that allowed administrators to contrast supposed European vitality with perceived Indian rigidity. David Arnold argues that in colonial discourse in India, "darzi became a byword for technological inertia, the unimaginative repetition of customary skills and imitative practices."[30] Similarly, in her study of the use of the sewing machine in Sri Lanka, Nira Wickramasinghe argues that Europeans across Asia often saw tailors as "hostile to change," unresponsive to changes in style, demand, and especially technical practice.[31]

It was this narrative that spurred the introduction of sewing courses in state-run and religious schools, as well as in jail workshops and other state-led projects. Because educational administrators saw the work of *darzīs* as simplistic and saw *darzīs* themselves as resistant to technological and stylistic change, they increasingly argued for the use of state-led institutions to create new classes of tailors. However, just as British administrative cadres never held uniform views about whether *darzīs* constituted a "caste," they also articulated a wide range of perspectives on how their work should be integrated into colonial educational institutions.

Specifically, educational administrators debated whether sewing ought to be taught in formal industrial schools set up by the state or whether the state might create new forms of apprenticeship and lineage-based training to create a new class of flexible, technologically adept tailors. An 1880 education department report proposed that Eurasian children—those of mixed European and Indian descent—should be educated in trades like tailoring, though its author admitted that they might be disadvantaged because they did not work as part of an established family trade. Therefore the author suggested that they be "brought into" state-run workshops, where they might train as apprentices and eventually "hand down to their children the taste for this work," creating new, presumably superior, lineages of tailors who would come to dominate "private enterprise."[32] Other educationalists disagreed, viewing industrial schools as the appropriate venue for the training of new cadres of tailors and noting approvingly the proliferation of sewing courses in formal state- and missionary-run schools, especially, but not only, schools for girls.[33]

Despite these differences, educational administrators concerned with sewing broadly agreed on two points. First, they maintained that as a trade, sewing was uniquely appropriate for women because it could be done within the home and did not require participation in a public space.[34] They often framed women as "seamstresses" rather than tailors or *darzīs*, but at least in colonial educational writing, the skills expected of each were often indistinguishable.[35] The exception to this overlap was that male *darzīs* were seen as more inclined toward design than women. Although colonial ethnographers dismissed male *darzīs* as not sufficiently creative to design within new fashion trends, these reports still placed male *darzīs*' design skills above those of women in the trade. Seamstresses were assumed to work from patterns designed by men, rather than engaging closely in design work themselves, an expectation that minimized the actual creative labor performed by women. Sewing, colonial educationalists argued, was accessible for women who observed forms of purdah, and it could provide economic opportunity for women whose religious, class, or social norms prevented them from working in public.[36]

Second, educational and industrial administrators were particularly concerned with adoption of sewing machines, both hand- and electric-powered, into the trade. They argued that as schools trained new, flexible cadres of tailors and seamstresses, they should emphasize the use of sewing machines. Atul Chandra Chatterjee, an Imperial Services of India official and the author of an expansive 1907 report for the colonial state on the industries of the United Provinces, suggested that "the use of knitting and sewing machines, in addition to ordinary knitting and sewing," be taught at all girls' schools in the region.[37] For state educationalists, sewing machines represented the potential for flexibility and change in the trade, with tailors who did not use sewing machines derided as rigid and backwards. The tailor or seamstress seated at a sewing machine became a key image in the colonial imagination of the technological and social modernization, contrasting sharply with the image of the tradition-bound *darzī* bent over his needle.

GIRLS' SCHOOLS AND THE MAKING OF THE IDEAL SEAMSTRESS

Colonial state educational and industrial officers expressed interest in both boys' and girls' schools and educational programs that would create more flexible tailors and seamstresses, distinct from North India's *darzī*s, whom they held to be tradition bound. But the most significant interventions in training in sewing came, not through state programs, but through charitable and religious institutions. Initially, these schools were led primarily by Christian missionaries, but by the 1880s they were joined by both Hindu and Muslim reformist groups.

Missionary schools, particularly those aimed at girls, invested in sewing machines and mandated the study of sewing as a central part of the curriculum. The leaders of missionary schools argued that they could train seamstresses and tailors who were more efficient and detailed—and therefore higher paid—than their non–missionary school trained counterparts. In doing so, they sought to attract poor families not only to their schools but also to Christianity.[38] For instance, by the mid-1860s the American Methodist Episcopal Church Mission founded orphanages and industrial schools for both girls and boys in Bareilly. Sewing was among the primary skills taught at the girls' orphanage, and the 1870 mission report on the orphanage noted that it aimed to become self-sustaining through profits from "fancy work and plain sewing" undertaken by the girls.[39] As Charu Gupta has shown, sewing was also important to missionaries who hoped to distinguish "the 'seminude' outcaste [Hindu] women" from their converted Christian counterparts, "clad in 'decent' clothes, fit for clean Christian souls."[40] Missionary reports expressed a conviction that the economic opportunity and the potential social status conferred by sewing would serve to attract the poor residents of Bareilly to Christianity.

Missionary efforts to spur conversion through industrial change prompted a backlash among both Hindu and Muslim elites, particularly those associated with "reformist" trends in each religion. By the 1890s, Christian missionary groups in North India complained of the "competition" their schools and charitable organizations faced from the Arya Samaj, a prominent Hindu reformist organization founded in 1875. Indeed, the orphanage-industrial school of the Bareilly Arya Samajists explicitly aimed to challenge the American Methodist mission there and was founded in part to stem conversions of Dalits and lower-caste Hindus to Christianity.[41]

Muslim reformist organizations likewise worried that the outreach of Christian missionary orphanages, industrial schools, and other charitable institutions would lead to the conversion of poor Muslims. Like the Arya Samaj and other Hindu revivalist organizations, Muslim charitable groups sometimes adapted the missionaries' own emphasis on the importance of training in sewing for poor Muslims, especially girls. They consistently asserted the potential power of sewing for economic and social uplift.[42] In Punjab, at the Maryam Muslim Orphanage in Sirhind—founded by the custodians of the shrine of the Naqshbandi Sufi Ahmad Sirhindi—the principal lamented that "the Christians proselytize through industry!"[43] The solution, he argued in a 1918 publication that sought support for his orphanage from Muslims across India, was to train Muslim artisans who could earn "higher wages." He argued that with greater financial support, his orphanage could train Muslim boys as "tailors, carpenters, and blacksmiths" who were successful enough to run their own small workshops and stores.[44] Girls, he wrote, should likewise learn sewing, so that they could "avoid the ills of poverty," ensuring their economic uplift and the preservation of their virtue.[45]

For Muslim founders of girls' schools and orphanages, efforts to educate the Muslim poor also often centered on whether it was possible to inculcate values of middle-class social respectability into working-class girls. As Shenila Khoja-Moolji has shown, the question of how and whether Muslim women should be educated was intimately tied to middle-class, *ashrāf* conceptions of propriety and respectability. Elite Muslim men debated whether educating a *sharīf* woman outside of the home would diminish her—and her family's—social respectability or, conversely, contribute to her status by enabling a woman to "reproduce her own and her family's social standing."[46] Those who believed that education conferred social respectability on women and their family sometimes sought to extend charity to poor women by offering them the promise of social respectability through charitable schools, orphanages, and other institutions.

Shabihunnisa wrote her 1907 *Muft kā darzī* in this context of competition between religious organizations in North India and the work of some elite Muslims to inculcate middle-class values into poor and working-class Muslim girls. Her book was intended, she explains in her introduction and conclusion, as an educational tool to be used at a wide range of girls' schools across the region. The very existence of a state-aided Muslim-led girls' school in the village of Belahra, located thirty-five kilometers from the small city of Barabanki, suggests the rapid geographic spread of narratives and practices of Muslim institutions of girls' education in the early twentieth century, as well as the spread of shared understandings of what characterized an upstanding Muslim woman. A conclusion to Shabihunnisa's book noted that, as the accomplished and educated wife of a *moulvi* in Belahra, Shabihunnisa was seen as the most suitable women to teach Muslim girls. Explaining that her "nature was inclined towards knowledge and skill since childhood" and that she had learned "reading, writing, sewing" to the "necessary degree," the text positioned Shabihunnisa as a model *sharīf* woman, able to demonstrate both social respectability and the useful skill of designing, cutting, and sewing clothing.[47]

In addition to drawing on her familial status as a member of the Muslim landed elite of the United Provinces, Shabihunnisa was clearly adept at negotiating the preferences and beliefs of regional colonial administrators. She noted with pride that her school had passed inspection by regional education directors.[48] The school was given "aided" status, meaning it received government grants. As Muslim-led charitable and girls' schools expanded in geography and popularity, many engaged more closely with the interests of the colonial state. In this case, that meant the desire of regional British administrators to create new classes of technologically and stylistically adaptable tailors and seamstresses. Indeed, the conclusion noted that the text itself was commissioned partially to fulfill the needs of state-funded girls' schools in the region, suggesting the fluid movement of models of women's engagement with sewing between Muslim girls' schools and other educational institutions in the region.[49]

SEWING AND EXPERTISE IN A MUSLIM GIRLS' SCHOOL

Shabihunnisa was explicit about her efforts to contribute to new forms of expertise about sewing and to help create new classes of tailors. In an introduction, she lamented that no other text like hers existed, likely because in the past tailors had passed on the trade from father to son. The lack of school books on sewing, in her view, not only limited the spread of knowledge and expertise about sewing but also kept the trade inert. What she desired, she wrote, was to see "new branches of industry emerge."[50]

Shabihunnisa's text rejected the centrality of a male *ustād* to sewing education, as well as the lineages of training that were central to *Risālah-yi Idrīsiyah*. However, the book was not designed to be used without guidance, and like other technical manuals it reflected the intersection of oral, illustrative, and textual knowledge in artisan education. The introduction noted that one of its purposes was to make the work of teachers in girls' schools easier, suggesting that Shabihunnisa's descriptions of sewing and illustrative patterns were, like the explanations of many other artisan manuals, used in combination with forms of oral education and training.[51]

For students in Shabihunnisa's school, as for those in government-run and Christian missionary schools, an aptitude with sewing machines was central to this conceptualization of a new class of women tailors. Providing a sketch of the hand-powered sewing machine, Shabihunnisa suggested that facility with the machine, far more than formal training under a master *darzī*, would allow one to make a living as a seamstress.[52] To an even greater degree than the sewing machine, however, Shabihunnisa positioned patterns and scissors as technologies that would create economic stability for Muslim women. Because cutting and designing were seen as marks of a highly skilled (and usually male) master tailor, Shabihunnisa emphasized these physical practices as the route to economic stability and social respectability.

To measure, sketch, and cut material, a seamstress using Shabihunnisa's book would have required a degree of extant knowledge of sewing, and likely also oral

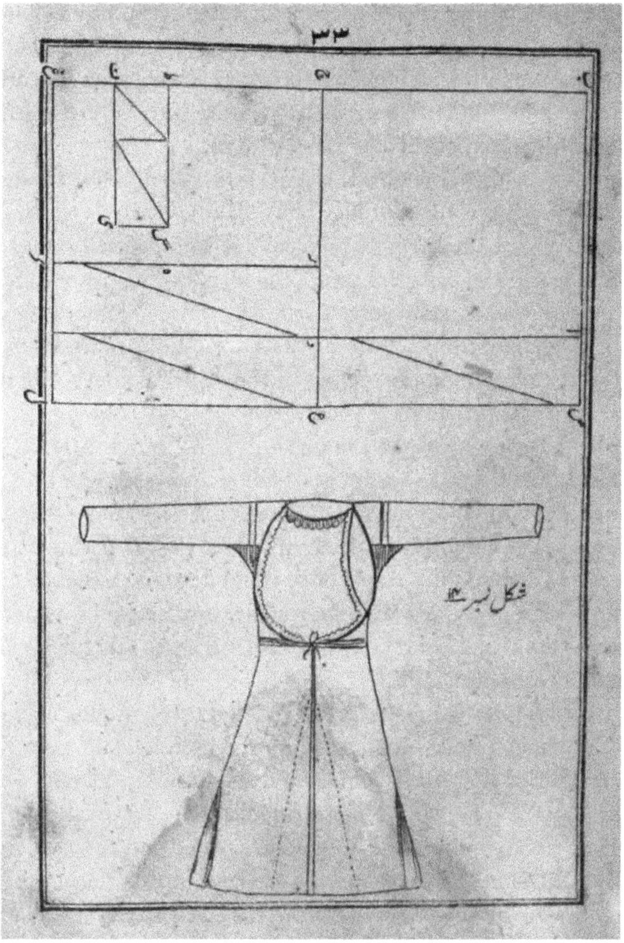

FIGURE 6. A pattern for an *angarkhā,* a style of men's outer coat, in Shabihunnisa's *Muft kā darzī* (Lucknow: Isnā ʿAsharī Press, 1907). (Rekhta)

engagement with a teacher or mentor. The text also assumed that readers would consult the attending images as they worked, or be shown them by a teacher. Introducing a section titled "Rules for Cutting an *Angarkhā*" (a men's outer coat), Shabihunnisa wrote, "If a cloth is 2 ¼ *gaz* [yards] in length and 20 *girah* [one-sixteenth of a *gaz*] in width, provided the lower waist is 16 *girah*, then you can make a 2 ¼-*gaz*-long *angarkhā*, always in the style of sketch number 12."[53] Shabihunnisa's sketch provided an outline of the *angarkhā*, as well as a model of where the tailor should cut (figure 6). Her instructions reflect a broader assumption often embedded in artisan technical manuals: the written word would be used alongside, rather than in place of, oral and visual education.

Shabihunnisa hoped to create a technologically adept and adaptable class of women who might compete with male *darzīs*, but male tailors continued to receive significantly higher pay than their female counterparts through the early twentieth century and beyond.[54] Indeed, even as training for women expanded, the terms *darzī* and *tailor* often remained associated with men in both colonial and postcolonial South Asia, with women portrayed as less skilled "seamstresses."[55] Despite colonial hand-wringing about the inflexibility of Indian male *darzīs*, and despite the efforts of women like Shabihunnisa, both colonial administrators and Indian consumers continued to express suspicion of the idea that women possessed enough creative expertise to design and cut patterns for more elaborate clothing.[56]

To this end, Shabihunnisa's book suggests at least one radical departure from the gendered assumptions about sewing and labor in colonial North India. Using *darzī* in the title and providing a wide variety of models that girls and women were expected to use and expand upon to design clothes, *Muft kā darzī* positioned women as real competitors to male tailors, not a secondary class of seamstresses. The text adopted colonial narratives about how tailors and seamstresses should train to become technologically modern, as well as the popular charitable understandings about the role of sewing education for poor and laboring women. But it also expanded these narratives insofar as it positioned women as the inheritors of the trade of tailoring, rather than as marginal participants in the trade and its economies.

Ultimately, however, the experiences and claims on technical authority that may have circulated among women tailors themselves—and even those of the pupils in Shabihunnisa's school—remained absent from the manual. Shabihunnisa and her elite Muslim contemporaries were dedicated to the creation of new classes of Muslim workers. Women tailors were to be created and cultivated from among the mass of the Muslim poor and working classes. The experiences of women who already engaged in tailoring seem to have been largely irrelevant, aligned with the technologically inert world of male *darzīs*.

ELITE MUSLIMS AND THE REFORM OF THE RELIGIOUS PRACTICES OF TAILORS

Shabihunnisa's frustration with male lineages of *darzīs* was likely informed by a colonial discourse that portrayed male *darzīs* as technologically and socially inert, hoarding knowledge of the trade while contributing to its lack of development. At the same time, it was also influenced by elite Muslim efforts to spread *ashrāf* models of social respectability to the working classes. As I explore in greater detail in chapter 4, elite Muslim *anjumans* opened a range of schools, including orphanages and charitable industrial schools, to train the poor in how to be religiously and socially upstanding Muslims, and to compete with Christian charitable institutions.

An 1895 report of a Bareilly orphanage-industrial school founded by the local Anjuman-i Islāmiyah (Islamic Association) noted, for instance, that "the elders of the community and supporters of the faith" had secured funding for the "books, meals, and clothing" used by the orphans. Anjuman members donated this funding with the expectation that the students would receive "rigorous" religious and moral education, and in doing so spread the Anjuman's interpretation of how a Muslim should behave and worship.[57] Implicit in this framing was the idea that the *ustād-murīd* relationship and apprenticeship training upheld by tailors such as Khwaja Muhammad had failed not only to inculcate technological adaptability but also to teach religiously "correct" forms of Muslim piety and worship.

CONFRONTING MUSLIM RELIGIOUS AUTHORITY THROUGH TAILORS' COMMUNITY HISTORIES

Despite limitations on tailors' social mobility and perceptions of their religious marginality, some Muslim tailors did successfully engage with both the colonial state and Muslim elites, contesting their exclusion from definitions of piety and orthodoxy. In some cases, they even negotiated forms of colonial authority to press for their religious and economic interests vis-à-vis members of the Muslim elite. In the realm of law, Julia Stephens notes that a Muslim tailor from Tajpore, in Bihar, then part of the Bengal Presidency, contested the prayer practices of the *imām* of a local mosque in colonial courts after the *imām* brought a civil case against congregants for "interfering" with prayers.[58] Stephens argues that the decision of the Privy Council, which ultimately heard the case, set a standard for a "hands-off approach to governing ritual differences" among Muslims.[59] Still, the ability of a Muslim tailor to assert his piety and religious knowledge in court, and to muster proof of the "correct" nature of his position, suggests that some engaged with shifting sites of political authority to press for their own status and beliefs as Muslims.

Khwaja Muhammad's engagement with print, and his efforts to disseminate knowledge of tailors' intrinsic piety through the *Risālah-yi Idrīsiyah*, can likewise be understood as a negotiation of an emerging site of South Asian authority represented by the printed word. Print facilitated the ability of tailors like Khwaja Muhammad to address readers across North India. It enabled him to contribute to the creation of a translocal, shared ideal of what it meant to be a pious tailor. At the same time, because community histories like the *Risālah-yi Idrīsiyah* were publicly available, print contributed to the efforts of tailors and other *kārīgars* to counter elite writing that excluded Muslim workers from ideals of piety. The *Risālah-yi Idrīsiyah* highlights what Tortsen Tschacher has described as "a heightened concern with authenticity" among Muslim communities that are accused of practicing "syncretic" or "popular" religion.[60]

LOCAL ENGAGEMENTS AND ARTISAN RESPONSES TO ELITE IDEOLOGIES

Although the *Risālah-yi Idrīsiyah* circulated translocally, across North Indian cities, it was also written in the specific context of early twentieth-century Allahabad. In his work and his writing, Khwaja Muhammad likely negotiated specifically Allahabadi claims on Muslim religious authority asserted by members of the Allahabadi Muslim elite. The city of Allahabad—from which Khwaja Muhammad published his community history—was an especially notable center of Muslim reformist efforts to address the urban working class.[61]

Like colonial administrators, many Muslim reformist intellectuals argued that the practices of working-class Muslims, including *darzīs*, were informed by Hindu religious pasts. Indeed, colonial ethnographers often drew on elite and reformist narratives of "orthodoxy" in their framings of the religious failures of Muslim artisans, with ethnographic practices shaped by elite Indian interlocutors. However, Muslim reformist scholars promoted discourses of how working-class Muslims should demonstrate piety that were more capacious and nuanced than the simplified dichotomies between orthodoxy and unorthodoxy that were reimagined by the state.

For instance, the scholar Maulana Muhammad Husain (d. 1904) was among the most prominent Muslim public lecturers in turn-of-the-century Allahabad and contributed to reshaping local conceptions of orthodoxy that Khwaja Muhammad may have encountered. Key reference points in the *Risālah-yi Idrīsiyah*, such as Khwaja Muhammad's insistence that piously tailored clothes had adorned the Prophet during his night ascension, or *miʿraj*, seem to reflect his influence on both popular and elite Muslim practice in Allahabad. Muhammad Husain is often credited with contributing to the popularization of public celebration of *miʿraj* night, which had previously been a primarily private, elite affair.[62] As a member of a scholarly family associated with a prominent local Sufi shrine, he delivered public addresses on the virtues of the Prophet that attracted Allahabadis from across social classes.[63]

Along with many other prominent Muslim scholars of the era across divergent reformist movements, Muhammad Husain viewed Muslim worship at shrines and sites of pilgrimage that were shared with Hindus with suspicion and consternation. But this did not mean that he, like some of his contemporaries, abjured the public worship of birth and death anniversaries or even popular practice at processions and Sufi shrines as intrinsically colored by contact with Hindu neighbors.[64] On the contrary, he was fundamental to the development of new forms of public worship, celebration, and commemoration that targeted working-class communities, including the celebration of *miʿraj* night.[65]

In early twentieth-century Allahabad, the night of the *miʿraj*—which had previously been marked primarily by elite Muslim families—became an important public celebration for Muslims from across class backgrounds. The public commemoration of events like *mi'raj* grew to incorporate large numbers of working-class Muslims and became a space for public lectures and processions, in part because of the intercession of scholars like Muhammad Husain.[66] Khwaja Muhammad's decision to center *mi'raj* in his narrative of the Muslim past of tailors, therefore, reflects not only his integration of tailors into a narrative of the Muslim past but also his potential engagement with the efforts of prominent Allahabadis to speak to Muslim laborers.

THE *RISĀLAH-YI IDRĪSIYAH* AND THE MUSLIM PASTS OF TAILORS

The *Risālah-yi Idrīsiyah* suggests the interpenetration of some of the elite and laboring-class Muslim narratives of piety and practice. But it also reveals artisan efforts to assert that their communities, by virtue of their labor, had distinctive claims on Muslim piety. Khwaja Muhammad integrated tailors into contemporary understandings of important moments in the Muslim past—such as the *mi'raj*—and provided a lineage of education and training for Muslim tailors that began with Idris but wound through Sufi saintly lineages in Allahabad and the surrounding regions. He suggested that a Central Asian Sufi saint from Samarqand had brought the knowledge of the Muslim precepts of sewing to North India and that local Sufi-tailor *ustāds* had trained *murīds* in the Islamic practice of their trade.[67] For Khwaja Muhammad, *ustād-murīd* relationships—condemned by both the colonial state and some Muslims elites as reflective of the inflexibility of the trade—were fundamental to protecting the distinctive Muslim past and piety of tailors.

Moreover, throughout his trade history, Khwajah Muhammad attributed his advice to that given by the prominent members of the Sufi-*darzī* lineage that he outlined in his introduction. In doing so, he suggested that his work was not his alone but representative of his community and his history. Indeed, while the title page of the book listed Khwajah Muhammad as its author (*muṣanif*), in the text he claimed he was more of a translator, making older bodies of knowledge accessible to contemporary tailors. He attributed the knowledge of the *Risālah-yi Idrīsiyah* to a Persian *kasbnāmah* (a book describing a craft of trade).[68] "It should be clear," he wrote, "that this advice was a translation [*tarjumah*] from a *kasbnāmah*."[69]

As I explore in chapter 5, the ability to adapt and vernacularize technical knowledge and terminology—usually between English and Urdu—often became a mark of authority among upwardly mobile *kārīgar*s in North India. In this case, however, the authority vested in the author-as-translator was based on the prestige of Persian and its association with knowledge of South Asian (and transregional) Muslim pasts. Although the use of Persian in India was in decline in the late nineteenth and early twentieth centuries, it retained authority and prestige as a language of historical South Asian dynasties, courts, and literature, claimed especially but not just by Muslims.[70] By referencing his translation and vernacularization of tailoring knowledge from a Persian *kasbnāmah*, Khwajah Muhammad positioned tailors as the inheritors of a specific and distinctly pious Muslim tradition.

PIETY AND GENDER IN THE *RISĀLAH-YI IDRĪSIYAH*

Khwaja Muhammad did not just counter the narratives of both elite Muslims and the colonial state about *darzīs* by offering Muslim pasts that centered the work of tailors and their lineages of descent and training. He also disputed the idea—present in the writings of both Shabihunnisa and the Anjuman-i Islāmiah—that sewing was incidental to a worker's religious identity. The authors of these texts hoped that sewing, like other forms of industrial training, could be used to help laboring Muslim women become socially respectable in an *ashrāf* model of femininity. However, they framed this work as a means to an end, not a form of piety in itself.

Conversely, Khwaja Muhammad tied the practice of Islam to the practice of sewing. He suggested that to fail to adhere to the norms of the trade—the "rules of the work"—would bring both religious and professional disrepute, and indeed that the religious and the professional were one and the same. He explained that tailors must maintain both "outer and inner purity" as they sewed. To be outwardly pure meant cleansing oneself and performing ablutions as one would for prayer, while inward purity meant to "work honestly, without theft." He argued that hadith taught that completing one's "daily work" without complaint was a *farẓ*, or religious duty.[71]

The *Risālah-yi Idrīsiyah* placed tailors at the center of a Muslim past and contemporary Muslim piety. In doing so, its author argued that knowledge of Islam was central to the correct practice of one's trade and that the correct practice of a trade could secure one's status as a pious and respectable Muslim. Khwaja Muhammad referenced the role of tailors and sewing in the creation of not only the "tunic of the Prophet Muhammad" worn on the night of the ascension, but also the "cloak" (*kisā'*) of the Prophet.[72] This was a reference to a well-known hadith that was particularly prominent within the Shia tradition but also recognized and well known among Sunnis. It held that the Prophet wrapped the members of his family "under his cloak" and in doing so purified them and removed their sins.[73] For Khwaja Muhammad, the hadith revealed the importance of the piety of tailors, implying that the cloak of the Prophet, like the Prophet himself, must have been pure. In other words, it showed not only that the labor of tailors had shaped and informed early Islamic history but also that the piety of tailors was central to the continued well-being and improvement of a wider Muslim community.

Khwaja Muhammad did not remark explicitly on the influence of the colonial state, and he was likewise silent about the relationship between his community and the charitable projects promulgated by elite Muslims. But he wrote in a moment when middle-class Muslims, many associated with religious reformist movements, sought to articulate moral standards and norms for Muslim artisans.[74] Khwaja Muhammad's silence about the efforts of middle-class Muslims to provide moral and practical education in trades such as sewing does not reflect a failure to recognize these projects. To the contrary, my contextualized reading of the *Risālah-yi Idrīsiyah* suggests that his religious, moral, and historical claims about the work of tailors were written in conversation with the rising influence of new, elite-led forms of artisan training aimed at tailors.

Khwaja Muhammad sought to distinguish the forms of training offered by artisan lineages from those proffered by both the colonial state and schools led by elite Muslims. Sewing, he argued, was central not only to tailors' laboring identities but also to their religious identities. He asserted that performing tailoring without a rootedness in its specific forms of Muslim piety risked exposing the tailor to both material and moral ruin. Conversely, learning to be a tailor without guidance from a pious (implicitly male) *ustād* meant that young tailors risked practicing the trade in an un-Islamic way. Rather than adopting colonial or middle-class narratives about what it meant to be a pious or modern Muslim tailor, Khwaja Muhammad argued that training within the community would always produce tailors who were both more adept and more pious.

In countering the claims of the colonial state and middle-class Muslim organizations about the nature of Indian tailors, Khwaja Muhammad also asserted the masculinity of his trade. He allowed limited space for the work of Muslim women tailors, masculinizing the work of tailors in a context where women were increasingly positioned as potential competitors. This suggests an important broader shift in how male tailors experienced the social and gendered spaces of sewing. Many likely continued to work alongside their wives and female relatives in family-run shops, a practice that was common across a wide range of artisan trades.[75] But they also aimed to limit the most lucrative spaces of tailoring to male authority and to claim the primacy of implicitly male forms of training and piety within the trade, in a context where forms of female training had expanded.

TECHNOLOGICAL CHANGE AND ARTISAN CREATIVITY IN THE *RISĀLAH-YI IDRĪSIYAH*

Given the degree to which technological ineptitude and a resistance to the sewing machine featured in colonial depictions of artisans, it is initially surprising to not find the sewing machine mentioned explicitly in the *Risālah-yi Idrīsiyah*. But Khwaja Muhammad portrayed his text as timeless, reflective of knowledge that had been revealed by God to Idris, passed down from *ustād* to *murīd* over millennia, and recorded in an earlier Persian *kasbnāmah*. In this understanding of sewing, addressing the technological change represented by the sewing machine, or the material change represented by colonial styles, could have diminished Khwaja Muhammad's ability to claim religious authority for his community.

Still, the pressures of economic, material, and technological change were not wholly overlooked in the text. Among Khwaja Muhammad's chief claims was that God had given the tailor the power of creativity and design. "The tailor's purpose," he wrote, "was created by almighty God, and as if by a flash of lightning, he gave [tailors] the power of creation, to make clothes fall into [the tailors'] hands."[76] To sew, to create new designs, and to embrace the creative force given by God was, for Khwaja Muhammad, to respect God's intentions for tailors. The type of clothes one sewed—or indeed, the specific tools one used—became secondary in this understanding of tailoring. Although the sewing machine itself remained unaddressed, the emphasis on creativity, or even flexibility, suggests that it was not necessarily prohibited.

Although the sewing machine was not prohibited or disdained in Khwaja Muhammad's understanding of his trade, it was not a key part of the education of a tailor at the feet of his master. As noted in the introduction to this chapter, the central conflict between texts published by elite Muslims, like *Muft kā darzī*, and community histories like the *Risālah-yi Idrīsiyah* was a difference in a fundamental understanding of the role of education. For Khwaja Muhammad, the education of a tailor at the feet of his *ustād* was a form of religious education, a chance to learn to be a good *Muslim* tailor. While the elite Muslims who founded new girls' schools were invested in the education of both good Muslims and good tailors, these categories remained distinct from each other. The sewing machine, for Khwaja Muhammad, may have been part of the practice of sewing and the embrace of the creative potential gifted by God, but it was not, in his understanding, fundamental to the practice of tailoring as a Muslim, so it remained absent from his *Risālah-yi Idrīsiyah*.

COMMUNITY HISTORIES IN A COMPARATIVE PERSPECTIVE

Khwaja Muhammad's *Risālah-yi Idrīsiyah* was far from being the only community history produced by a member of an artisan or working-class community or trade in the early twentieth century. Partly because of the increased accessibility of print, members of many economically or socially marginalized communities—with varied religious identities—published community histories that sought to improve their social status both vis-à-vis their coreligionists and vis-à-vis the colonial state. Badri Narayan argues that among Dalit and marginalized communities within a Hindu caste context, efforts to improve social standing included claiming "narratives of social origin" and community histories that both mirrored and undermined upper-caste claims. This process relied on—and perhaps even contributed to—the rise and popularization of print technology in the early twentieth century.[77]

Within Muslim communities, the early twentieth century also saw a rise in print production of community histories by laboring groups. Santosh Kumar Rai has shown that Muslim weavers from *jūlāhā* caste backgrounds in early twentieth-century North India asserted new social identities and forms of social prestige by claiming Arab origins, an identity usually seen as restricted to the *ashrāf*.[78] This included forming associations for social, religious, and economic uplift that published works about the community's history and correct religious practice. Leading members of Muslim butcher communities in early twentieth-century North India likewise used print to circulate community histories. One such work, the *Risālah-yi banī Quṣṣá* (Treatise of the children of Qussa), published in Delhi in 1925, was similar to the *Risālah-yi Idrīsiyah* in that it provided a lineage of practice and a set of moral and social precepts for butchers. It laid out a set of behaviors, rooted in an Islamic past and a Quranic tradition, that were indicative of a butcher's morality and piety.[79]

The *Risālah-yi banī Quṣṣá* also emphasized ancestral lineage and bloodline descent in a more direct way than the *Risālah-yi Idrīsiyah*. It argued that Delhi's Muslim butchers could claim ancestors who were members of prominent Arab families that had shaped the early Muslim world. In focusing on a narrative of community descent and Arab ancestry, *Risālah-yi banī Quṣṣá* more explicitly used the language of the *ashrāf* for laboring-class Muslims.[80] Its use of genealogy mirrored the late nineteenth- and early twentieth-century publications of family trees and narratives of descent by elite Muslims across the region, suggesting the spread and assertion of some elite assumptions about social respectability among Muslim laboring communities.[81]

The diversity of tactics represented by the work of *jūlāhā* weavers, as well as *Risālah-yi banī Quṣṣá* and the *Risālah-yi Idrīsiyah* highlights the fact that Muslim artisans and laborers in colonial India had differing opinions about how to assert social respectability in contexts of marginalization. One important element that was shared was an emphasis on the transmission of knowledge about their trade. Both the *Risālah-yi banī Quṣṣá* and the *Risālah-yi Idrīsiyah* highlighted Sufi regional lineages that the authors claimed had contributed to the transmission of knowledge across centuries. Just as Khwaja Muhammad traced knowledge about tailoring through a Sufi saintly lineage to Allahabad, so too did the author of the *Risālah-yi banī Quṣṣá*. He asserted that shrines and saints in Delhi were connected to Muslim butchers' histories.[82] Transmission through Sufi lineages, the authors of both the *Risālah-yi Idrīsiyah* and the *Risālah-yi banī Quṣṣá* argued, had allowed information about how to piously practice one's trade to move across languages and geographies. This emphasis on the process of transmission not only served to historically root the community histories but also suggested how their authors expected their printed texts to be used.

PRINT, LITERACY, AND ORALITY IN THE CIRCULATION OF COMMUNITY HISTORIES

An obvious problem with using community histories such as the *Risālah-yi Idrīsiyah* to reconstruct early twentieth-century artisan social identities is the question of literacy. We do not have detailed records that reflect, for certain, the percentages of artisans who could read and write in Urdu or any other language. We know, however, that overall literacy rates across British India remained around

10 percent through the early twentieth century and that literacy rates among artisan and laborer communities were usually much lower, with a few exceptions.[83] Therefore, when we read the *Risālah-yi Idrīsiyah*, we must do so with careful consideration of its intended audience and the ways that they may have accessed the text, even without high rates of literacy.

Khwaja Muhammad himself referenced this question in his conclusion to the *Risālah-yi Idrīsiyah*. He noted that the history was meant to provide blessings and moral edification for "anyone who reads it, or hears it read by another."[84] He clearly wrote with an assumption that literacy and orality intersected and that knowledge about sewing was transmitted between master and pupil—and within the community more broadly—through both methods. While not all tailors could read or read well, Khwaja Muhammad recognized that literate people read aloud to others and that those who were read to remembered and passed on knowledge to others. Indeed, while the *Risālah-yi Idrīsiyah* was a short, concise manual that did not make extensive use of poetry, other community histories, such as the *Risālah-yi banī Quṣṣá*, were written with large portions in verse, indicating that the author may have intended the text to be partially memorized to ease circulation.[85]

Moreover, Khwaja Muhammad attributed similar levels of authenticity to knowledge transmitted orally and through text. After all, he noted that the knowledge that he published through the *Risālah-yi Idrīsiyah* had itself reached him through a combination of oral and literary transmission. Although he cited from, and claimed to have translated portions of, a Persian *kasbnāmah* aimed at tailors, he also attributed his knowledge more broadly to the *ṣāḥib-i fan* or masters of the art, emphasizing his own, presumably orally transmitted, education.[86] And while he used the presumed textuality of the older *kasbnāmah* to support his authority on the trade and its history, he did not explicitly prefer textual knowledge over oral knowledge. He wrote that Idris had learned to tailor, not through a process of reading or writing but instead through God's revelation and command.[87]

It is in this context of mixed print and oral transmission that we should consider the religious traditions proposed by trade and community histories such as the *Risālah-yi Idrīsiyah*. For Khwaja Muhammad, print offered the opportunity to promulgate an alternative narrative of Muslim practice and belief that centered his own trade. But this promulgation relied on not only individual, literate leaders but also on processes of oral community transmission. Indeed, the popularization and transmission of trade histories that centered the narratives of Muslim laborers in the Islamic past was also informed by consolidating spaces of labor, including the development of large-scale urban workshops and factories. Processes of urbanization, migration, and industrialization, spurred by both the state and the consolidating Indian capitalist classes, contributed to intensifying social marginalization. At the same time, they also contributed to the ways that artisans circulated narratives about their histories and religious practices, enabling, in the case of Khwaja Muhammad, engagement with the printing press and translocal forms of oral and printed circulation. In chapter 4, I turn to these consolidating spaces of work as spaces of social interaction, asking how artisans circulated localized narratives of the Muslim pasts of their trades through processes of migration.

. . .

Shahid Amin has argued that the "siring of communities through print and the affixing of history to persistent memories" contributed to the consolidation of oppositional religious identities in India.[88] And indeed, emphasis on an exclusively Muslim past and claims on religious orthodoxy in the *Risālah-yi Idrīsiyah* and other similar community histories likely contributed to the elision or erasure of shared pasts. Because religiously shared pasts and practices were decried by both Muslim reformists and the colonial state as evidence of low status and a lack of orthodoxy, the community histories of Muslim artisans did often emphasize an exclusively Muslim social identity. But reading the *Risālah-yi Idrīsiyah* in its contemporary social context also highlights the fact that it was not a purely responsive text that adopted middle-class norms, colonial narratives, or reformist ideologies. It sought instead to "sire communities" and "affix history" to assert community identity for marginalized Muslims in a way that challenged exclusive elite and middle-class claims on Muslim pasts.

Ultimately, the publication of the *Risālah-yi Idrīsiyah* reflects efforts within established Muslim artisan communities to contest state and elite understandings of their trades, in part by positioning their work within narratives of the Muslim past. Muslim tailors like Khwaja Muhammad recognized their own marginalization within the ethnographic and educational projects of the colonial state, which often depicted them as unorthodox Muslims incapable of technological adaptation. Likewise, they understood that middle-class projects aimed at creating new classes of tailors were built on the fact that many *sharīf* Muslims viewed existing communities of Muslim tailors to be of poor social, familial, and educational backgrounds. As suggested by *Muft kā darzī*, schools led by elite Muslims sought to create new models of artisanal expertise. In doing so, they often excluded the forms of training that were most dominant within extant artisan communities, even as they asserted conceptions of the trade that made space for women's economic participation and professional authority. In response, the authors of trade histories placed their own work at the center of a Muslim tradition. They argued that their trade practices reflected, not technological or educational inflexibility, but their piety and connection to the Muslim past.

This chapter focuses on individuals like Khwaja Muhammad, who circulated their claims on the Muslim past through an expanding North Indian print economy. Chapter 4 turns to the circulation of artisan religious and material practices through migration. Drawing on analyses of migrant carpenters in Lahore and

Kanpur, it highlights the exchange of localized traditions within new urban workshops. Just as the *Risālah-yi Idrīsiyah* and the *Muft kā darzī* reflect a competitive knowledge economy about sewing, the carpentry manuals reflect multiple understandings of how to practice carpentry and how to practice Islam. Drawing on an Urdu-language manual of carpentry knowledge, as well as records of labor migration, chapter 4 traces how knowledge of carpentry moved and changed through processes of artisan urbanization.

4

Migrant Carpenters, Migrant Muslims

Religious and Technical Knowledge in Motion

A WOODWORKING MANUAL IN EARLY TWENTIETH-CENTURY KANPUR

Around 1910, the Islāmī Press in Kanpur released a series of Urdu-language manuals on artisan practices, attributed to the *kārkhānahdārs* (workshop owners) and *kārīgars* of the city. Among the most popular and widely promoted of these was a text on decorative woodwork. The book, titled *Lakṛī kā kām sikhānewālī kitāb* (The educational woodworking book), opened with an admission that "to write of all the types of woodwork would require too much time, and demand pages upon pages of text." For this reason, the author explained, he had chosen to confine himself to "wondrous and strange practices that the people of Europe have invented."[1] Over the subsequent twenty-two pages, the anonymous author showed how to emboss, lacquer, and ebonize wood, how to draft designs for woodcarving, and how to repair rotting wood, among other "wondrous practices."[2] While the author attributed these practices to European invention in his introduction, in subsequent descriptions he was more circumspect, referencing both "Hindustani" and "European" models of many of the practices he described.[3]

The unnamed author of *Lakṛī kā kām* positioned the city of Kanpur—and more specifically its *kārkhānahs*, or workshops—as a source of authority and regional prestige to assure readers of his knowledge of the wonders of woodwork. By the turn of the twentieth century, Kanpur featured in the North Indian popular imagination as a site of steadily expanding industrial development, home to workshops employing the newest technologies and producing goods in popular, modern styles.[4] The city was not, however, widely associated with carpentry or woodwork. Instead, it was known as a center of textile mills and tanneries, many of which had initially produced goods for the expansive colonial military and police contingents based in the city in the wake of 1857.[5] Although Kanpur lacked a popular regional reputation for carpentry, colonial reports and Indian newspapers noted that it was among the largest employers of carpenters in North India.[6]

Woodworkers—people who design and create wooden goods—and carpenters—those who construct, repair, and install wooden structures—flocked to Kanpur from towns across North India, adapting their skill sets for local employment. From at least the 1860s, they were drawn to the city because its textile mills, tanneries, and railway workshops relied on carpentry skills to build and repair machinery, and because they offered some of the highest wages for carpenters in the province.[7] Many migrants in Kanpur continued to labor within these spaces for decades. But others eventually established their own small workshops in the city, contracting for state and private projects or producing items popularly associated with their hometowns.

The author of *Lakṛī kā kām*, therefore, positioned his text as a repository of the latest knowledge of woodworking associated with bustling, modern *kārkhānahs* in Kanpur. Many of the skills described in the book were, by 1900, closely associated not with Europe but with regional centers of small-scale and decorative artisanal woodworking such as Saharanpur, Bareilly, Fatehpur, and Nagina, near Bijnor. As a result of migration from these cities and towns, Kanpur became an urban center where practices were brought together by different communities of woodworkers, and where woodworkers from across North India were brought into conversation with each other. In the process, these artisans exchanged material practices and, in many cases, narratives about their religious identities.

In Kanpur, migrant carpenters and woodworkers exchanged technical knowledge and skills with a wide range of counterparts, many of whom asserted differing religious identities. But the publication history of *Lakṛī kā kām* suggests that migrant Muslim woodworkers in the city exchanged not only technical knowledge but also knowledge about how to practice their religion. *Lakṛī kā kām* was printed by the Islāmī Press, a prominent publisher of Muslim religious and educational texts in Kanpur. It printed Urdu translations of the works of the eighteenth-century theologian Shah Waliullah Dehlvi, along with mathematics and chemistry primers for Muslim-run schools, which were advertised at the end of *Lakṛī kā kām*.[8]

By publishing with the Islāmī Press, the compilers of *Lakṛī kā kām* and the other artisan manuals in the series asserted a religious propriety and Muslim social character for the practices of artisanship that they profiled. Although the author of *Lakṛī kā kām* was not named, the cover page thanked Sayyid Muhammad Abdullah, a "knowledgeable merchant of Kanpur," for funding the compilation of the series.[9] As the owner of the Islāmī Press, along with several other workshops in Kanpur, Muhammad Abdullah was dedicated to what he saw as the proper religious and social comportment of North Indian Muslims. Through his press, he released self-authored books that were meant to educate upwardly mobile Muslims in the region—including potential urban migrants—on topics ranging from how to perform ablutions and pray to how to dress and eat.[10] Muhammad Abdullah and his press sought to contribute to the development of a community of urban Muslim readership that cut across class and economic difference and held shared interests in the religious and the industrial.

Lakṛī kā kām is an ambiguous text. Unlike many of the other technical manuals examined in the book, neither its author nor its intended audience are made explicit in its contents. The ambiguity of *Lakṛī kā kām* means that we must consider a range of possibilities, including its potential circulation among artisans, as well as its potential use among middle-class hobbyists or consumers eager to understand the models of woodwork available. Even with these ambiguities, however, *Lakṛī kā kām* demonstrates that the migration of artisans to Kanpur in the late nineteenth and early twentieth centuries spurred an exchange of models of woodworking. Whether we read the text as indicative of practices that artisans hoped to learn, or of the practices current in the city and available to hobbyists and consumers, *Lakṛī kā kām* reveals that diverse regional styles of woodworking coexisted in Kanpur. The practitioners of these styles likely jostled and competed for space in the market and, in some cases, may have guarded their practices. But they also encountered each other and likely circulated practices in the city's rapidly expanding industrial workshops.

Moreover, when read in the context of the Islāmī Press, *Lakṛī kā kām* suggests that through migration, Muslim carpenters also encountered plural forms of knowledge about what it meant to be Muslim and to labor as a Muslim artisan. In many cases, as reflected in the other publications of the press, this meant that members of the consolidating Kanpuri Muslim middle class sought to define pious Muslim comportment and behavior for the new migrants. But an analysis of the neighborhoods, workshops, and factories where Muslim carpenters settled and worked also highlights alternative spaces and forms of knowledge exchange. Migrant carpenters and woodworkers maintained and expanded localized and artisan-centric narratives about how to practice both Islam and carpentry.

• • •

This chapter asks how Muslim artisans exchanged and reoriented knowledge about their labor and their religious traditions, drawing on the experiences of migrant woodworkers and carpenters in rapidly industrializing cities of the United Provinces and Punjab. It focuses primarily on Kanpur and Lahore. Both Kanpur and Lahore were cities where carpentry and woodworking skills were in especially high demand. The rapid, late nineteenth-century growth of major workshops, factories, and mills in these cities necessitated the migration of growing numbers of carpenters, who contributed to the building and repair of wooden machines as well as to architectural woodwork and production of rail carriages. Migrant woodworkers and carpenters in Kanpur and Lahore were often beholden to emerging classes of wealthy *kārkhānahdār*s and dependent on wage labor, but growing demand for their specialized skills kept their wages high compared to other industrial laborers.[11] And as migrant carpenters built livelihoods in these industrial cities, some even opened independent workshops, selling wares and styles associated with their regions of origin and contributing to continuing migration from their hometowns.[12]

This chapter explores how technical and religious knowledge circulated within the artisans' adopted cities by analyzing how Muslim carpenters negotiated the economic pressures that led to migration to urban industrial centers. Migration spurred exchange between Muslim artisans from across North India and occasionally beyond. This exchange of knowledge through migration reshaped both technical practices of artisanship and Muslim religious narratives about the trade. As we saw in previous chapters, artisan religious traditions were often locally inflected. In some cases, this meant attachments to local Sufi shrines and lineages, and the assertion of a connection to the trade that emphasized localized practices and styles. In other cases, it meant that artisans claimed local Muslim pasts that contested their social marginalization by both the colonial state and Indian elites.

The migration of woodworkers and carpenters to large cities necessarily brought multiple artisan traditions of both woodwork and Islam into conversation with each other. For many carpenters, Kanpur and Lahore represented what Nile Green has termed a "religious economy" in which understandings of Islam were "changed in [their] very act of reproduction."[13] Simultaneously, migration to Kanpur and Lahore meant that Muslim artisans encountered new middle-class urban projects of religious reform. Focusing on Bombay, Green depicts the city as a space where migration spurred a turn toward a "comfortably familiar" Islam based on a "theology of intervention" via "holy men."[14] Conversely, in Lahore and Kanpur, there was flexible coproduction of multiple religious narratives and practices. Migrant carpenters learned new technical practices and material traditions that they applied in response to industrial demands; they also flexibly engaged with plural Muslim religious narratives for their trade.

Like print, migration placed Muslim artisan communities in conversation with each other, spurring Muslim artisans to assert translocal narratives of artisan Islam. Multiple artisanal and Islamic traditions intersected through widespread migration, most often from smaller provincial towns and cities to growing urban centers. Likewise, dependence on wage labor in cities such as Kanpur and Lahore meant that many Muslim carpenters and woodworkers encountered new technical expectations and new religious movements, which were often promoted to them by members of the emerging Indian Muslim capitalist classes.

After an overview of the pressures driving carpenter migration to Kanpur and Lahore, the chapter analyzes workshops, schools, and neighborhoods as sites of interactions among woodworkers. Muslim carpenters and woodworkers did not just engage with different regional or localized traditions of woodwork but also reimagined and reasserted localized inflections of their religious traditions. In its final sections, the chapter turns to the influence of the Muslim middle class and their efforts to reshape both carpentry work and artisan practices of Islam. I position these interventions as part of a wider economy of religious and material knowledge. Ultimately, I propose that the knowledge and religious narratives that migrant Muslim carpenters negotiated in Kanpur and Lahore contributed to the development of both Muslim political identities and class-based solidarities.

WHY MIGRATE? THE ECONOMIC PRESSURES OF WOODWORKING

By the turn of the twentieth century, the cities of Kanpur and Lahore were each home to over eight thousand carpenters and woodworkers.[15] Neither of these cities, however, was portrayed in colonial reports as a center of a major carpentry industry, though Lahore was often praised as a home to distinctive Mughal- and Sikh-era architectural woodwork. Cities such as Bareilly and Saharanpur in the United Provinces and Jullundur and Gujrat in Punjab were known across the region for the production of wooden goods, praised in colonial reports for the fine skill of their woodworkers.[16] Kanpur, in contrast, was portrayed as bereft of "traditions" of woodwork but in constant need of carpenters, while Lahore was said to boast a small number of skilled carpenters who had come to the city in earlier periods of migration. Colonial industrial reports regularly noted that demand for carpenters exceeded their numbers in these cities and that migrants therefore received relatively high wages.[17]

Carpenters both complicate and conform to some of the broad trends in early twentieth-century North Indian labor migration. Both before and after the First World War, migrant woodworkers and carpenters in large North Indian cities were often drawn from the artisan classes of smaller cities, towns, and *qasbahs*. This set them apart from many other migrants to urban industrial centers. As Douglas Haynes and Nikhil Rao note, prior to the 1920s, most other migrant laborers to industrializing Indian cities were drawn not from smaller cities but from "impoverished" rural "labor catchment areas."[18]

In 1906, S. H. Fremantle, an Indian Civil Service official responsible for several labor department and industrial reports in the United Provinces and Bengal, summed up a popular colonial position on the causes of woodworkers' migration in the region:

> At Cawnpore, the common cry is the short supply of workers in the shops. . . . There is no doubt that the supply of mechanics in Upper India has not kept pace with the demand created by the expanded use of machinery for industrial purposes and a liberal programme of public works. In Allahabad and Lucknow where there are old established shops there is a fairly good supply of trained men, but the other towns are as badly off in this respect as Cawnpore.[19]

The report went on to explain that "the greatest difficulty of all" was experienced by the owners of cotton gins and presses, because "these require constant adjustment and therefore necessitate a large staff of fitters."[20] The proliferation of wooden gins and presses necessitated the employment of carpenters, joiners, and woodworkers with the skills to adjust and fit the machines.[21]

In the United Provinces, some woodworkers were drawn to large cities such as Kanpur by the high demand for labor in the cities' growing factories and workshops, both private and state run, and the relatively high wages that they could command there. At the same time, many experienced economic marginalization in the towns, *qaṣbahs*, and small cities of the province, further spurring migration, informing a process that Christopher Bayly has described as the "redistribution and dislocation" of both mercantile and artisanal interests.[22] A 1921 industrial report described the pressures that woodworkers across the United Provinces had faced over the previous four decades. Its report from Etah district noted that one town in the district, Marehra, had been associated with the production of "office boxes, ladies toilet cases (singardan), and qalamdans (pen cases)" throughout the nineteenth century.[23] By the turn of the twentieth century, the town's woodworkers faced increased competition from items imported from Europe and large Indian cities, and their prices for household items were no longer competitive. The town also suffered a series of epidemics of "plague and influenza," contributing to a broader decrease in population.[24] As a result of these pressures, the report explains, "Many carpenters have migrated to other places and only a few are left. . . . Even the best *mistrī* is thinking of leaving Marehra for want of work."[25]

Like other labor migrants, woodworkers migrated to cities such as Kanpur through the intervention of "jobbers"—intermediary recruiters—who coordinated their employment within factories. As Chitra Joshi demonstrates in the context of textile workers in the Kanpur mills, laborers' connections with jobbers were often based on kinship networks, with locality and other social connections also spurring migration.[26] Moreover, within carpentry, jobber-laborer distinctions were often flexible, and laboring carpenters acted as recruiters for other individuals from their cities, towns, and kinship networks.

Despite frequent suggestions that migrants left smaller cities and towns in United Provinces for work in large cities such as Kanpur, colonial reports rarely identified urban migrants by their town of origin unless they were from outside the province. The 1906 labor report, for instance, specifically noted migrant carpenters who had arrived in the United Provinces from "Ahmedabad and Bombay."[27] But census records suggest that the largest communities of migrants in large cities of the United Provinces and Punjab were likely from cities and towns within the same province, rather than recruits from across the subcontinent. This meant, in the case of Kanpur, that they moved from towns such as Marehra, Nagina, and Fatehpur, and occasionally also cities such as Bareilly and Saharanpur.[28]

Workers from Saharanpur were especially attractive to large-scale workshop managers because Saharanpur itself boasted wagon shops and repair workshops for the North-Western Railways, which employed approximately three hundred people as of 1908.[29] As a result, workshop managers believed that Saharanpuri carpenters were likely to be trained in "modern" practices of carpentry. This perception was shared and promoted by colonial officials, such as J. L. Maffey, the Indian Civil Service officer who compiled a 1903 report on wood carving in the United Provinces. Maffey both praised Saharanpuri woodworkers for adapting new forms of inlay and lamented that their traditional skills were in decline because of their engagement with machines. He reinforced this narrative with a posed portrait of a Saharanpuri workshop where some artisans worked by hand but others labored with a fret-saw (see figure 7). While Maffey decried the fret-saw as an

FIGURE 7. Woodworkers engaged in carving and brass inlay in Saharanpur, in J. L. Maffey, *A Monograph on Wood Carving in the United Provinces of Agra and Oudh* (Allahabad: Government Press, 1903). (© British Library Board, IOR/V/27/942/20, plate 3)

"abomination" responsible for the decline of local traditions, the reputation of Saharanpuri woodworkers for engaging with new machines and practices likely endeared these workers to recruiters.[30]

However, Saharanpuri carpenters were also difficult to recruit to larger cities. This was due to the availability of work and high wages in their home city, as well as the proximity of Saharanpur to Roorkee, home to large public works department workshops offering high wages.[31] In contrast, workers from the small town of Nagina faced greater local precarity and fewer local options for migration. They were regionally renowned for manufacturing and carving "tables, chests, screens, and panels."[32] But workshops were usually family run, and there were limited alternative sites of employment for woodworkers. Woodworkers and carpenters from family workshops that fell on hard times had few options besides migration if they wished to continue in their trades.[33]

In contrast to Kanpur, where many migrants were drawn from towns and *qasbahs*, Lahore relied heavily on migration from midsized cities in other parts of Punjab, drawing in workers from these cities to labor in rapidly expanding railway workshops. Census reports from Lahore note the migration of artisans from Gujrat, Sialkot, and Gujranwala, three cities that were all characterized in colonial reports as home to significant carpentry traditions. As early as 1881, twenty thousand residents of Lahore *tehsil* were drawn from Sialkot alone.[34] While only a fraction of these migrants worked in carpentry or woodworking, industrial reports suggest that Sialkoti woodworkers were in high demand in Lahore's railway workshops and were well regarded in carriage and wheel-making factories, both state run and private.[35]

Because the woodworkers most frequently recruited for migration to Lahore were from midsized regional cities, many were embedded in multigenerational histories of migration. The increased demand for European-style furniture in the province with the consolidation of colonial rule after 1849 had led to a consolidation of woodworkers and carpenters in a few regional cities, particularly Gujrat, which became well known for its manufacture of wooden chairs.[36] Woodworkers migrated to Gujrat from nearby villages throughout the second half of the nineteenth century to join relatives and community members in the growing furniture industry. In many cases, however, a second or third generation of migrants moved from midsized cities in Punjab such as Gujrat to larger cities such as Lahore. This was spurred by a combination of factors, including community recruitment by jobbers and intermediaries, family connections, and periods of temporary economic downturn in local industries such as the furniture trade in Gujrat.[37] For instance, during the famine of 1896–97, many carpenters in cities including Gujrat, Sialkot, and Gujranwala were unable to sustain workshops because of decreased demand. While some secured positions as overseers in state famine relief projects, others migrated to Lahore to seek work in the city's rapidly expanding railway workshops.[38]

Underscoring processes of migration in both Punjab and the United Provinces is the fact that woodworkers and carpenters regularly shifted between fields within the larger trade, despite colonial claims to the contrary. British Indian monographs on industry distinguished sharply between practices of carpentry and woodworking. Their categorization and classification of subfields implied that a turner could hardly ever become an architectural woodworker and that a carpenter who made agricultural tools would never turn toward furniture or carriage manufacture.[39] But the growth of new trades—furniture manufacture, railway work, and new styles of architectural woodwork, for instance—belied these assumptions. Indeed, colonial administrators' own notes on the expansion and contraction of subfields within carpentry and woodworking reveal that Indian artisans moved flexibly between manufacturing practices.[40]

CARPENTRY AND RELIGIOUS COMMUNITY IN KANPUR AND LAHORE

Encounters between migrant Muslim carpenters gave rise to new understandings of their trade, their technologies, and their religious practices in Kanpur and Lahore. It is important to note that similar processes of knowledge exchange also took place among carpenters who identified as Hindu or Sikh and that religious communities often shared places of work and trade practices. The migrant carpenters who traveled to both Lahore and Kanpur identified with a variety of religious practices and beliefs. In the United Provinces, most woodworkers from Nagina, Saharanpur, and Fatehpur identified themselves in colonial census reports as Muslim, but Kanpur also drew in migrants from Bareilly and Gorakhpur, where most woodworkers identified as Hindu.[41] Likewise, while most carpenters and woodworkers from Gujrat, Sialkot, and Gujranwala identified as Muslim in the colonial census, others who migrated to Lahore from Jullundur and Hoshiarpur more frequently identified as Hindu or Sikh.[42]

These religious identities and communities were never hermetically bounded, and urbanization likely contributed to the creation of new shared spaces of religious practice as people negotiated and reimagined extant sites of veneration, memorialization, and worship.[43] Woodworkers and carpenters of varied religious identities exchanged technical practices in the context of new urban workshops, and they also may have exchanged knowledge about how to practice their trade piously. However, both the vernacular and colonial records present significant challenges for fully tracing potential exchanges of religious knowledge across communities.

As I explored in the introduction to this book, colonial administrators often dismissed Muslim artisans as not Muslim at all because of overlaps with Hindu spaces and practices of worship. We must be wary, therefore, of colonial claims of so-called syncretic practices that dismiss practitioners' own understandings of their traditions, particularly because, in their own publications, Muslim artisans often defended their practices as reflective of an Islamic orthodoxy.[44] Likewise, many contemporary Urdu publications aimed at artisans—such as, potentially, *Lakṛī kā kām*—were sponsored by members of the Muslim middle class who were invested in promoting what they saw as normative Muslim practices among laboring communities. Given these limitations, this chapter maintains a narrower focus on knowledge production among Muslim carpenters while noting, when possible, instances of engagement beyond a Muslim religious or social space.

LOCALIZING ISLAM AND CARPENTRY IN NORTH INDIA

The cities and towns that provided many of the migrants for the urban industrial projects of Kanpur and Lahore were home to distinct Muslim traditions that centered woodworking and carpentry. In a few cases, these traditions were shared across South Asian geographies. For instance, just as blacksmiths sometimes asserted a connection to Prophet Dawud, and tailors to Prophet Idris, Indian Muslim carpenters and woodworkers occasionally laid claim to a prophetic past. In the case of woodworkers, references most frequently invoked Nuh (Noah), with an emphasis on the idea that God revealed carpentry skills to Nuh to enable him to build a wooden ark capable of surviving the great flood. As was the case with blacksmiths and their association with Dawud, association with Nuh was one of the few forms of Muslim woodworker community identity that the colonial state recognized.[45]

The practice of tracing carpentry and woodwork to Nuh was also recognized and even promoted by Indian elites, both Muslim and non-Muslim. *Yādgar-i Bahāduri* (Memoir of Bahadur), an 1834 North Indian Persian compendium of regional histories that included descriptions of artisan trades, traced carpentry to Nuh. Its author, Bahadur Singh, a Kayastha, wrote in Lucknow during the reigns of the nawabs Ghaziuddin Haidar (1818–27) and Nasiruddin Haidar (1827–37). In his notes on carpentry and woodworking, Bahadur Singh noted the widespread belief that God had revealed carpentry skills to Nuh and argued that specific practices associated with Nuh were protected and transmitted by the carpentry "masters of Egypt."[46]

Middle-class and elite Indian interest in the relationship between Nuh and woodwork continued well into the twentieth century.[47] By the 1920s, prophetic histories provided a model to valorize artisanship and industry as members of the Muslim middle class increasingly positioned themselves as potential industrialists interested in scientific and material change.[48] Members of the middle class sought to appropriate and reorient artisan claims on a prophetic tradition to a greater degree than other—often localized—narratives about the Muslim pasts of artisan trades.

However, for carpenters and woodworkers in North Indian towns and small cities, other narratives were often more relevant to their day-to-day practice and social positionality. Many of these narratives were local, focused on specific technical or material practices and regional traditions, including attachments to regional shrines and Sufi lineages. As Hussain Ahmad Khan has noted, in the towns of central Punjab many carpenters professed an attachment to the Chishti Sufi Sheikh Bahauddin (d. 1628), who had reportedly "wandered the Punjab and other parts of India, head[ing] a group of carpenters."[49]

In other contexts, such as the town of Marehra, carpenters claimed connections to local shrines, not only as spaces of Muslim piety, but also as centers for the economic growth of their trade. Marehra is a major center of pilgrimage because it hosts seven sacred tombs, the most notable of which is that of Sayyid Shah Barkatullah Marehrvi, the founder of the Qadri-Barakati *silsilah*.[50] As Brannon Ingram has shown, mass pilgrimage to Sufi shrines expanded following the construction of new railway lines in the North-Western Provinces. In the case of the *ʿurs* of Sayyid Shah Barkatullah, Ingram notes, "Custodians of the shrine would advertise the event up and down the railway route and string lights from the station to the shrine."[51]

The expansion of these annual events in the mid-nineteenth century brought worshippers and celebrants—both Hindu and Muslim—from across the region to the shrine, and they also became important commercial events for the artisans of Marehra. In addition to woodworkers, the *ʿurs* of Sayyid Shah Barkatullah Marehrvi attracted glass bangle-makers from the town and district. Both groups built a regional reputation for handiwork in part by selling their goods to the attendees of the *ʿurs*.[52] The carving work of the Marehrvi carpenters, along with their skill in making wooden trinkets that travelers could take with them, meant that they became important economic and social participants in the *ʿurs*. While the carpenters of Marehra did not trace their trade to Sayyid Shah Barkatullah or other members of the Qadri-Barakati *silsilah*, they became prominent figures at the *ʿurs*. Their material and religious relationships with the shrine became intertwined, with the *ʿurs* providing both economic and spiritual benefit.

Other local traditions centered forms of descent from prominent regional ancestors who were cited as the source of skills in woodwork. For instance, the woodcarvers of Nagina maintained a community tradition that they were the descendants of Muslim artisans from Multan who had been brought to Nagina as arms manufacturers for the Mughal emperor Aurangzeb.[53] Having developed skills in intricately carving the wooden handles of knives and guns, they shifted to decorative woodwork as the regional market for weapons declined.

In Nagina, as across North India, association with a history of arms manufacture, particularly for the Mughal Empire, commanded a degree of prestige among nineteenth- and early twentieth-century Muslims. A connection with arms manufacturing sometimes allowed artisans to ascend in the caste-like social hierarchies explored in chapters 1 to 3, as they were considered more likely to be of Mughal—largely Central Asian—descent and to have accompanied the empire's armies across the Hindu Kush mountains. But even when Muslim weaponsmiths did not claim Mughal descent and accompanying status, their claims to patronage from former regional Muslim dynasties afforded them a degree of social prestige beyond that available to most artisans. As a result, for carpenters from Nagina, claims on a weaponsmithing past assured improved social positionality vis-à-vis other local Muslim artisan communities.

Reflecting the association between carpenters' claims on a past of weapons manufacture and Muslim social identity, Hafiz Muhammad Rahmatullah, a member of the Sufi Naqshbandi-Mujaddidi *silsilah* from Nagina, published a text on weapons and styles of fighting in 1904. Titled *Islāmi akhāṛā* (The Islamic arena) and published in Bijnor, the text argued that methods of fighting and styles of weapons had long Islamic lineages, passed down from *ustād* to *murīd*.[54] Though not written on behalf of the Muslim carpenters of Nagina, the text reflected their local social milieu in which a weaponsmithing past provided social status.[55] For a woodworker in Nagina, social, religious, and economic capital were bound together with this assertion of a distinct Muslim past for their trade and localized community.

MIGRATION AND KNOWLEDGE AMONG WOODWORKERS IN KANPUR AND LAHORE

When they migrated to major cities such as Kanpur or Lahore, Muslim carpenters brought with them these distinct religious and social associations, as well as material and technical knowledge. As a compilation of technical knowledge that drew its authority from the workshops of Kanpur, *Lakṛī kā kām* suggests the types of exchanges that took place among Muslim migrant carpenters there. I first explore how and why artisans exchanged material and technical knowledge, and then ask whether Muslim religious traditions also circulated among migrant carpenters.

Among the first practices described in *Lakṛī kā kām* is how to ebonize, or chemically darken a light-colored wood to make it appear more like black ebony.[56] Ebony carving was, by the late nineteenth century, closely associated with Nagina, but Maffey's 1903 report on wood carving noted that the high price of natural ebony, which was imported from the Central Provinces, limited the profitability of the trade.[57] As a result, Maffey lamented, carpenters from Nagina sometimes used alternative woods unless they were carving a commissioned ebony project, and he featured a posed photograph titled "Nagina 'ebony' carving," suggesting that most of the wood was not in fact ebony (see figure 8).[58] Alternative materials included rosewood (*shīsham*) and sandalwood, which were sometimes colored to resemble ebony. *Lakṛī kā kām* provided a "recipe" for ebonizing these alternative woods, explaining how to create a dye from madder (*majīth*), oak nuts (*māzū*), copperas (*hīrā kasis*), and fungal rust (*zangār*). Prepared over the course of three days, the dye would allow carpenters to make "ordinary" woods appear "as dark as ebony."[59]

FIGURE 8. "Ebony" woodcarvers in Nagina, featured in J. L. Maffey, *A Monograph on Wood Carving in the United Provinces of Agra and Oudh* (Allahabad: Government Press, 1903). (© British Library Board, IOR/V/27/942/20, plate 7)

As Eugenia Lean notes in her study of "vernacular industrialism" in early twentieth-century Chinese cosmetics production, workers who had "long produced" materials and goods described in technical manuals "may not have had much need" for such texts.[60] A woodworker trained in Nagina almost certainly did not require *Lakṛī kā kām* to learn a recipe for ebonizing wood. Upon migrating to Kanpur, however, he may have been expected to expand his repertoire of work. Whether this expansion of technical knowledge was achieved in conversation with other woodworkers or through texts such as *Lakṛī kā kām*, it reflected the circulation of knowledge within a context of urban migration.

For many migrant woodworkers, the first step in expanding one's repertoire of work was learning skills to secure wage labor repairing wooden machinery in private factories and mills, or in the railways and public works. Colonial reports that characterized carpentry and woodworking as inflexible trades expressed skepticism that artisans from small towns with specialized woodworking traditions were well suited to this type of industrialized labor. But even these reports admitted that specialized carvers or toymakers often also engaged in turning, in furniture manufacture, or in tool repair.[61] Artisans' knowledge of woodworking and carpentry often went beyond the specific practices for which they were renowned, and in periods of economic pressure it was these broader skill sets that enabled both a diversification of the trade and migration to large urban centers such as Kanpur.

Moreover, when migrant woodworkers and carpenters in Kanpur founded their own workshops, they were expected to sell goods that reflected not only specific practices of their hometowns but also a wider range of decorative styles that were in demand among urban consumers. Woodworking families who specialized in a specific style of work before migration expanded to other practices to succeed in a market that was less explicitly associated with specific localized styles, a process suggested by *Lakṛī kā kām*, with its description of varied regional and global styles and practices.[62] A woodworker from Nagina, for instance, might depend on the regional reputation of his hometown in ebony work to secure consumers for an independent workshop in Kanpur. But in the context of Kanpur, consumers would have also expected him to be proficient in practices such as lacquering and polishing—practices also described in detail in *Lakṛī kā kām*.[63] While some migrants to the city may have specialized in this work before their migration, others likely built on knowledge that they exchanged in contexts of wage labor.

For a migrant woodworker or carpenter, the situation was somewhat different in Lahore. In Kanpur, privately owned factories demanded the highest number of woodworkers and carpenters by the turn of the century, with railway and public works workshops supplementing this demand. In Lahore, by contrast, demand for woodworkers and carpenters was driven foremost by railway workshops. These were first established near the Lahore Junction station after the construction of the city's railway lines in 1860.[64] In 1904, the city's railway labor demands expanded, as colonial railway administrators founded additional workshops in Mughalpura, located approximately four kilometers to the east of Lahore Junction. Mughalpura became the site for the manufacture and repair of coaches and wagons for the North-Western Railways, a project that required hundreds of additional carpenters and woodworkers.[65]

Migrant carpenters to Lahore were therefore expected to be competent in practices ranging from fitting, joining, and sawing to polishing, sanding, and painting. Those who worked to build, expand, and maintain the city's stations were also expected to know practices of decorative architectural woodwork, such as fretwork. By the 1910s, the state emphasized the importance of new electrical tools for carpentry, especially for coach and carriage builders, and carpenters at Mughalpura were expected to become proficient with electric-powered circle saws and other tools.[66]

As was the case in Kanpur, migrant carpenters and woodworkers may have arrived in Lahore with several of these skills, while learning others on the job likely from other laborers in the workshop. Lack of familiarity with the technologies and materials used in railway workshops—particularly after the expansion of the use of electrical tools—could be dangerous. Throughout the 1910s and 1920s, most workplace injuries and deaths reported in Lahore took place at the railway workshops, both those located near the city station and those at Mughalpura. In 1922, 233 injuries occurred within the railway workshops at Mughalpura, making up over 70 percent of reported factory injuries in Punjab that year.[67] While most injuries were categorized as "minor," the next year, in 1923, the state factory act report noted that at Mughalpura, "a carpenter, whilst fixing a facie board to a coach, fell from its roof and sustained a fractured skull, as a result of which he died."[68]

Given the threats posed by railway labor for carpenters, the exchange of technical and material knowledge in the workplace was central not only to wage earning but also to physical survival. Knowledge about different practices of work circulated within workshops as well as in the neighborhoods where workers settled, through networks of migration and even jobber-laborer relationships. Moreover, as I argue in chapter 2, many of the so-called industrial arts did not conform to colonial assertions that Indian artisans were obsessed with secrecy and protecting trade knowledge. This was especially true for fields such as woodworking, carpentry, blacksmithing, and other trades that were in high demand in urban centers in the late nineteenth and early twentieth centuries. There were, of course, specific styles associated with regional cities and towns that a woodworker may have been loath to reveal if they secured him customers in a privately run workshop in Kanpur or Lahore. But in many other cases, the fact that demand for workers exceeded the number of skilled carpenters in major cities meant that migrants could earn higher pay by combining regional practices. Because many migrants initially focused on building and repairing wooden machinery for mills, tanneries, and railways, they had incentives to exchange knowledge that could enable the mutual improvement of wages and conditions.

MUSLIM SOCIAL IDENTITIES AND REMAKING OF COMMUNITIES AFTER MIGRATION

Lakṛī kā kām can thus be read as reflective of an urban context where migrant carpenters and woodworkers from different localities circulated technical practices and knowledge. This exchange occurred through the development of new neighborhoods, workshops, and other spaces of both socialization and labor where carpenters from different regions encountered each other in an industrializing city. Within these spaces, did carpenters exchange only information about how to carry out physical and technical processes? Or might these forms of association have also contributed to the circulation of religious modes of being, knowing, and asserting status?

In Lahore, new settlements around the Mughalpura workshops became centers where migrant carpenters and other artisans exchanged knowledge about how to be a pious Muslim. The railway administration had purchased the land around Mughalpura in the 1880s, establishing worker colonies and residences there well before the new carriage workshops opened in 1904. As Laura Bear notes, colonial railway administrators were initially reluctant to build housing colonies for Indian railway workers, though Europeans and Eurasians were housed through many railway projects from the 1860s. But the settlement of large numbers of Indian workers around the workshops convinced these administrators to construct small huts and basic housing for other Indian laborers by the 1890s.[69] As early as 1892, Mughalpura was home to approximately four thousand men who labored in the railway workshops, and this number expanded further after the establishment of the carriage workshops.[70] The influx of workers in Mughalpura spurred new forms of religious association and knowledge exchange between Muslim carpenters who had migrated from other regions of the province.

To meet the religious needs of the laborers in Mughalpura, small mosques, temples, gurudwaras, and churches were erected within and around workshop complexes. In 1909, as railway administrators sought to expand the marshaling yard in Mughalpura, they noted that a mosque used by laborers and residents stood on the newly acquired land. Following an inquiry, which demonstrated that the mosque was in regular use, railway administrators concluded that the only way to avoid conflict with the workers was to design the marshaling yard around the mosque.[71] While specific actions that laborers at Mughalpura took to protect the mosque are not recorded, the state fear of violence suggests that the workers may have successfully communicated discontent, or perhaps that railway administrators were aware of other instances of protest and conflict. In either case, for migrant carpenters in Lahore, religious spaces within the railway settlements and workshops and their accompanying mosques likely contributed to what Naveeda Khan characterized as "experimentation," "striving," and "Muslim becoming."[72]

Khan, in her study of post-Partition Lahore, emphasizes the actions that Lahori Muslims take as they lay claim to, or assert ownership over, local mosques, often for a specific community or *maslak* or pathway within Sunni Islam.[73] These claims are laid under "the shadow of the state," as worshippers work to prove the legitimacy of mosques that they have constructed on lands that are often marked for other purposes. Contemporary practices of state negotiation and efforts to demonstrate the legitimacy of a place of worship echo the experiences of carpenters and other laborers who worked in the railway workshops and worshipped in the marshaling yard mosque. Despite—or perhaps because of—their employment through a state project, these workers were able to negotiate under the "shadow of the state," even sparking a colonial reconsideration of railway design plans.[74]

TECHNICAL AND INDUSTRIAL SCHOOLS AS SITES OF MUSLIM EXCHANGE

In addition to workshops, residential settlements, and mosques, other spaces where members of woodworking families from various regional backgrounds exchanged knowledge and engaged in projects of "Muslim becoming" included colonial technical and industrial schools. Most artisans in colonial India were trained through family structures and apprenticeships.[75] But in both Kanpur and Lahore, the late nineteenth century saw a rapid expansion in formal industrial educational institutions. These institutions sought to reorient woodworking and carpentry training to the aims and preferences of the state. Nonetheless, they unintentionally provided spaces where migrant Muslim artisans—or their sons—exchanged both religious and technical knowledge with each other.

Overwhelmingly, scholarship on state-led artisan education in Lahore has focused on the Mayo School of Art (established 1875) and the projects of John Lockwood Kipling, including his engagement with the Arts and Crafts Movement. Much of this scholarship notes Kipling's interest in recruiting members of artisan communities to the school, as well as the fact that so-called hereditary craftsmen approached the school practically, often sending their sons for a year or two before withdrawing them and putting them to work.[76] But for a far larger number of woodworkers in Lahore, exposure to state-sponsored education was through the city's Railway Technical School, founded in 1889, not through the Mayo School.

Scholars have positioned the Railway Technical School as reflective of the type of training received by Anglo-Indian families who worked for the railways.[77] But in practice, annual reports show that students were overwhelmingly from Muslim artisan backgrounds, with few Anglo-Indian students. As of 1900, nearly 90 percent of enrolled students—299 out of 334—were Muslim.[78] This is an important distinction because students educated at the Railway Technical School were among the literate artisans who wrote and circulated the types of periodicals and manuals that argued for a shared social identity for *kārīgar*s. As I show in chapter 5, the contributions of these individuals to laboring identities, and the degree to which their engagement with Islam may have shaped those contributions, have often been understated.

In the early twentieth century, carpentry was by far the most popular course of study at the Railway Technical School. The year 1904 saw a significant growth in the student body, from 382 to 441 students. Of these, 75 percent, or 331 students, were enrolled in the carpentry program, with the remainder primarily studying metalsmithing. Predominantly Muslim, overwhelmingly from artisan families, with most students focused on carpentry and woodwork, the school was a key center for the education of the sons of Muslim carpenters and woodworkers who had migrated to Lahore to work for state projects.

The Railway Technical School also hosted small evening classes, primarily aimed at "apprentices and illiterate artisans" working within the railways but open to other working artisans in the city as well.[79] As was the case with the day students, most of the evening students identified as Muslim; in 1900, the student body was 85 percent Muslim. Classes met three times a week for two hours each, although colonial reports noted that attendance was sometimes sporadic.[80] The evening classes are especially notable because they did not focus primarily on carpentry or other artisan trades. Instead, artisans who already worked in these trades used the evening classes to learn basic literacy, math skills, and sometimes drawing.

Despite colonial administrative emphasis on the 3 Rs (reading, writing, arithmetic) and drawing at the Railway Technical School evening classes, it is likely that carpenters and other artisans also used the classes as a community space.[81] Aside from a few unusual instances, night schools provided limited access to improved wages or status in the industrial workplace.[82] They reflected, instead, the efforts of workers to access knowledge and community, a process that was especially important for migrants who may have lacked access to other forms of local community in urban Lahore. Railway workers seem to have chosen to attend to pursue what Tobias Higbie, in the American context, has termed "networks of other learners, communities, [and] organizational cultures" of "self-education."[83] The Railway Technical School and its evening classes were bound up in the railway administration's efforts to teach or coerce ways of laboring that conformed to their expectations of modern carpenters and woodworkers. Nonetheless, voluntary participation, especially in the evening classes, suggests that carpenters and woodworkers repurposed this educational space to exchange knowledge that they found relevant to their own lives and work.

In both Kanpur and Lahore, projects of "Muslim becoming" and claims on religious infrastructure thus grew in tandem with the exchange of technical knowledge in spaces such as the Railway Technical School. As woodworkers and carpenters congregated in new workshops, new spaces of worship, and new centers of education, they exchanged narratives about the pious nature of their work. These exchanges and encounters encouraged carpenters and woodworkers to emphasize certain traditions about their trades over others.

REORIENTING LOCAL TRADITIONS

Assertions of the divine revelation of carpentry to Nuh, for instance, may have contributed to a consolidation of shared Muslim identities in the workshops and factories, as this narrative did not assume connections to shrines or saintly lineages associated with specific localities. *Asrār al-ṣanʿat* (Secrets of industry)—a 1927 Urdu compendium of artisan trades and practices authored by ʿAlimuddin Nairang Hashmi, a state employee of princely Bhopal—proclaimed in one of its concluding verses that "the great carpenter [*najjār*] Nuh cultivated a new sweetness in industry."[84] It positioned Nuh alongside Adam, who "cultivated the ḥalal trades" as a progenitor of artisanal knowledge within prophetic tradition.

Hashmi's book was not aimed exclusively at artisans, and its multiple potential audiences highlight the fact that artisan traditions about prophetic forebearers for trades also circulated among other Muslims in the early twentieth century. Hashmi was born into an elite Muslim family in Bareilly and had secured work and income as a state adviser in the quasi-autonomous state of Bhopal. The *Asrār al-ṣanʿat* was partially aimed at members of his own class: Muslim elites who might aspire to direct or to patronize modern industrial workers. His lengthy and extensively illustrated compendium, which cost a rupee, was more expensive than most artisan manuals and profiled a wide range of trades. It was likely most useful to aspiring industrialists who hoped to learn enough about various trades to employ artisans. However, Hashmi did anticipate at least some artisan readers; his introduction noted that the compendium hoped to teach carpentry, woodworking, and blacksmithing to *kārīgar*s who lacked *rozgār* (employment) and sought to secure it in the growing cities of North India.[85]

The verses referencing Nuh suggest that by the mid-1920s, the revelation of carpentry to Nuh held multiple resonances for varied audiences. It provided a means for valorizing artisanship and industry for members of the Muslim middle class as they sought to socially justify their turn toward industrial production in the colonial capitalist economy.[86] For artisans and laborers, however, it provided a site for shared social and religious identity and a means of asserting a Muslim character for their trade that did not depend on shared descent or attachment to shared local shrines or Sufi lineages.

Conversely, emphasis on descent from prominent or especially skilled forebears, such as those claimed by woodworkers of Nagina, may have become more exclusionary, especially if they were asserted by artisans seeking to establish independent workshops. Migrant artisans experienced social exclusion in part because, as Kanpur expanded, middle-class Muslims who claimed *ashrāf* lineages became more engaged in asserting that status and in contesting the perceived fabrications of others. Soheb Niazi argues in a study of Amroha that "genealogy functioned as a tool to establish and legitimize social hierarchies."[87] From the 1890s, periodicals printed in Kanpur and sponsored by local merchants sought to define the prominent Muslim lineages of the city's residents. One monthly periodical, the *Tuḥfah-yi Muḥammadiyah* (Gift of Muhammad), sponsored by the merchant Muhammad Sayyid, routinely profiled prominent local Muslims and highlighted their lineages and forms of *ashrāf* descent.[88]

Artisans were never included in these discussions, as they were assumed to be from familial backgrounds lacking in prestige and status. Nonetheless, for migrant carpenters like those from Nagina—who based their claims of expertise on a narrative of a prestigious Muslim past and community descent from Mughal-era weaponsmiths—this context likely shaped their engagement with potential customers and other residents of the city. Association with an elite Muslim past likely helped distinguish these workers in a market crowded with migrant woodworkers, where genealogy and lineage provided powerful markers of inclusion and status.

Regardless of whether Muslim artisan traditions about carpentry and woodwork became more capacious or more exclusionary, they were reshaped through encounters with other Muslim carpenters and woodworkers in periods of intense migration to industrializing cities. At the same time, the entrenchment of carpenters and woodworkers in new workshops, neighborhoods, schools, and places of worship also meant that middle-class religious organizations targeted these communities and sought to reorient their practices.

MIDDLE-CLASS KNOWLEDGE AND THE REMAKING OF ARTISAN PRACTICES

The colonial state sought to reorient carpenter labor and education to suit its industrial demands in the late nineteenth century. Simultaneously, newly founded Muslim *anjumans*, or civic associations, sought to intervene in both industrial training and religious education. C. Ryan Perkins argues that members of new *anjumans* conceptualized "volunteerism" as "part and parcel of a modern sharif Muslim identity in the post-1857 period."[89] In this context, industrial education was framed as a form of community uplift, a means of improving the status of Muslims within India by teaching poor and working-class children to be pious Muslims and disciplined workers. For some members of these groups, such as Muhammad Abdullah, the sponsor of *Lakṛī kā kām*, educating carpenters and woodworkers may have offered economic benefits, as they employed these laborers in their workshops.[90] For many other members of the Muslim middle class, however, charitable giving to industrial education offered an opportunity to reshape the religious, social, and material practices of their poor and laboring coreligionists.

As migration and industrialization led to the congregation of large numbers of Muslim workers in urban centers like Lahore and Kanpur, members of the Muslim *anjumans* debated the best ways to "uplift" laborers and their children. By this, they meant disciplining laborers' religious practices, which middle-class Muslims often characterized as unduly influenced by Hindu traditions.[91] They also sought to provide economic uplift for Muslim laborers, arguing that this would increase the respectability and influence of the Muslim *qaum* (community).[92]

Large *anjumans* in both Lahore and Kanpur settled on the foundation of charitable orphanage-industrial schools as one of their most important investments. The schools were partially created in response to Christian missionary institutions aimed at orphans and the urban poor, which likewise emphasized industrial training as part of their conversion efforts. By the 1880s, both Hindu and Muslim educational and reformist organizations sought to counter Christian influence by training poor children and orphans in trades. Carpentry was among the most promoted trades at these schools, as it was seen as a consistent path to a stable livelihood, but also one that required less investment in materials and space than trades such as blacksmithing.[93]

In Lahore, the most prominent orphanage-industrial school was sponsored by the Anjuman-i ḥimāyat-i Islām (Association for the Defense of Islam, or AHI), an organization founded in Lahore in 1884 with an initial membership of over nine hundred people.[94] Its members emphasized their commitment to charity and industrial training that inculcated "correct" Muslim practices and behaviors in workers. The group opened its first orphanage-industrial school in Lahore in 1887. Similarly, beginning in 1894, the members of the Anjuman-i Islāmiyah (Islamic Association) of Kanpur raised funds and support for a local *yatīmkhānah*, or orphanage, which also functioned as an industrial school and workshop. In both cases, woodworking training was the most significant form of boys' industrial education at the schools, and both schools developed internal carpentry workshops to make the schools partially self-sustaining by selling goods produced by pupils. To this end, the schools, like their Christian and Hindu counterparts, were sites of coerced labor, where poor boys were compelled to work for the benefit of the institutions but rarely received more than nominal income from the items that they produced.[95]

Moreover, while these schools sought to create new models for what it meant to be a pious, disciplined, and modern Muslim carpenter, their influence over the laboring lives of woodworking communities remained limited. The Anjuman-i Islāmiyah orphanage in Kanpur educated only twenty-six boys and seven girls as of 1913, and only the boys were trained in carpentry. The AHI orphanage was larger, with approximately 220 boys and 15 girls as of 1913, but only about half of the boys trained in carpentry.[96] Its larger numbers reflected the policy of the state of Punjab of sending the indigent or orphaned Muslim children to orphanage-charitable schools run by Muslim *anjumans*, which took on increased importance during the First World War.[97] Both institutions also grew in the 1920s and 1930s as they increasingly sought to attract potential carpentry students who were not indigent or orphaned. By 1934, the institution of the Anjuman-i Islāmiyah of Kanpur was recognized by the state administration as primarily a carpentry school for both orphans and others, and received state grants-in-aid for carpentry education.[98] But far larger numbers of youths were trained in carpentry at home, in apprenticeships, or through state-run schools.

The orphanage-industrial schools are important both because they were centers of carpentry training and because they reflected broader efforts by elite and middle-class Muslims to reorient how artisans practiced their faith and their trades. One founder of a small orphanage-industrial school who published a treatise on the subject through a Kanpuri press in 1918 explained that his aim was to provide both "material education" (*taʿlīm-i māddī*) and "religious education" (*taʿlīm-i dīnī*).[99] The author, a descendant of the prominent Naqshbandi Sufi saint Ahmad Sirhindi (1564–1624), founded an orphanage that taught carpentry near the shrine of his ancestor and sought to improve the quality of religious and industrial training in orphanages across India.[100] He lamented that wealthy Muslims assumed that poor boys "did not require high levels of religious education," asserting to the contrary that if the "Muslim *qaum*" hoped to advance in India, even "the poorest orphan" needed a full education in his faith.[101]

Most carpenters did not encounter these projects of religious education and ideals of material and spiritual uplift in orphanage-industrial schools. Nonetheless, they were an important part of the religious economy that migrant carpenter communities inhabited and negotiated in cities such as Kanpur and Lahore. The influence of these ideals is reflected in texts such as *Lakṛī kā kām*. While profiling the decorative woodworking practices current in Kanpur's workshops, the author and publisher assumed that their urban Muslim readership shared religious and industrial interests across class boundaries. The publishers of technical manuals imagined a Muslim readership composed of both members of the industrial middle class and artisans themselves, all of whom they positioned as committed to the social uplift of the *qaum*.

The imagination of a shared Muslim identity, education, and commitment to the social and economic uplift of Muslims is implicit in *Lakṛī kā kām*, accessible primarily through its publication history. In other technical manuals that addressed woodworking and carpentry, however, it is far more explicit. The *Asrār al-ṣan ʿat*, the 1927 manual that referenced Nuh's influence on carpentry, was published in Agra but circulated across North Indian cities. Its introduction positioned "industry and trade" as central values of the Muslim *qaum* in North India. It admonished Muslims who lacked interest in artisanship, asserting that God had created man and in turn had given him the powers of industry and material creation.[102] By tying industriousness in artisan trades—including carpentry and metalworking—to Muslim piety and belief, the author emphasized the values that members of the *anjumans* sought to inculcate in both their own class and communities of laboring-class Muslims.

The *Asrār al-ṣan ʿat* integrated these moral assertions about industriousness with practical tips on topics ranging from how to design wooden trunks and chairs to how to prepare and apply lacquers. As noted earlier, the *Asrār al-ṣan ʿat* explicitly addressed *kārīgar*s in its introduction but may have been too expensive or unfocused to reach a wide working-class audience. Still, even if it was not widely read in workshops, artisans may have encountered its expectations and narratives from their managers and workshop owners. Both *Asrār al-ṣan ʿat* and *Lakṛī kā kām* reflect the integration of middle-class ideals of Muslim industriousness with technical and material knowledge in texts that at least partially addressed woodworkers and other artisans.

Elite-led charities and social reformist movements sometimes also sought to reorient laboring family and marital practices alongside their efforts to inculcate new forms of Muslim industriousness. As noted earlier, new residential settlements contributed to the remaking of workers' religious and social communities, including through familial and neighborhood relationships. Some male migrant laborers in early twentieth-century India maintained families in their home regions, where their wives continued to engage in agricultural and household labor.[103] Colonial policy makers fretted that labor recruitment—of both men and women—from rural regions would weaken bonds of marriage among poor Indians, particularly Muslims, whom they characterized as being prone to "transient" marriage customs.[104] In response, some Muslim social reformers sought to empower Muslim men to economically sustain a family, while simultaneously promoting middle-class ideals of gendered respectability to women from laboring communities, often through *ajuman*s such as the AHI.[105]

In the case of many carpenters and woodworkers, relatively higher wages in comparison to most other industrial migrant laborers often enabled them to bring families to the city or to identify marriage prospects among their larger endogamous networks. Women and girls in these families thus encountered shifting urban socioreligious norms surrounding their public presence and labor, including the efforts of Muslim reformist *anjumans* to promote their own concepts of gendered respectability. The creation of consolidated settlements of workers and their families provided new sites for the intervention of social reformers in local debates about familial and marital comportment. While organizations such as the AHI focused much of their internal debate about Muslim women's education on the propriety of formal education for elite women, they also explicitly claimed to attempt to change the perspectives of "*ajlāf* [laboring class] men."[106] Through educational programs and social outreach—including industrial schools aimed at both men and women—these middle-class social reformers sought to remake norms of marriage and women's economic participation in new artisan urban settlements. The AHI, for instance, promoted crafts education for the wives, daughters, and widows of artisans, arguing that "it is only ignorance that has made women incapable," even as they also encouraged women to work primarily within the home to maintain consolidating urban norms of social respectability.[107]

MIGRATION, KNOWLEDGE, AND EMERGING SOCIAL SOLIDARITIES

While middle-class visions for Muslim artisanship are often the most well attested in the archive, they formed only one part of a broader exchange of technical, religious, and material knowledge among migrant carpenters and woodworkers. In the wake of migration to Lahore and Kanpur, Muslim carpenters exchanged, debated, and reasserted their technical knowledge and relationship with Islam in urban workshops, places of worship, and educational contexts. As Thomas Chambers has argued in his ethnographic study of Saharanpuri woodworkers and twenty-first-century migration, "Various forms of continuity persist within both the material and the imagined," even when "migrations create shifts" in the self-assertions of migrants.[108] In the context of late nineteenth- and early twentieth-century migration, this meant that forms of technical and religious continuity interpenetrated reimagined and redefined practices, including those that were shaped by middle-class movements or colonial demands on production.

The knowledge, skills, and religious narratives that Muslim artisans negotiated in large cities such as Kanpur and Lucknow contributed to the consolidation of both Muslim political solidarities and class-based identities. Through the exchange of these forms of knowledge and skill, migrant Muslim carpenters and other artisans built new communities and urban social identities, which they engaged for a range of political purposes. In Kanpur, for instance, the lead-up to the 1913

Machchli Bazaar Masjid massacre suggests that Muslim elites and members of the middle class saw a degree of success in their efforts to engage with Muslim workers. In 1913, the Kanpur Municipal Board decided to demolish the perimeter and *wuẓū* (ablutions) area of the Machchli Bazaar Mosque to widen a roadway.[109] The mosque was a site of worship for many of the city's laboring-class Muslims, especially workers in textiles and leather, but also groups such as carpenters and blacksmiths who maintained machinery in the mills and tanneries.[110] On August 3, 1913, thousands of Muslims from across class communities marched to the mosque, symbolically restoring it by piling up bricks over the demolished area. In response, the magistrate of Kanpur ordered the police to open fire on the protesters, resulting in at least sixteen deaths, with twenty-eight others reported injured.[111]

Sana Haroon argues that Muslim agitation for the Machchli Bazaar Masjid was not simply a reflection of "instrumentalist" efforts among elite Muslim political actors who sought to promote anticolonial agitation within their community. Instead, the Muslims who protested the demolition of the mosque's perimeter and exterior spaces asserted social and spiritual connections to the building and its surroundings.[112] But despite the cross-class nature of the protests, Muslim laborers were excluded from negotiations with the colonial state in the wake of the massacre. Some colonial administrators attempted to "appease" the "respectable Muslims" of Kanpur, but they evoked the involvement of urban workers in the events to characterize these groups as "fanatical."[113] Likewise, Muslim lawyers rallied behind the most prominent arrested Muslim activists—members of the middle class—while sidelining the popular nature of the protest. Even when elite and laboring-class Muslims participated in the same forms of mass organization, state and elite response to each group differed significantly, contributing to an ongoing sense of social difference and alienation among migrant laboring communities.

And indeed, Muslim laborers sometimes resisted the efforts of elite and middle-class Muslims to co-opt or reorient their forms of protest, for instance during the 1920 Railway Strike in Lahore. Ahmad Azhar notes that Muslim participants in this large-scale labor agitation made recourse to their religion by emphasizing the "poverty" of the Prophet Muhammad's early companions.[114] This language explicitly limited the space and influence for middle-class Muslim industrialists, some of whom sought to reorient the strikers toward participation in the ongoing Khilafat movement and critiqued the strikers for protesting for "bread" rather than "God."[115]

In chapters 5 and 6, I expand my analysis of the ways in which the exchange of artisan knowledge and religious narratives spurred new solidarities and forms of social and political organization. Likewise, I ask how labor within colonial infrastructure—such as the railway workshops in Lahore—presented specific challenges for Muslim artisans who sought to assert Muslim pasts and traditions for their technologies and practices of production. In these spaces, I argue, Muslim artisans expanded the technical and religious traditions that they circulated through migration and print. Some Muslim artisan communities engaged with colonial technologies—such as the steam engine—as a way of building new social and economic solidarities in a context that diminished their technical authority. Simultaneously, others positioned new materials—such as the new plasters preferred by the British Indian public works—within long-standing artisan traditions of Muslim piety and practice. Chapters 5 and 6 elucidate the plurality of Muslim artisan responses to the technologies that they encountered through employment on state projects.

PART THREE

Muslim Artisans, State Projects, and Hierarchies of Technical Knowledge

5

The Steam Engine as a Muslim Technology

Boilermaking and Artisan Islam

THE STEAM ENGINE AS THE "KEY TO INDUSTRY"

In 1890, Hakimuddin, the head fitter for the North-Western State Railways Locomotive Department in Sukkur, Sindh, published a manual on the steam engine. Titled *Kalīd-i ṣanʿat* (The key to industry) and published by the New Imperial Press in Lahore, the text provided notes on the use of steam engines and described how to maintain them. It explained the principles behind locomotive steam engines, focusing especially on boiler repair and use within railway workshops, and guiding Indian workers on how to move up in the locomotive workshop hierarchy.[1] The text proved popular. Following an initial print run of 350 copies, it was republished by the Khādim al-Ṭaʿlīm Press three times over the subsequent thirty years.[2]

Hakimuddin was the son of Daswandi, a *mistrī* from a small town in Amritsar district, Punjab, and he framed his text as aimed at others from *kārīgar* and master artisan backgrounds who hoped to transition to roles in locomotive workshops. These roles focused on boilermaking, which in late nineteenth-century India primarily meant the maintenance and repair of steam engines. Educated both at home and at a colonial industrial school, Hakimuddin was part of a small cadre of upwardly mobile hereditary artisans who secured salaried or supervisory state employment through the colonial railway locomotive department, and he sought to position his text as accessible to others from artisan backgrounds. He complained that other Urdu texts on boilermaking were inaccessible to Indian *kārīgar*s because they neglected the workers' social contexts and were written in unfamiliar registers of Urdu. To counter this problem, Hakimuddin claimed to have written his text "without eloquent turns of phrase or idiomatic expressions," relying partially on English loanwords that were popularly used in railway workshops, since "the Urdu terms for this [boilermaking] knowledge are still not widespread."[3]

In a lengthy introduction, Hakimuddin laid out his understanding of the role that the steam engine should play in Indian society and his hopes for the future of Indian artisans, though he began by acknowledging the divine "true mechanic." "Infinite praise is due to the true mechanic, who, with only divine power, unrestrained by tools or measurements, created the perfect human engine, making it the origin of a thousand tomorrows."[4] For Hakimuddin, the steam engine allowed humanity to draw forward the "train of endless progress" begun through divine creation.[5]

Hakimuddin characterized divinely inspired technical progress as a boon for all mankind but also, specifically, as a route to economic and social stability for India's skilled but impoverished artisans. "The poor man," Hakimuddin maintained, was "terrified" to make demands or changes to his work, for he lived in "fear of a loss of wages."[6] But, he claimed, knowledge of the steam engine could counter such oppression. Artisans, in his view, required access to forms of training and encouragement to adapt their knowledge to the manufacture and maintenance of new tools, which would allow them to secure higher wages and improved social status.

For instance, while describing steam injectors that were used to provide cold water to the boiler from exhaust steam, Hakimuddin explained that the principles behind the injectors could be confusing but that an understanding of their use was necessary to their maintenance, repair, and use. He provided an evocative metaphor of a hookah to explain how an injector functioned:

> Let us think of [the injector] as if it were a hookah, in which the base will always keep its form. Blowing into the hose of the hookah will produce a fountain of water in the base and steam out of the other hose, which will disperse, so long as there are no obstacles at the mouth of the hose. But if a stone is placed on the mouth, then the steam will only be able to come out if the force of our breath overcomes the weight of the stone. . . . In the same way, the water from the injector flows into the boiler. There are many obstacles in the way, so now we must provide the formula that overcomes the obstacle and clears the way for the water to enter the boiler.[7]

The description of the steam injector as hookah served less to fully explain its mechanical properties than to make the steam technology accessible to artisans who possessed related technical skills but limited experience with boilers. Similarly, Hakimuddin provided a sketch of the injector (figure 9), which he referenced repeatedly in his description. While the sketch was useful as an overview, Hakimuddin's text recognized that artisans would need to physically engage with the injector to fully understand its use. Hakimuddin thus supplied familiarity with the properties of the steam engine to artisans seeking railway positions, while also recognizing that much of their physical engagement with steam technology would be learned through their job.[8]

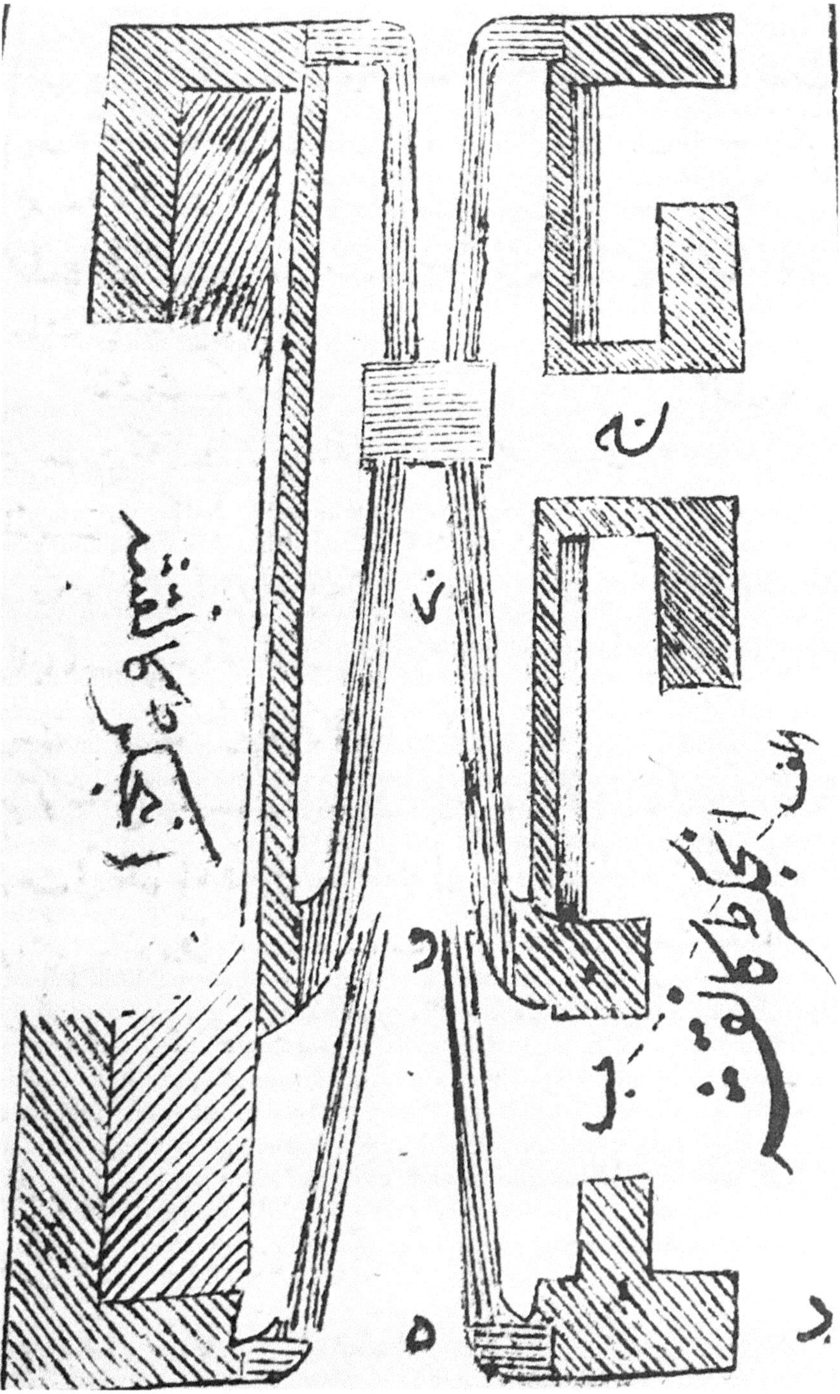

FIGURE 9. A sketch of a steam injector from the 1922 edition of Hakimuddin's *Kalīd-i ṣanʿat* (Lahore: Khādim al-Ṭaʿlīm Press) (Punjab Public Library)

The positions and labor described in the *Kalīd-i ṣanʿat* differed significantly from many of the others described in this book, in that they did not primarily involve making or building new items for sale or for patrons. Rather, these workers focused on the repair, maintenance, and use of boilers and other machinery associated with locomotive workshops. But for Hakimuddin—a master artisan who had secured upward mobility and economic stability through railway employment—railway workers remained *kārīgar*s, skilled workers whose labor reflected divinely inspired ingenuity. This perspective hinted at the often-overlooked centrality of repair and maintenance, while also reflecting the relative fluidity with which some North Indian artisans moved between artisanal production and railway industrial labor.

Hakimuddin's treatise also differs from the other materials explored in this book in that he was not significantly concerned with Muslim religious narratives of labor and technology. Indeed, the only explicit mentions of God in the text is Hakimuddin's introductory evocation the "true mechanic" and his "divine power," a phrase he transliterated from English as "dīvāyin pāvar."[9] Hakimuddin framed his text as intended for Indian *kārīgar*s, broadly defined, emphasizing their shared social positionalities and decrying the religious conflict and "separation" that he saw as preventing economic and industrial growth.[10]

Despite these differences, I read *Kalīd-i ṣanʿat* as a record of Muslim artisan negotiation of the colonial industrial economy. When read alongside colonial records of railway labor and middle-class Muslim efforts to claim technological authority for members of their own class, the *Kalīd-i ṣanʿat* suggests the ways that Muslim artisans like Hakimuddin sought to raise *kārīgar*s' social standing. To this end, the steam engine can be studied as a Muslim technology, not because Hakimuddin or other Muslim master artisans offered a religious past or tradition for it, but because it was a technology through which Muslim artisans asserted their visions for the economic and social futures of their communities.

Within two decades of the publication of the *Kalīd-i ṣanʿat*, Muslim railway laborers, including boilermakers, blacksmiths, and others employed in the maintenance of steam engines, founded organizations aimed at the social uplift of their communities. The evocation of *kārīgar*s' authority in the *Kalīd-i ṣanʿat* suggests a potential historical lineage for Muslim artisan efforts to assert shared class and social identities, both within and across religious communities. Ultimately, a contextualized reading of the *Kalīd-i ṣanʿat* and its insistence on artisanal ingenuity may help trace the influence of Muslim artisan identities on the influential railway labor solidarities and movements of early twentieth century.

. . .

This chapter focuses on the relationships between communities involved in the labor and oversight of boilermaking and the maintenance and use of steam engines in the railways of Punjab and the United Provinces. Hakimuddin wrote at a moment of significant upheaval and realignment in the hierarchies of control and application of technical knowledge. Ajantha Subramanian characterizes this shift in the social hierarchies of technical knowledge and authority as one "from guild to state, shopfloor to classroom, and lower to upper caste."[11] Hakimuddin occupied an ambiguous position in this shift. He was the son of a blacksmithing *mistrī* who had trained with his father but subsequently enrolled in a colonial technical school and secured state employment. He was part of a small cadre of artisans, from varied religious backgrounds, who made this transition to supervisory railway intermediary in the late nineteenth century. But by the time he published his text, this group was increasingly marginalized by an emerging middle class of technical overseers from landholding, service gentry, and other elite backgrounds.

The chapter argues that artisans—and artisan-intermediaries like Hakimuddin—did not simply acquiesce to the displacement and devaluation of artisanal skill within railway hierarchies over the course of the late nineteenth and early twentieth centuries. Instead, they developed narratives of *kārīgar* solidarity, based on both shared religious pasts and shared skill. They promoted and, in the words of Kenneth George and Kiran Narayan, "exalted" their distinctive physical skills as a form of technical authority.[12] The exaltation of *kārīgars*' knowledge seen in the *Kalīd-i ṣanʿat* was ultimately not successful in preserving hereditary artisans' technical authority within the railways. Nonetheless, I argue that it informed the social and religious solidarities that became increasingly prominent among railway laborers over the subsequent decades. I read the *Kalīd-i ṣanʿat* as reflective of a form of artisan Islam because it attempted to cultivate shared Muslim laboring and social spaces within locomotive workshops, not because it proposed a specific Muslim past for new technologies.

This chapter positions the late nineteenth-century *Kalīd-i ṣanʿat* at a key moment of upheaval in the forms of technical authority that commanded influence among Indian employees of the railway locomotive departments. After an overview of the rise of Indian boilermaking and locomotive workshops, it turns to the social, laboring, and religious spaces of Muslim artisan-intermediaries such as Hakimuddin and their relationships with the laborers they oversaw. Subsequently, the chapter examines the displacement of Hakimuddin's class of artisan-intermediaries by new cadres of overseers drawn primarily from upper-caste Hindu and Sikh and *sharīf* Muslim backgrounds. I argue that middle-class Muslim technical overseers promoted their own visions of Islamic technical modernity for railway labor, which often diverged from those popular among artisan laborers. Finally, the chapter asks how artisans challenged the marginalization of their forms of technical authority and traces the ways that these challenges contributed to the laboring identities asserted by Muslim boilermakers, locomotive repairmen, and other laborers through the 1920s and 1930s.

INDIAN ARTISANS AND THE RISE OF BOILERMAKING

Starting around the late nineteenth century, colonial railway authorities began to "Indianize" railway labor and oversight, a process that Ian Kerr traces from its origins in the 1860s but that gained significant momentum around the turn of the twentieth century.[13] While "Indianization" created new spaces of employment for educated Indians, colonial railway administrators often enforced class, caste, and social hierarchies through this process. By the early twentieth century, even as Indians were recruited for a wider range of positions within the railways, the social hierarchies of positions open to Indians became more ossified.

Though many positions remained open only to Europeans (and sometimes Anglo-Indians), from the second half of the nineteenth century, mid- and low-level supervisory positions such as "head fitter," "subinspector," "overseer," and "chargeman" recruited "natives."[14] In many cases, these positions were filled by middle-class Indian men, the sons of the so-called service gentry who leveraged colonial higher education to secure state employment. But between the 1860s and the turn of the twentieth century, a small number of young men from artisan families with training in trades such as blacksmithing and carpentry also secured these positions. The number of master artisans like Hakimuddin who were able to access even supervisory positions was never large, but the possibility of upward mobility became even more remote around the turn of the century as growing numbers of middle-class Indians sought railway employment. Indian railway intermediaries—whether from artisan or middle-class backgrounds—oversaw larger cadres of Indian artisan laborers who transitioned to railway labor. This class continued to perform the lowest-paid and most physically taxing work of boiler use and repair throughout the early twentieth century.

In Hakimuddin's view, labor within the railways was a potential route not only to prosperity but also to forms of industrial authority and social status for Indian artisans. More specifically, he argued that knowledge of steam engines and boilermaking would allow artisans to adapt their extant knowledge to a trade that was in high demand. But which artisan communities transitioned into boilermaking, and what forms of social and educational access did they require to make that transition possible? In nineteenth-century India, practices such as boilermaking were often not recognized as distinct trades dependent on distinct skills. The term *boilermaker* did not reach widespread use even in Britain until the mid-nineteenth century.[15] Laborers were, instead, often recorded simply as "blacksmiths" or sometimes as "machinists," reflecting the broad nature of their skills and sometimes the trade from which they had been recruited.[16] Nonetheless, it is possible to identify the centers of the growth of boilermaking as a trade and, in doing so, to consider the adaptation of specific artisan communities to its technologies and forms of labor.

Much of the earliest demand for boilermakers in the late eighteenth and early nineteenth centuries centered on the dockyards of port cities, particularly Calcutta and Bombay. There the construction, inspection, maintenance, repair, and use of steamships necessitated a growing labor force familiar with boilers. The development of small-scale iron foundries, textile factories that relied on steam power, and a variety of saw, oil, and paper mills also spurred demand for boilermakers in mid-nineteenth-century urban India.[17]

The rapid mid-nineteenth-century expansion of colonial railway infrastructure represented a second stage in the growth of boilermaking as a distinct trade in India. As suggested by Hakimuddin's manual, laborers were required to maintain, repair, and use the boilers for steam-powered locomotives. The railways in India were initially constructed by private, Britain-based companies that were guaranteed a 5 percent minimum return on investment by the East India Company, contributing to financial extraction from the colony to the metropole.[18] Constructed for industrial transport beginning in the 1830s, and then for the movement of passengers from the 1850s, early railways in India relied on extant boilermaking knowledge to run and repair steam locomotives. European boilermakers were recruited to these projects, but as in the case of steamships an Indian labor force quickly developed—often drawn from artisans in related trades—to address the repair and maintenance of steam locomotives. By the 1870s, railway boilermaking was a trade with considerable demand and was increasingly incorporated into colonial industrial schools.[19]

The 1870s also saw a reorganization of the Indian railways, contributing to the rise of large-scale, consolidated locomotive workshops. Several of the smaller Indian railway lines merged, creating a system of five major railway companies that crisscrossed British Indian territory. In the North-Western Provinces, most of the rails were controlled by the East India Railway Company, which had initially aimed to connect Delhi and Calcutta.[20] In Punjab, most of the lines were consolidated under the administration of the North-Western Railways from the 1880s, connecting Punjabi cities such as Lahore and Amritsar to Sindh, Baluchistan, and the Afghan frontier.[21]

Boilermakers were employed by all the railway companies in India. As was the case with carpenters, they migrated to major centers of railway construction and production, and in many cases consolidated in communities around the largest locomotive workshops. The largest locomotive workshops of the Eastern Railways were in Jamalpur, present-day Bihar, with other significant locomotive workshops near Calcutta and in Lucknow. For the North-Western Railways, the largest sites of employment for boilermakers in the locomotive workshops were Lahore (Mughalpura) and Rawalpindi in Punjab, and Karachi and Sukkur in Sindh. Other boilermakers migrated to or were trained in workshops that combined a smaller amount of locomotive repair and maintenance with work like carriage construction.[22] Hakimuddin's own employment trajectory reflects this mobility: raised and trained in Punjab, he worked as a boilermaking fitter in a smaller workshop in Jacobabad, Sindh, before being appointed "head fitter" in Sukkur.[23]

Despite the rapid expansion of the trade, boilermakers and others who labored on steam technology in the Indian railway context have received limited scholarly attention. This is in part because the "design and construction" of steam locomotives for the Indian railways were overwhelmingly carried out in Britain, so the history of Indian engagement with steam engines as a technology may seem limited.[24] But Indian laborers nonetheless developed their own technical practices around steam locomotives, even if they focused primarily on maintenance and repair rather than construction.

Hakimuddin portrayed boilermaking as a site of potential upward mobility, but like many technical trades in colonial India, it was rigidly and hierarchically organized along racial lines, with only specific, lower-paying positions open to Indians before the 1920s.[25] Throughout the nineteenth century and as late as 1935, lead railway boiler inspectors—often trained engineers—were almost always Europeans. Most district boilermakers who were responsible for the oversight of "three to five engine houses" were European or Anglo-Indian, though other Indians were also permitted to apply for these positions. Suboverseers, chargemen, and other Indian intermediary positions were responsible for coordinating between these inspectors and the *mistrīs* who carried out most of the technical work. Indian *mistrīs* were employed for the day-to-day labor of boiler repair, including "the renewing of strays, caulking of firebox corners, foundation rings, or other work coming under boiler or firebox repairs."[26]

Following several high-profile accidents, most Indian provinces, beginning with Bombay Presidency in 1873, required forms of certification for the people who inspected or maintained steam boilers. A divide emerged between colonial administrators who believed that such laws should certify engineers—who led the inspections—and those who believed that they should certify lower-level supervisors or even *mistrīs* themselves, who were responsible for most of the daily maintenance and repair.[27] In the United Provinces and Punjab, which adopted boiler inspection certification laws in 1899 and 1902 respectively, the former position eventually dominated.[28] This partially deprived Indian boilermaking *mistrīs*—and even some Indian supervisors—of the authority they might have held in the workshop by making their work dependent on the oversight and authority of an inspecting engineer.

Despite limitations in authority and prestige for *mistrīs* within the locomotive departments, Hakimuddin identified an important economic reality. Boilermaking provided some of the highest wages available to Indian artisans and laborers within the railways, as well as in other sites of labor recruitment such as public works departments, shipyards, and private mills and factories. By the turn of the twentieth century, locomotive shop boilermakers in Punjab and the United Provinces could earn up to forty-five rupees per month, placing them among the highest earners of the "skilled," "native" laborers in the railway infrastructure.[29]

In some cases, the artisans who were trained and recruited for boilermaking were part of multigenerational artisanal railway labor cadres. As chapter 4 shows, the sons of railway workers in Lahore often trained in the Railway Technical School.[30] There they learned skills specifically related to railway labor, with some learning boilermaking and repair. In many other cases, however, blacksmiths and workers from other aligned trades learned boilermaking on the job, within the locomotive workshops. In the 1920s and 1930s, this ad hoc form of "training" and the organization of boiler shops was repeatedly decried by railway administrators as leading to unsafe working conditions and injuries.[31] Nonetheless, it reflects the fact that many Indian artisans used extant skills to secure positions in the locomotive workshops that required the adaptation of technical practices but also the potential for higher wages.[32]

BOILER WORK AND THE QUESTION OF ARTISANSHIP

Most of the work carried out by Indian artisans within locomotive workshops would not have been categorized as "artisanal" or "craft" work in colonial monographs on industry. It led, not to the making of distinctively "Indian" goods or items, but rather to the repair of materials that had often been brought in from abroad. But boiler repair, maintenance, and even use, built on what Joshua Grace, in the context of East African car repair, framed as the "accessible infrastructure of expertise." Accordingly, this infrastructure reflected the "material places, things, and knowledge" often associated in India with blacksmiths and other skilled artisans.[33] When artisan-intermediaries like Hakimuddin expounded on the new technologies and materials that an artisan would encounter in a locomotive workshop, they did so secure in the knowledge that artisans had access to previous training and embodied skill in a related trade.

Indeed, in praising *kārīgar*s' skill, Hakimuddin went beyond boiler repair and maintenance to highlight a wide range of embodied knowledge of the steam engine. He profiled, for instance, the role of the fireman, responsible for stoking the boiler fires within the steam engine. This was a physically taxing trade with a high rate of injury and low rate of pay compared to mechanical work but was nonetheless central to the safe running of locomotives.[34] While many firemen were Anglo-Indian, the position was open to other Indian workers and, despite its dangers, was seen as a potential path to better-paid railway positions.[35] Indeed, Hakimuddin noted that when a fireman had demonstrated mastery of his work and distinguished himself in his diligence, he might "climb the ladder" of his trade and take an exam to qualify him to work as a driver.[36] Hakimuddin offered an overview of what the fireman's day might look like, as well as praise of his embodied knowledge and skilled diligence. After a description of how the fireman should lay out his tools, take the directions of the train driver, and check the levels of water and oil, he described the fireman's role on the moving train:

> When the train has left the station, [the fireman] opens the small damper and lights a few coals on the coal fire. This coal will burn in a dull flame. And now he must

> check to see if the steam is still blowing. And this is where it is seen how useful the starting fire was, as it could get the light engine up to full speed in roughly fifty miles. Care must be taken that when the boiler is filled with steam, the needle of the steam gauge or pressure gauge is not pulled out of its place. . . . It is never possible to gain complete control over such a base substance as fire. . . . But if he keeps at his work bearing in mind moderation, then he will be up to the challenge. He will begin to see the excellent quality of his work everywhere, such as in the boiler, which is full of steam today and will be so tomorrow as well. . . . As he protects himself, so will he preserve his shovel.[37]

By including laborers like firemen in his depiction of the skill and knowledge of Indian *kārīgar*s, Hakimuddin suggests important shifts in the types of social and laboring identities and solidarities claimed by Indian artisans around the turn of the twentieth century. Their location within locomotive workshops spurred new associations and affiliations. These new *kārīgar* identities were based on the ability to make, or repair, and also on shared engagement with the material and technology of the steam engine. Hakimuddin envisioned a future in which laborers employed in the locomotive workshops would enjoy upward mobility, distinguishing themselves as in roles like firemen and sitting exams to become well-paid and respected locomotive drivers. To this end, he even provided a guide to key questions on the locomotive driver exam.[38] While he explained that a driver did not necessarily need to be a *kārīgar*, he maintained that any effective driver would have "appreciation for the work of industry" and competency in the "artistry" of the locomotive workshop.[39]

But while Hakimuddin may have promoted locomotive workshops as a site of upward mobility, many workers found themselves blocked from these paths by strictures of race, caste, and education that governed railway hiring and promotion. As artisan laborers were pushed downward within technical hierarchies of railway employment from the late nineteenth century, shared identities and values among railway *kārīgar*s took on contours that Hakimuddin did not predict. In many cases, they were ultimately relevant, not for securing promotions, but instead for building social and economic solidarities among workers.

MUSLIM ARTISANS AS BOILERMAKING INTERMEDIARIES

Scholars of colonial-era South Asia have emphasized the racially segregated and hierarchical nature of technical education and employment in the nineteenth and early twentieth centuries. Aparajith Ramnath, for instance, recently examined the "prevailing [colonial] view of Indians as lacking technical aptitude" and the exclusion of Indians from many forms of engineering education prior to the 1920s.[40] David Arnold describes the "clear hierarchy of authority" that gave Europeans authority over science and technology and "fixed India"—and Indians—"in a position of dependence and subordination."[41] But colonial administrators also enforced a second hierarchy in technical education from the mid-nineteenth century. Upper-caste Hindus and Sikhs, *sharīf* Muslims, and Anglo-Indians were recruited to engineering and arts schools, creating a "native" level of technical oversight under European direction. Conversely, the state recruited children from artisan families to trade-based technical schools, often funneling them into large-scale railway workshops and public works labor.[42]

Prior to the consolidation of middle-class Indian technical oversight, nineteenth-century artisan-intermediary communities had distinct experiences of social and economic mobility, which were rarely generalizable to broader artisan experiences. Nonetheless, some, like Hakimuddin, attempted to speak for artisan interests within state railway and public works department workshops. By tracing the careers and experiences of members of the small cadres of Muslim artisan-intermediaries we can identify ways that their backgrounds informed their engagement with both labor and Islam or the spaces of Muslim sociability.

Hakimuddin's own career reflects moments of both distinction and engagement with broader artisan communities. He noted his hereditary artisan background, describing his father as a *mistrī* in Hoshiar Nagar, in Amritsar district.[43] After joining the North-Western Railways, he was posted to Jacobabad, Sindh. Jacobabad was home to a small locomotive workshop that, unlike large locomotive shops in North-Western railway centers such as Lahore and Rawalpindi, adjoined a wagon and carriage shop.[44] This meant that Hakimuddin was likely responsible for oversight not only of boilermakers and others engaged in engine repair but also for a cadre of carpenters, blacksmiths, and other artisans who built and repaired the rail carriages. Apparently distinguishing himself—and beginning his composition of the *Kalīd-i ṣanʿat*—there, he was sent to the larger locomotive workshop in Sukkur, where he was employed as head fitter by the time the first edition of the book was released.[45]

Hakimuddin's assignments in Sindh also reflect an important social difference between artisan-intermediaries and the laboring cadres that they oversaw. While many artisan laborers migrated to secure railway positions, these migrations were frequently—though not always—within the same province or region; even when they occurred across larger distances, they were coordinated by kinship and social networks mediated by jobbers. Supervisory or salaried intermediaries, however, were assigned on the basis of the needs of the North-Western Railway administration overall. Hakimuddin, who had been born in Amritsar district, was thus sent to Sindh, where he may have encountered some Punjabis who would have migrated there for work. It is more likely, however, that he oversaw workers who had migrated from cities and towns in the surrounding regions of Sindh and Baluchistan.

Despite these social differences with the laborers that he oversaw, Hakimuddin asserted his social connectedness to the world of artisanship within the railways.

In the text, he described his social circle, with whom he shared his concerns about the future of Indian artisans and artisanship, as railway workers "in the fields of industry and crafts [*ṣan ʿat-o-ḥirfat*]." These friends, he complained, were "like parrots in a gallery," constantly lamenting the dominance of European engineers and inspectors over Indians skilled in *dastkārī*, meaning handicrafts or artisanship.[46] Hakimuddin saw his role as building "consensus" (*itifāq*), among his fellow Indian employees, including those in both intermediary and laboring roles. He explained: "If you try to take one step forward in the field of industry without *itifāq*, you risk falling flat on your face [*munh ke bal girnā*] for the next fifty steps."[47]

Like many of the *obreros ilustrados* (enlightened workingmen) described by Jorell Meléndez-Badillo in his analysis of the knowledge produced by early twentieth-century Puerto Rican workers, Hakimuddin envisioned potential solidarities "on behalf of" a broader cadre of artisans and workers.[48] Though he possessed a higher status and a more well-renumerated position within the workshop, he positioned himself as responsible for building connections among Indian workers, including *mistrī*s, other laborers, and his fellow intermediaries. He argued that these solidarities were required both to improve the technical abilities and social status of Indian *kārīgar*s and to restore Indian authority over industry.

BOILERMAKING ARTISAN-INTERMEDIARIES BEYOND THE RAILWAYS

Prior to the release of the second edition of his book in 1899, Hakimuddin left the railways to work as an "in-charge" in a European-owned ginning and pressing factory in Okara, Punjab, where he supervised the maintenance of the boilers and other machinery.[49] This transition out of railway employment reflected the fact that there was high demand for boilermakers in a variety of different industrial contexts, not just privately owned factories but also government military and public works projects.

Hakimuddin's career is not traceable beyond his move to Okara, as later editions of the text continued to list his role as "in-charge" at the ginning and pressing factory.[50] However, the experiences of other artisan-intermediaries engaged in boilermaking and in positions of oversight likewise suggest the ways that members of this class engaged with labor beyond the railways. Like Hakimuddin, a father and son named Muhammad Bakhsh (d. ca. 1890) and Muhammad Hanif (d. 1915) were members of an artisan family who secured salaried employment, working for the public works department of the princely state of Rampur.[51] The father, Muhammad Bakhsh, trained in the family trades of metalwork and weaponsmithing, learning to make cannons and artillery for the state armory and other patrons. But British military paramountcy and new restrictions on weaponsmithing drove Muhammad Bakhsh to pursue alternative employment. He was employed in the state's icehouse (*barf khānah*), an innovation that was adopted in princely states in the 1850s following earlier trends in the import, production, and storage of ice in major British-administered Indian cities.[52]

Muhammad Bakhsh became known in the state for his skill in repairing the icehouse's boiler, a skill he used to secure an official role as a state public works department subinspector.[53] He trained his son, Muhammad Hanif, in both metalsmithing and the technical skills that he had developed through his work on the icehouse boiler. Muhammad Hanif used these skills to gain a position overseeing the repair of engines and boilers for several state workshops.[54] He was selected to accompany the state's British chief engineer to the 1883 Calcutta International Exhibition, where he studied displayed steam-powered lathes. Upon his return to Rampur, he manufactured his own power lathes for state use.[55] Both Muhammad Hanif and Muhammad Bakhsh thus successfully negotiated an emerging system of state technical oversight to secure formal positions, despite training within familial artisan apprenticeships rather than state institutions.

In the first decade of the twentieth century, many princely states like Rampur had slightly more flexible requirements for supervisory public works employment than the railways or the public works departments of directly administered British Indian regions. The fact that neither Muhammad Hanif nor Muhammad Bakhsh had studied in colonial engineering or industrial schools was therefore less of an impediment to their employment than it may have been in British India. Nonetheless, Muhammad Hanif, like Hakimuddin, was likely representative of a final generation of state-employed artisan-intermediaries.

By 1915, the time of Muhammad Hanif's death, employment in Rampuri public works oversight was increasingly limited to the graduates of colonial engineering and arts schools.[56] Although colonial administrators often expressed a desire to recruit the sons of artisans to these schools, they overwhelmingly became sites primarily for the training of middle-class boys from nonartisan backgrounds by the early twentieth century. This consolidating class of state-educated, middle-class intermediaries—composed primarily of upper-caste Hindus and Sikhs, *sharīf* Muslims, and some Anglo-Indians—pushed artisan-intermediaries downward in the hierarchies of technical oversight. This process took place not only within the railway locomotive workshops but also across a wide range of spaces where artisan-intermediaries had overseen and engaged with boiler repair and maintenance.

THE MUSLIM SOCIAL SPACES OF ARTISAN-INTERMEDIARIES

As new cadres of middle-class Muslims displaced artisan-intermediaries in positions of oversight in the railways and other contexts of boilermaking, they brought with them narratives about the relationship between technology and Islam. These new understandings about the relationship between technology and Islam did not supplant artisan engagement with Islam in the workshop but did contribute to the marginalization of Muslim artisans' understanding of their work and religious practice. I examine whether, and how, artisan-intermediaries such as Hakimuddin participated in or made space for artisan Islam in contexts of boilermaking and railway workshops before I turn to the new Muslim middle-class *ashrāf* of technical intermediaries and their efforts to discipline the religious practices of Muslim laborers.

Hakimuddin's treatise did not conform to many of the conventions of writing about the pious labor of Muslim artisans. At nearly 150 pages, it was far longer than most technical manuals and community histories, and Hakimuddin showed limited interest in integrating the Muslim past into his explanation of new technologies and trades. Many of the narratives of artisan Islam that I have explored so far—such as references to a prophetic past or emphasis on the pious nature of physical labor—seem notably absent from the *Kalīd-i ṣan ʿat*. Nonetheless, in his claimed inspiration for the text, as well as his theory of translation, Hakimuddin reflected a Muslim sociability of railway work, in which skilled workmanship and Muslim social identities intersected to contribute to new laboring solidarities among *kārīgar*s. His work suggests an artisan Islam that included not just narratives of religious piety or practice but also the cultivation of shared social and intellectual worlds among Muslim workers.

Hakimuddin's initial impetus for writing the text, he claimed, was conversations with his colleague Nur Muhammad Khan, a railway water inspector. The two lamented to each other, "Why is it that the industry and craft of our country declines day by day, even in this modern era of development and growth?"[57] Hakimuddin castigated both "Europeans" and the "Indian gentlemen who follow in the footsteps of the English in most matters" and held them responsible for this "decline" in Indian artisanal and industrial skill. He concluded that the solution was for Indian workers to collaboratively cultivate these skills for themselves.[58] Hakimuddin's account of his conversation with Nur Muhammad Khan painted an image of two Muslim railway intermediaries who identified with the challenges of the artisanal laborers employed in their workshops and saw themselves as distinct from the "European" and "Indian gentlemen" supervisors with whom they likely interacted. It suggests that a community of Muslim intermediaries used their social connections with each other to imagine new forms of technical authority for *kārīgar*s.

Hakimuddin's theory of translation likewise reflected a Muslim laboring sociability, in which shifting technologies were articulated through localized forms of knowledge, including religious and cultural knowledge. In his introduction, he criticized British Indian industrial and technical institutions for relying primarily on direct translations of European works. "Most translators," Hakimuddin lamented, "do not consider that they must bring a book new life. . . . They reject the idea of taking parts out and putting new parts into the book."[59] Conversely, he wrote, his technical manual was one through which "everyone might find satisfaction in its *faiẓ*." *Faiẓ* is often translated as "grace" or "bounty," and Paul Losensky characterizes it as the "infinite inspiration" that writers and thinkers take from the divine.[60] Hakimuddin contrasted his own manual—suffused with *faiẓ*—with technical manuals that had been translated from English, which, he claimed, "follow[ed] the rules" of language but failed to communicate knowledge. By communicating with and through *faiẓ*, Hakimuddin wrote, "we have compiled the book for this community, in which there is no need for ostentation and pretentiousness [*ṣūrat parastī aur 'ibārat-ārā'ī*]."[61]

Hakimuddin's reference to the *faiẓ* of boilermaking knowledge did not necessarily suggest a specific form of divine inspiration. But it did reflect a mode of writing common among Muslim artisans in which the "divine power" of new technical knowledge was made accessible through reference to artisan experiences, be they material, religious, or social. Even the use of the hookah as a metaphor for the steam injector might, in Hakimuddin's terms, contribute to a reader finding "satisfaction in [the] *faiẓ*" of mechanical knowledge. Hakimuddin was, of course, just one representative of the small but diverse cadre of Muslim artisan-intermediaries who attained positions of oversight in the late nineteenth century. But his emphasis on the *faiẓ* inherent in knowledge of steam engines suggests that he expected artisans to engage creatively with both processes of physical production and knowledge of the "divine power" that inspired this production in the workshop.

The degree to which Hakimuddin or other artisan-intermediaries led their workshops in ways that encouraged the adaptation of artisan religious practices in the context of industrialized labor remains opaque. Nonetheless, Hakimuddin's writing hints at a Muslim parallel to the world of Hindu "technophany" described by George and Narayan, in which skilled mechanic-technicians often claimed "special discerning authority and understanding" of the relationships between technology and divinity.[62] Hakimuddin's aims for Indian *kārīgar*s extended beyond the boundaries of religious identity, but they were articulated within a Muslim social world and through Muslim imaginaries of divine knowledge.

EDUCATIONAL HIERARCHIES AND THE MARGINALIZATION OF MASTER ARTISANS

The marginalization of artisan-intermediaries—and their social and religious spaces and imaginaries—within the railways took place gradually. It was a result of the slow rise of a new middle class and accompanying practices of technical oversight, which were, in turn, shaped by emerging systems of colonial technical education and employment preferences. Although individuals like Hakimuddin and Muhammad Hanif secured positions of technical oversight in the waning years of the nineteenth century, they were members of a diminishing cohort of artisan-intermediaries. Artisans of diverse religious backgrounds continued to find employment in railway workshops and through public works contracts. But while master artisans occasionally rose to positions of oversight in the nineteenth century, by the 1910s these positions went almost exclusively to members of a new middle class. *Sharīf* Muslims and upper-caste Hindus and Sikhs dominated the positions of oversight permitted to Indians, alongside the Anglo-Indian workers who were often most closely associated with the railways and who were sometimes preferred for higher-paid positions.[63]

While Hakimuddin was optimistic about the ability of Indian artisans to assert authority over knowledge of steam engines, he also recognized the strengthening of social hierarchies that marginalized artisanal authority. He was especially suspicious of evolving systems of employment and patronage that gave "gentlemen" technical authority over artisan skill. Describing Indian social hierarchies that were strengthened through the colonial organization of railway workshops, he wrote: "Assuming I am well versed in industry and craftsmanship, and even know how to make sketches, and I have endured hard work to make complete and useful items, I still cannot trust that a nobleman [*raīs*] or other wealthy Indian will treat me well and will respect my work in a way that will encourage me to make something even better in the future and to expand my knowledge."[64] Hakimuddin thus highlighted the social hierarchization that had dominated boilermaking and engine repair and their oversight from the rise of these trades in the 1850s. He expressed hope that artisans might disrupt these hierarchies through their technical mastery—or through the *faiẓ* of boilermaking knowledge. Nonetheless, he also seemed to recognize that, around the turn of the twentieth century, these hierarchies were strengthening, not diminishing.

One reason for the ossification of social hierarchies of technical oversight was that middle-class boys—from across religious backgrounds—were increasingly likely to engage with colonial technical education. The most prestigious site for technical training in North India was Thomason Civil Engineering College in Roorkee (founded as the College of Civil Engineering circa 1847).[65] Education at Roorkee was segregated along racial lines. Small numbers of Indians were admitted into "engineering" and "upper subordinate" courses, but they were educated separately from their European counterparts. Prior to the twentieth century, most Indian graduates from the college studied in the "lower subordinate" courses.[66] Nonetheless, Roorkee and other engineering colleges provided a springboard from which Indians—primarily with upper-caste and Muslim *ashrāf* backgrounds—secured provincial public works and railway jobs.

Reflecting some of the earliest associations between *ashrāf* identities and technical training at institutions like Thomason College, a list of graduates in 1852 showed that of the ten Indians who completed lower subordinate training, five—all Muslims—had previously studied at the Anglo-Arabic Delhi College.[67] Delhi College had its origins as a center for the education of regional Mughal nobility, but in the 1820s, under British East India Company direction, it became a prominent site for the education of regional elites in "Western" knowledge. Moreover, while the college's mid-nineteenth-century students were religiously diverse, Delhi College became an embodiment of the new middle-class *ashrāf* mode of education and comportment for many Muslim students.[68]

The associations between the emerging middle class and government positions of low-level technical supervision grew over the course of the late nineteenth century. The expansion of engineering and technical education to regional universities and schools made it a viable option for members of Muslim middle-class *ashrāf* families across the United Provinces and Punjab. Members of this class, along with their upper-caste Hindu and Sikhs counterparts, often framed technical work as both the most secure form of salaried, government employment and an appropriate use of middle-class skill and education. An 1895 article in the Urdu-language journal *Indian Architect* (transliterated in Urdu as *Inḍiyan arkitīkt*), published from Lahore, reflected this perspective. Writing about the local engineering school, the author praised "those parents who enroll their sons" in the school as "invested" in both the "progress of the province" and the children's "future employment."[69] Emphasizing that the school "combined book learning with practical knowledge," the author framed technical education as a suitable path to salaried state employment for middle-class families who hoped to encourage both the economic and intellectual development of their sons.[70]

British administrators of colonial engineering and technical schools sometimes expressed a desire to reorient their educational institutions away from the education of the sons of wealthy and middle-class families to attract students from artisan families instead. Records on Thomason College and other engineering, technical, and arts colleges are replete with British lamentations about artisan "lack of interest" in the "special courses" that they had opened in fields like woodworking.[71] Some administrators blamed artisans themselves for these "failures," citing a supposed lack of technical and social adaptability among Indian artisans. The more circumspect noted the loss of wages and the lengthy nature of programs.[72]

But the predominantly wealthy and middle-class makeup of technical training also reflected an enforced colonial hierarchy of technical education. The massive demand for physical labor in urban public works departments and railway workshops meant that artisans who did engage with state-led training were usually recruited for industrial schools associated with these workshops, such as the Lahore Railway Technical School.[73] Efforts to train a large-scale wage labor force belied colonial administrators' stated desire to educate artisans in ways that would enable them to secure salaried state employment. Colonial hierarchies of technical education—including the recruitment of urban artisans primarily into workshop-based technical schools—created conditions in which members of the Indian middle classes dominated salaried technical positions and claimed authority over technical knowledge.

In this context, master artisans were increasingly restricted to wage labor positions under these new middle-class overseers on the railway and in public works department service. Though artisans were often still employed as *mistrīs* under these new intermediaries, they lacked opportunities for promotion into the ranks of technical oversight. Reflecting this hierarchy, an Urdu-language treatise, published in 1913 in Shahjahanpur, in the United Provinces, listed wage rates that the railways would provide to salaried, middle-class overseers and contractors for the various artisans they hired. The text, titled simply *Engineering Book* (*Injinīring buk*) and authored by a middle-class Muslim railway contractor, Sayyid Tasdiq Husain, was aimed at overseers in locomotive workshops in addition to others. It provided information on new materials, methods of measuring and drawing, and styles of construction for middle-class technical overseers, including those who may have overseen boilermakers.[74] The treatise assumed that members of this middle class were responsible for "*mistrīs*, blacksmiths, carpenters, masons, and menial servants."[75]

"MECHANICS AND MUSLIMS": MIDDLE-CLASS INTERMEDIARIES AND GOLDEN AGE NARRATIVES

The skills of master artisans were still in demand on the railways and in public works departments, but these artisans were pushed downward in a colonial hierarchy of "native" employment that demanded new forms of middle-class oversight, such as that outlined in the *Engineering Book*. Muslim members of the new middle-class overseer cadres brought with them new narratives about the ways that Muslims should engage with technological change. Many members of this class also read and debated the works of Indian Muslim scholars who sought to integrate the study of "Western" science and technology into "Islamic" models of education.

This trend, represented most famously by Sayyid Ahmad Khan and his educational institutions in Aligarh, made explicit efforts to address members of the technically educated Muslim middle class.[76] Sayyid Ahmad's *Aligarh Institute Gazette*, a bilingual paper published in Urdu and English through the Aligarh Scientific Society, occasionally noted developments in steam technology and boilermaking, most notably improvements in safety mechanisms.[77] At the same time, while Sayyid Ahmad Khan was adamant that the Aligarh Scientific Society's most important work was in "practical technology," including "mechanics," many of their publications focused on debates about the causes of perceived Muslim "decline" or "backwardness" vis-à-vis European technology.[78]

The writings of Muslim scholars often diverged from artisan-intermediary representations of technology because scholars sought to establish Indian Muslim rootedness in a supposed Islamic "golden age." A short article by Allamah Shibli Nuʿmani (1857–1914), a prominent North Indian Muslim scholar and educator, is representative of this "golden age" discourse and its impact on elite Muslim technical writing.[79] Published in 1898 in Amritsar, just eight years after the first edition of the *Kalīd-i ṣan ʿat*, the article, titled "Mechanics and Muslims," traced the history of Muslim ingenuity in the "art of mechanics."[80] "Among Muslims," Shibli wrote, "this art began with the translation of Greek treatises under the Abbasid Caliphate" (AD 750–1258).[81] He emphasized that Muslim mechanics had improved on Greek ideas and that Europeans had appropriated "Muslim" knowledge, creating circulatory exchanges. By way of example, Shibli profiled the work of Abbasid-era clockmakers. He told his readers of the "wonderous art" of Abbasid clockmaking under the Caliph Harun al-Rashid (786–809), recounting a story of the caliph's exchange of gifts with Charlemagne (800–814). The caliph sent Charlemagne a brass water-powered clock with hourly chimes, and according to Shibli this "miraculous" technology sparked renewed European interest in mechanics.[82]

"Golden age" discourse—and its accompanying narratives of decline—asked how Indian Muslims might create a new era in which European Christians coveted "Muslim technologies," rather than the reverse. It sought to reclaim for Muslims an intellectual heritage associated with the Abbasids that Europeans had often erased through their own projects of translation.[83] In reclaiming the Arab-Islamic pasts of "European" technologies, Indian Muslim scholars imagined a future in which "Islamic" technical ingenuity was recognized and coveted in the "West." At the same time, it often sidelined the position of artisans and laborers within material production and diminished their technological authority by assuming that the rejuvenation of Islamic science and technology was the responsibility of patrons and scholars. Any role for Muslims who made and repaired mechanical objects was subsumed under an imagined revival of elite Muslim authority over technical knowledge.

Ideals of the restoration of an Islamic golden age through elite engagement with technology were cultivated through Muslim reformist institutions such as the Aligarh Muhammadan Anglo-Oriental College. But they did not remain confined to these spaces, and over time they became relevant to locomotive department workshops and other sites of railway labor. Middle-class Muslim supervisors in these spaces likely read and circulated periodicals such as *Taraqqī* (Development)—published in Lahore in the first decade of the twentieth century—which echoed "golden age" narratives about the need to cultivate elite Muslim authority over technology. Indeed, *Taraqqī* reflected the interests of the Muslim middle class in both developments in locomotive construction and debates among religious scholars about how to engage with technological change. Some articles profiled the scientific principles behind technologies, including steam engines.[84] Others, however, focused on the efforts of Indian Muslim scholars to explain what they saw as a "decline" in Islamic civilization, and through this narrative of decline to explain why Muslims seemed to lag Europeans in technical capabilities.[85]

MUSLIM ARTISANS UNDER MIDDLE-CLASS TECHNICAL OVERSIGHT

The popularization of this discourse of "decline" among new middle-class Muslim cadres of overseers engaged in railway oversight had several important implications for Muslim artisans, including those who participated in boilermaking. The discourse of decline suggested that a reason for Muslim "backwardness" in technological development was the dominance of "custom" over both technological creativity and theology. Muslim artisans were often assumed to be the culprits of both sources of decline. Muslim scholars—borrowing, in some cases, from colonial writing—characterized Indian artisans as lacking in technological adaptivity and creativity. At the same time, as I noted in chapter 3, Muslim reformist scholars often characterized laboring-class Muslims as participants in what Francis Robinson termed "indigenous customs that had come to be incorporated into Islamic practice."[86] These scholars critiqued popular practices that reformists saw as insufficiently supported by Quran and hadith, often directing their attention and criticism to practices that were most widespread among Muslim artisans and laboring communities.[87]

Middle-class narratives left little room for an exaltation of boilermaking. As Muslim middle-class overseers who were conversant in discourses of decline, revival, and purification took up intermediary positions in the railways, they sought to distinguish themselves, socially and religiously, from the workers they oversaw. As a result, forms of Muslim artisan sociability—and the understanding of the divine that may have accompanied them—were pushed downward in the hierarchies of knowledge and status within locomotive and other railway workshops.

Nonetheless, artisan-intermediary insistence on the creativity and divine inspiration of technical labor such as steam engine repair and boilermaking did not disappear from railway workshops. Instead, it seems to have contributed to the consolidation of class solidarities and identities within the workshops, occasionally even inspiring forms of labor agitation similar to those analyzed in chapter 1.

MUSLIM BOILERMAKERS AND THE POLITICS OF CLASS AND LABOR

The strengthening of social hierarchies and limitations on opportunity for advancement for artisans in the locomotive workshops around the turn of the twentieth century contributed to rising participation in labor agitation and organizing. By the late 1910s, the transition that Hakimuddin made—from artisan family to supervisory technical intermediary—was rare. Even as his text remained popular and was repeatedly reprinted, the potential for artisans to attain his level of supervisory authority had largely waned. This alienation of artisans from technical oversight spurred Muslim master artisans to articulate new community identities in the early twentieth century, and these identities sometimes—though not always—emphasized laboring-class solidarities within the workshop.

Hakimuddin's writing itself, with its assertions of *karīgars*' solidarities and its frustrations with both British and Indian "gentlemen" who controlled the capital of boilermaking, reflected an awareness of and a desire to align with laboring-class identities.[88] At the same time, although Hakimuddin worked for colonial state projects, his aims for Indian artisans in some ways also echoed the emerging swadeshi movement, which would gain significant traction and popular support following the first partition of Bengal in 1905. His writing is evocative of what Aashish Velkar terms the "swadeshi spirit of combining indigenous enterprise, local traditions, and Western technologies."[89] Hakimuddin dreamed that "we might keep our needs confined to Indian products" and argued that "it is not possible for our industry and crafts to progress until the existence of the nation is fully implemented."[90] Unlike the leaders of the swadeshi movement, however, he did not primarily frame this potential turn toward Indian products as a political tool for pressuring the colonial state. Instead, he argued that it would push Indian artisans to "develop," claiming that "as a result, Indian artisans will become more attracted to [making] modern products." In the long run, he opined, this would both free Indian artisans from the authority of colonial capital and improve the social status of artisan labor.[91]

By the end of the first decade of the twentieth century, the limitations placed on the mobility and authority of master artisans in the railway workshops, including those engaged in boilermaking, spurred many to explicitly assert class identities and even organize as laborers. Among the most notable organizations founded in this period was the Anjuman-i muṣlaḥ-i qaum-i āhangarān (AMQA), or Organization for the Uplift of the Community of Blacksmiths.[92] Although the AMQA used the term *āhangar*—"blacksmith," drawn from Persian—in its title, it sought to represent the social, economic, and technological interests of members of a variety of aligned trades in the railways, including boilermakers.[93]

The AMQA was founded in Lahore around 1909 by two blacksmiths, Firozuddin and Ziauddin, who seem to have been employed at the Mughalpura workshops. According to colonial reports, the organization published a monthly periodical, the *Risālah-yi roīdād-i jalsah-yi ʿām anjuman-i muṣlaḥ-i qaum-i āhangarān* (Report of the events of the general meeting of the AMQA). The periodical grew to a circulation of approximately eight hundred by the end of 1911 from an initial circulation of about two hundred copies. It circulated primarily but not exclusively within Lahore and its surrounding regions in Punjab.[94] The ability of the AMQA to command eight hundred monthly readers suggests that its projects attracted significant interest in the growing artisan and laboring communities around Mughalpura and other regional locomotive workshops. Moreover, whether the periodical was read aloud or simply passed among literate workers, it likely circulated beyond those who subscribed or purchased it.

Reflecting the high level of demand for organizations and publications that addressed Muslim artisans and laborers, the AMQA was one of two organizations that were founded in Lahore between 1909 and 1911 and that aimed to speak for this community. The second, the Anjuman-i mu᾽ayyid al-ṣanʿat (AMS), or Organization for the Strengthening of Industry, was likewise founded by a railway blacksmith, Muhammad Din, who worked under the office of the district traffic superintendent in Lahore. Beginning in 1911, AMS published a monthly periodical, *Ṣanʿat* (Industry), although the periodical seems to have been focused more on explaining technical knowledge and processes than on cultivating laboring-class identities among workers. Within a year of its foundation, *Ṣanʿat* had a circulation of approximately five hundred, and it provided special reduced rates to students, suggesting that its authors may have hoped that subscribers would be pupils of institutions such as the Lahore Railway Technical School.[95]

Neither of the periodicals published by these two organizations seems to have survived, a fact that reflects the piecemeal and endangered nature of the archive of materials written for and by Muslim artisan communities. Nonetheless, colonial reports suggest that the AMS focused on artisan education for railway and public works department positions, likely asserting some of the same goals as Hakimuddin.[96] The AMQA, by contrast, sought to "uplift" Muslim blacksmiths and grouped railway laborers as a social and class community. Even the choice of the term *āhangar* over the more commonly used Urdu *lohār* highlights the commitment of the organization to improving the social status of Muslim blacksmiths. By avoiding *lohār*, a term laden with caste connotations, and adopting *āhangar*, the group may have sought to avoid assumed placement in the low levels of a caste-like social hierarchy. Likewise, while *āhangar* was sometimes used as a synonym to *lohār* in Urdu, it was more common in Persian, and in choosing a Persian term for the organization's title the AMQA may have sought to evoke a transregional Muslim past.

These attempts at internal social "uplift" among Muslim blacksmiths and boilermakers were sometimes accompanied by projects of labor organization and agitation that sought to improve the wages and working conditions within the railways. By 1905, colonial records note that North Indian locomotive workshops were periodically shut down by strikes focused on improved pay and conditions.[97] Labor organization and agitation gained further traction in locomotive workshops and other sites of boilermaking in the wake of the First World War. Indian artisans, especially from Punjab and the North-West Frontier Province, were recruited as ironsmiths, carpenters, and other industrial workers as part of the war effort, with many assigned to ordnance factories in Britain.[98] In the postwar period, as Radhika Singha has shown, many of these workers transitioned to urban industrial projects in their home regions, particularly on railways and in public works departments. They faced, however, colonial reluctance to legislate improved wages and limited attempts to improve labor conditions. Colonial industrial reports accused Indian laborers of a lack of "commit[ment] to industrial and urban life" based on their supposed "inefficiency" vis-à-vis Western laborers but maintained that the solution was to teach Indian laborers to aspire to better standards of living, rather than raising wages.[99]

In addition to the large-scale railway strike of 1920 in Lahore, noted in the previous chapter, the immediate postwar period saw a series of smaller strikes across the locomotive workshops of both Punjab and the United Provinces.[100] As was the case with the press strikes and other instances of labor agitation discussed in chapters 1 and 4, strike organizers likely drew on narratives of Muslim labor and community that had been reimagined and reasserted by groups such as the AMQA. The AMQA—and to an extent, artisan-intermediaries like Hakimuddin before it—provided a language for social solidarities among Muslim blacksmiths, boilermakers, and other aligned workers. As Nitin Sinha argues, railway workers' politics were both contested and shared across racial, religious, and caste boundaries, with workers sometimes using these identities to build solidarities but rejecting solidarities in other cases.[101]

While strike and union organizers sought to assert class solidarities that cut across religious identities, they also recognized that workers in locomotive workshops and other sites of boilermaking engaged with a religious imagination of their trades and technologies. During prominent strikes and efforts at union agitation, these leaders called on Muslims to build a more egalitarian and equal society through rhetoric of both religion and class. At the same time, as Ali Raza has noted, many of the Muslim leftist organizers of the 1920s drew inspiration from the newly founded Soviet Union, with several engaging with Soviet publications and emissaries in Afghanistan.[102] The converging language of class and religion in railway strikes and other labor agitations of the 1920s thus likely had multiple antecedents and influences. But for Muslim laborers in locomotive workshops and other sites of boilermaking, these movements likely evoked social and religious solidarities that had been built on the "exaltation" of artisan technical knowledge.

. . .

Hakimuddin wrote his guide to the steam engine and boilermaking as a member of a small cadre of artisan-intermediaries who sought to promote what they saw as the interests of master artisans within colonial railway workshops. He imagined spaces where artisan technical skill and adaptability provided opportunities for upward social and economic mobility. At the same time, he seemed to recognize that he was a representative of a shrinking, small community of upwardly mobile artisan-intermediaries within the railways and that the hierarchies of oversight were increasingly closing these pathways to other master artisans. While expressing a degree of optimism, Hakimuddin's text recognized that many hereditary artisans within railway locomotive workshops experienced the marginalization of their technological authority. These shifts took place in a context in which, as Subramanian argues, "technical knowledge went from the purview of Indian lower-caste artisans to becoming integral to state power, economic development, and upper-caste status."[103]

To counter the ways in which they were pushed downward in colonial railway hierarchies, Muslim boilermakers and other skilled artisans employed in the railway locomotive workshops increasingly asserted class-based solidarities. But Muslim artisans negotiated these shifts not just by asserting class-based identities that drew on their sense of shared religious history as members of a trade. They also sometimes incorporated aspects of the religious expectations of their middle-class Muslim supervisors into their narratives of the Muslim past of their trades. In the next and final chapter, I examine these varied responses to changes in technical oversight and authority in the context of stonemasonry, particularly the construction of Muslim religious architecture. In doing so, I analyze the relationships between Muslim artisans and their supervisors or intermediaries and their negotiations with Muslim patrons as well as the patrons' understanding of the relationships between labor, technology, and Islam.

6

Building the Modern Mosque

Stonemasonry as Religion and Labor

STONEMASONS, PATRONS, AND ARCHITECTURAL KNOWLEDGE

In 1875, Riyasat ʿAli Sarshar, a master builder and lead mason from Lucknow, compiled a sixteen-page treatise on construction, titled *Tazkirah al-aiwān* (Compendium of buildings).[1] The text, like so many of the others in this book, focused explicitly on how to carry out a trade—in this case, stonemasonry and construction—as a pious Muslim. Sarshar and the masons and builders that he hoped to educate were engaged partially in the construction of religious architecture, building mosques, tombs, shrines, and other physical markers of Muslim religious practice and identity.[2] Like many of the master artisans analyzed in the previous chapters, Sarshar framed his labor as pious, informed by a Muslim past and Islamic practice. But unlike most of the others that we have studied, the structures that he produced were also received—by patrons and a wider public audience—as sites of Muslim religious piety.

Sarshar's authority as a master builder was based in part on his training under his father Muhammad Nizam, a lead mason who had worked maintaining the religious architecture of the nawabs of Awadh in Lucknow.[3] Prior to the deposal of the nawabs of Awadh by the East India Company in 1856, Lucknow was among the most prestigious sites of patronage and employment for those engaged in the construction of Muslim religious architecture.[4] For Sarshar, familial and educational ties to this site of displaced architectural prestige offered proof of his ability to write knowledgably about how to build and engage in stonemasonry piously. At the same time, Sarshar also based his authority on his experiences as a lead mason and master builder, noting that he had been employed by Sayyid Muhammad Ali Khan, the landlord of Shamsabad, near Fatehgarh in the North-Western Provinces, to construct an *imāmbāṛā* (a site for Shia commemoration) there.[5] His work was published by the small Dilkushā Press in Fatehgarh, suggesting that his work on the *imāmbāṛā* may have brought him local prestige.

Sarshar emphasized both the pious nature of the labor of stonemasons and the pious nature of the buildings that they might construct. Reflecting the norms of artisan manuals aimed at Muslim workers more broadly, Sarshar explained God's revelation of knowledge of construction and stonemasonry.[6] Written primarily in verse, the *Tazkirah al-aiwān* highlighted God's revelation of building to the immediate descendants of Adam, and through them to humanity. Referencing God's revelation of construction to Mahalalel, the son of Qaynan and great-grandson of Adam, Sarshar tied the origins of construction to the origins of humanity and the Prophets:

> God, who has created the Prophets,
> Has given each of them a task,
> And when God created the Prophet Mahalalel
> What was the order of God the Great?
> He started the construction of palaces
> And He propagated the methods of construction.
> From Him came forth the invention of houses.
> He remains the supreme *ustād* in this trade.[7]

Even as he centered God's revelation of knowledge of construction and stonemasonry, Sarshar maintained that some buildings were more reflective of God's intention for construction than others. His own claim to fame was in the construction of religious architecture, as represented by the *imāmbāṛā* of Shamsabad. But he did not suggest that the buildings that were most reflective of God's intentions were only those that served as sites of religious practice. Instead, he maintained that all buildings—palaces, homes, mosques, *imāmbāṛās*, even offices—could be designed in an "auspicious" manner that glorified God and his revelation of knowledge.[8]

Sarshar's text did not provide detailed patterns or training in the basics of masonry; it focused, instead, primarily on the ways a mason should perform his piety while building. It served as a trade history and manual of the religious practice of building. Still, he included notes on the properties of auspicious buildings, including the positions of their walls and the organization of their rooms. Sarshar's intended audience, therefore, consisted of members of his own class of apprenticeship-trained lead masons and master builders, artisans with a degree of authority over construction. For instance, he maintained that there were months and days when it was auspicious or inauspicious (*sa'd o naḥs*) to undertake the construction of new architecture, suggesting that his readers should have sufficient authority within their worksites to influence the days and order of work.[9]

Sarshar wrote primarily for Muslim master masons, people trained piously, at home or in a workshop, but with sufficient authority in their field to coordinate labor. But he also spoke to their patrons and employers, those who would pay for the materials and designs and would demand that work be completed within specific time frames. He aimed to ensure that these patrons and employers would understand why the construction of their buildings must follow certain principles.[10] As an accomplished master builder, notable for his contributions to Muslim religious architecture in North India, Sarshar sought to educate his potential patrons about the piety of the labor that they should expect from him and other Muslim masons and architects. For Sarshar, the piety of labor and the piety of buildings were intimately connected, and to dispense with the former would be to risk the latter.

By the late nineteenth century, texts like Sarshar's *Tazkirah al-aiwān* circulated in a crowded knowledge economy centered on practices of building and construction. For Muslim lead masons and the Muslim artisans who labored under their direction, materials like the *Tazkirah al-aiwān* were useful means of circulating knowledge about the pious practice of their trade. These manuals may also have been relevant in convincing patrons and overseers of the importance of recognizing artisan knowledge of the pious way to build. This was especially, but not only, true for structures that were popularly understood as sites of religious practice.

Simultaneously, lead masons were exposed to the shifting norms and preferences promulgated by colonial public works departments and British engineers. Even when they did not work directly for the British Indian public works departments or had limited interactions with British engineers, both patrons and technical intermediaries expected masons to follow a consolidating set of building practices. These building practices often centered the precise preparation of new plasters, as well as the application of new styles preferred by the consolidating Indian middle class. As a result, while many Muslim lead masons engaged with models of pious labor like those promulgated in Sarshar's *Tazkirah al-aiwān*, they also relied on translated and adapted British Indian textbooks about construction.[11] In contrast to their patrons, who often divorced technological change from the religious meaning of buildings, Muslim masons often integrated new technologies and materials into their religious narratives of construction. They adapted to shifting technical demands without necessarily adopting the distinctions between the religious and the technical asserted by many of their patrons.[12]

. . .

In chapters 2 and 3, I argued that Muslim artisans often maintained religious traditions and asserted Muslim pasts for their trades and technologies. In most cases, while artisans understood their labor and production as pious, patrons and consumers did not share this understanding. Producers experienced the religiosity of their work but consumers did not typically understand the final product as "Islamic" or reflective of Muslim practice—except for scribal work when it was used to produce religious texts.

In contrast, this chapter examines a trade in which both producers and consumers often understood the final product through a lens of religious experience and practice. The mosques, shrines, tombs, and other "religious architecture" that I analyze here reflect the pious labor of producers. Additionally, for the people who funded and visited them, they reflected what Anna Bigelow calls "Islamic materiality," functioning as "emplaced material objects . . . [that] facilitate or inhibit transactions between religious actors and their conceptions of the divine."[13] Focusing on stonemasons and the construction and repair of mosques, shrines, tombs, and *imāmbāṛās*, the chapter analyzes how patrons, technical intermediaries, and artisans understood the "Islamic materiality" of architecture. It asks how shifting practices of patronage and technical oversight influenced how master masons understood and practiced their trades.

I argue that Muslim stonemasons often maintained a more capacious understanding of "religious architecture" than their patrons or middle-class overseers. They did so both by integrating new technologies and materials into their narratives of pious labor and by applying their understanding of Muslim stonemasonry to a wider range of buildings. Through this chapter, I position artisan Islam within the argument that practices of construction and stonemasonry could reflect or even deepen the Muslim piety of the worker, regardless of whether the building itself was popularly understood as "Islamic." However, I am especially interested in the ways that Muslim artisan engagement with sites of worship and piety intersected with and diverged from elite conceptions of "religious architecture."

This chapter focuses on the patronage of religious architecture of two Muslim-led princely states: Rampur, which is surrounded by the North-Western Provinces, and Bahawalpur, in Punjab. In both Rampur and Bahawalpur, a class of Muslim lead masons engaged with the models of pious stonemasonry and construction recommended in the *Tazkirah al-aiwān*. At the same time, these masons necessarily negotiated shifting technical expectations of princely patrons and the technical intermediaries and engineers that they employed. Masonry work, even on architecture understood by patrons and the public as Islamic, was increasingly subsumed within princely state adaptations of what Gyan Prakash terms the "technologizing exercise of state power."[14] In the context of directly administered British India, Prakash notes that colonial administrators "represented colonial rule as a matter of improving technics," meaning "technical routines, knowledges, practices and instruments."[15] In their efforts to demonstrate their scientific and technical parity with British India, princely state rulers often adopted these same technics.[16] These princely patrons required local laborers—such as masons—to adapt materials, technologies, and practices that were promoted by the colonial state to a variety of princely projects, including religious architecture.

Muslim-led princely states were not the only or even the primary sites of Muslim patronage of religious architecture. Wealthy Muslim families in rapidly growing cities in British India, religious *anjumans*, and regional landholders were all also major patrons of new mosques, shrines, tombs, and *imāmbāṛās*. But princely state patrons—and the colonial administrators assigned to their states—left behind a wealth of records that offer unique insights into why and how they commissioned the construction and repair of religious architecture. Moreover, even outside of the geography of the individual princely states, members of princely families and their courts were among the most prominent funders of mosques and other forms of "Islamic architecture," exerting both stylistic and ideological authority. And when the members of Muslim *anjumans* and other institution in British India sought to build religious architecture, they often turned to princely patrons to raise sufficient funds, allowing these patrons input into the style and design of their buildings.[17] As a result, focusing on princely patronage offers important insights into the shifting expectations placed on master masons in the late nineteenth and early twentieth centuries.

The chapter turns first to a brief contextualization of how princely state elites understood and patronized architecture that they understood as "Islamic," before returning to knowledge production about masonry and construction. It examines not only the *Tazkirah al-aiwān* and similar manuals but also formal textbooks that circulated in colonial technical institutions, many of which were translated or adapted from English. Subsequently, I explore how these forms of knowledge may have been used by masons in Rampur and Bahawalpur. By the early twentieth century, masons in both states faced a deepening overlap of courtly patronage and state bureaucracies. I ask how artisan stonemasons circulated knowledge about their labor, religion, and technologies as they constructed representations of the Muslim authority of the courts of Bahawalpur and Rampur. How did Muslim stonemasons engage these multiple forms of knowledge about how to carry out the technical and pious work of stonemasonry? And to what degree did they integrate the shifting technical and ideological preferences of their patrons into their narratives of the Muslim practices of building?

CONTEXTUALIZING ISLAMIC ARCHITECTURE BETWEEN RAMPUR AND BAHAWALPUR

In his article "What Is Islamic Architecture Anyway?" Nasser Rabat argues that the academic category of Islamic architecture emerged through colonial power over much of the so-called Islamic world, solidifying in the late nineteenth century.[18] The category holds inherent contradictions. As Rabat notes, the "architectural historical discipline . . . cast Islamic architecture as a formal expression of Islam," even as it "shunned religion as a . . . classificatory measure and instead sought unity in culturally shared approaches to aesthetics and spatial sensitivities."[19] European orientalists of the nineteenth century usually located Islamic architecture in a supposed classical precolonial period, one from which living Muslims were excluded as part of the narrative of "Eastern" and Islamic decline.[20] However, in India as elsewhere, wealthy Muslims often sought to revive and revitalize Islamic architecture, even in cases where they accepted European narratives about its defining characteristics and its "decline." They were sometimes joined in these projects of revival by Europeans themselves, with one British state architect asserting in 1913 that regional Islamic architecture was "dormant" but "worth reawakening."[21]

In South Asia, Muslim-led princely states were a major site of this Islamic architectural revival. Many princely state leaders—be they Hindu, Muslim, or Sikh—sought to position themselves and their states as repositories of architectural traditions that had been lost in British India, even as they also hastened to demonstrate their technological parity with British-administered territory.[22] In Muslim-led states, this meant that stonemasons and other artisans who labored on architectural projects were expected to adopt materials and styles that were seen as evocative of a Muslim—often Mughal—past, even in cases where these materials and styles had limited local precedent. In the late nineteenth century, popular Indian accounts of the Mughal Empire and its architecture portrayed elite mosque construction as a means of developing the Muslim social, political, and architectural identity of the state, a form of both aesthetic and religious influence.[23] For Muslim princely elites who hoped to evoke Mughal authority, this was a powerful precedent, and one that they pursued not only by endowing mosques but also by determining the material and style of the mosque itself. Simultaneously, however, masons were expected to apply materials that were widely used by the British Indian public works departments and other British Indian projects to architectural projects that aimed to evoke a restoration of a prestigious Muslim past.

In the wake of 1857, the Indian subcontinent was divided into a patchwork of administrative territories. Regions outside of directly administered British India, known as native or princely states, were at least nominally ruled by local dynasties. Princely states formed approximately a quarter of India's population and nearly 40 percent of its territory.[24] This division of regional authority reflected the piecemeal conquest of India under the British East India Company. Rampur and Bahawalpur were both Muslim-led states with quasi-autonomous Indian rulership under British Indian governmental oversight and suzerainty, although their political histories differed notably.

Bahawalpur State was led by a dynasty that had established itself near the edge of the Cholistan desert in a primarily Saraiki-speaking region located geographically within the British province of Punjab. The Bahawalpuri dynasty had conquered a set of small local polities that together became Bahawalpur State in the mid-eighteenth century.[25] The dynasty successfully negotiated the rise of regional powers including the Afghan Durranis and the Sikh Empire, ultimately entering a subsidiary alliance with the British in 1833 to protect itself from its more powerful neighbors. The state retained quasi-autonomous status due to the support of its nawabs for the British during the Anglo-Afghan War of 1839–42 and the two

Anglo-Sikh Wars of 1846 and 1848–49.[26] Rampur, conversely, was a rump state, the remains of a larger polity of Rohilkhand that covered much of what is now Western Uttar Pradesh. Most of Rohilkhand was conquered by the British East India Company between 1774 and 1745, but a member of the deposed Rohilkhandi ruling family was installed as nawab of Rampur as part of a peace agreement with the Company.[27] Although they were descendants of Afghan Sunnis, the nawabs of Rampur embraced Shiism in the mid-nineteenth century, and their architecture sometimes sought to evoke the lost power of the Shia-led court of Awadh. Indeed, both states were home to courts that sought to assert political and religious authority through Islamic architecture, including through the construction and repair of local mosques, shrines, and tombs.[28]

Despite the differing histories and geographies, Rampur and Bahawalpur states shared sufficient commonalities to allow meaningful comparisons of their courtly patronage of architecture. Both were midsized states in terms of population. Unlike states such as Hyderabad and Mysore, neither was home to a massive population that would rival European nations.[29] Bahawalpur, with a population of approximately 720,877 in 1901, was more populous than Rampur, which was home to 533,212 residents. Bahawalpur was, however, far less dense. It was the seventh-largest Indian princely state by area and covered a much more expansive area—including much of the Cholistan desert—than geographically diminutive Rampur. Their titular capital cities—where the most notable state- and court-patronized religious architecture was constructed—were roughly similar in size, with just under eighty thousand people in Rampur city and just over ninety thousand in Bahawalpur at the turn of the twentieth century.[30]

What is most important for the purposes of this analysis is that both states also hosted public works departments modeled on those in British India by the 1870s. This was not the case in several of India's approximately six hundred princely states, many of which were tiny polities functionally closer to large landholdings or feudatories than states.[31] But both Rampur and Bahawalpur had a level of wealth and population that enabled their courts to develop bureaucratic markers of statehood and autonomy, even as they remained bound to colonial suzerainty and often hosted British advisers.

This meant that increasingly, in the late nineteenth and early twentieth centuries, major projects of religious architecture in each state were shaped not only by the interests and aims of individual patrons. The administrations of each state also used the technical expertise and manpower of their public works departments and related bureaucracies to direct the construction of important new mosques, shrines, and tombs.[32] And even when this was not officially the case, the workshops contracted for public works department projects were often also contracted by princely patrons, meaning that technical expectations common within the public works departments extended to these private projects.[33]

TRANSLATING AND CIRCULATING KNOWLEDGE OF CONSTRUCTION

Even before the consolidation of public works department technical oversight over architectural production in Rampur and Bahawalpur, regional masons negotiated patrons' changing preferences surrounding materials and technologies of construction. This was the case not only in princely states but also in directly administered British India, where masons often constructed Islamic architecture at the behest of landowners, Muslim *anjumans*, or princely patrons who wished to demonstrate their authority beyond their territory. In this context, Riyasat ʿAli Sarshar framed his 1875 *Tazkirah al-aiwān* as a guide to the pious labor of masonry. At the same time, as a lead mason and master builder in the North-Western Provinces, he was clearly aware of the demands of regional colonial public works departments, including the materials that they preferred and their processes of contracting and recruitment. His text highlighted the organization of rooms and internal walls and provided advice on the construction of external brick walls.[34] Sarshar wrote with the assumption that masons were familiar with many of the basic physical requirements of construction, gleaned either from their apprenticeship training, or from likely having contracted for regional public works department projects. In the latter case, masons would have been exposed to the regulations for building set out in translated textbooks used by Indian engineers and construction overseers, even if they did not personally read or use these textbooks.

English-language textbooks on construction and stonemasonry that focused on the standards of building for the colonial public works departments were first translated into Urdu beginning in the 1850s. Many of these early Urdu translations of textbooks were translated at Thomason College at Roorkee. As I have already shown, engineering education, including at Thomason College, was organized hierarchically by "race," with Indians excluded from the highest levels of training.[35] But beginning in the early 1850s, Indians were trained in "subordinate" classes to take up medial positions for both the railways and the public works departments. Thomason College's "native masters"—many of whom were Indians who had been educated there and stayed on as teachers—translated or adapted English-language textbooks and manuals on construction materials for the school's lower-level classes. For instance, an 1873 translation of a manual titled simply *Ta'mīr -i ʿimārat* (Construction of buildings) was produced by two "native masters" named Rai Mannu Laʿl and Lala Behari Laʿl and then reprinted with amendments by Lala Behari Laʿl four years later.[36] The text included precise recipes for various plasters, as well as directions on how to "build brick walls" and "create domed roofs."[37] Other contemporary translations, some undertaken by the public works departments themselves, addressed the use of lime and concrete plasters, as well as practices of whitewashing and inlaying.[38] These directions were aimed primarily at Indians trained to supervise public works department and railway labor, teaching them the expectations that they should hold for the masons and other laborers contracted to carry out the work of construction.

Institutional translations were not the only sources of printed knowledge for Urdu-literate technical intermediaries employed to oversee the construction of religious architecture in the late nineteenth and early twentieth centuries. Some members of this consolidating class of technical overseers also wrote and circulated periodicals that emphasized both technical knowledge and the social interests of Indians who had been educated in colonial engineering schools. Among the most notable of these was *Indian Architect* (*Inḍiyan arkitīkt*), the monthly Urdu-language journal printed in Lahore throughout the late 1880s and early 1890s. *Indian Architect* billed itself as "a journal of art, civil engineering, and building in the vernacular" providing "all types of engineering articles and drafts of old and new buildings, both English and Indian . . . rendered into the Urdu language."[39]

As Gail Minault has argued in the context of Urdu-language women's magazines aimed at middle-class Muslim women, late nineteenth- and early twentieth-century periodicals contributed to a sense of shared class identity. They enabled individuals who otherwise lacked easy or frequent direct contact with each other to develop cohesive norms.[40] Intermediary professionals working in different regions across India similarly developed shared practices and identities through trade periodicals. In the case of *Indian Architect*, this meant that trained architects, engineers, and other associated professionals maintained similar standards even as they found employment across the subcontinent, including in princely states such as Rampur and Bahawalpur.

Unlike most translated textbooks and public works department manuals, articles in *Indian Architect* also opined on the potential futures of Indian building and construction. Just as many princely state patrons sought to "revive" supposedly dormant Indian traditions of architecture using new materials and technologies, so too did the technical intermediaries who wrote and read *Indian Architect*. The journal was aimed at a religiously pluralistic audience, but throughout its run the architectural style and methods of construction used in the Mughal era and earlier periods of Muslim rule in North India were popular topics. It regularly featured sketches of mosques, tombs, and other Islamic architecture and extolled readers to study their dimensions and construction principles.[41] An article from 1894 titled "The Importance of Studying Old Buildings" argues that Indians should base their approach to new construction on that of the Swiss, who supposedly integrated historical styles with modern technologies.[42] The journal emphasized the aesthetics of an Indo-Islamic past as a source for the renewal of Indian building practices.

Even as they encouraged state technical intermediaries to learn from the past, periodicals and treatises such as *Indian Architect* framed new technologies and materials as "modernizing" in nature. They promoted a uniform middle-class professionalism that could be applied equally to colonial public works projects or the construction of a mosque, tomb, or *imāmbāṛā*. These new intermediaries increasingly understood their role as applying "modern" technological and material practices to construction, regardless of whether the buildings were meant to represent the power of the colonial state or the "traditions" of a presumed religious past.

MUSLIM STONEMASONS AND THE REINTERPRETATION OF COLONIAL KNOWLEDGE

Lead masons and apprenticeship-trained master builders may have used translations to learn the physical expectations of colonial public works departments to secure contracts and patronage. Likewise, some may have read periodicals like *Indian Architect* to understand the changing technologies and materials preferred by their patrons and the growing class of technical intermediaries who oversaw their work. But as reflected by the *Tazkirah al-aiwān*, lead masons and apprenticeship-trained master builders also reinterpreted texts and histories for themselves, integrating new technical and material expectations into narratives of pious labor.

For instance, one of the final segments of Sarshar's text laid out a series of rules and expectations for master builders. These rules indicated that builders were required to possess knowledge circulated through textbooks like the *Instructions on Building*, but this was not the only requirement. Of equal importance was builders' comportment, their ability to work with their hands, and their knowledge of the religious strictures of their trade. Entreating masons to understand the "perfect" practices of construction, Sarshar explained that they would never suffer "unemployment" (*baykārī*) if they followed these rules:

> It is first that you should be wise and prudent
> And second, do your craft [*dastkār*] with your own hands.
> Third, you should remember the principles of the plan.
> Fourth, you should be a participant in [the knowledge of] this treatise.[43]

For Sarshar, then, a master builder or lead mason was fundamentally an artisan or craftworker, someone who not only was capable of working with his hands but regularly did so. He was, moreover, educated in the knowledge of pious labor contained in Sarshar's own text. Following his concluding verses on the nature of such a builder, Sarshar listed a series of supplications that any builder should know, recite, and teach to the workers and apprentices in his workshop. Written in Arabic, the supplications centered the theme of God's protection of his creation and his intervention in the work of the mason. For instance, he wrote, "Oh God, protect the world and double the sustenance [in] my work," and "Oh God, provide us with sustenance and double the success of my work in the world."[44]

Sarshar's text was written in an Islamic idiom, emphasizing the prayers that Muslim master masons should perform over their work. But it also reveals the interpenetration of multiple Indian religious and visual imaginaries in the worlds of master masons. In a text with few images, he included a single sketch of an ouroboros (figure 10), labeled with the months of the year and cardinal directions, suggesting the auspicious months for starting work in construction.[45] While labeled with the Islamic, Hijri months, the image evokes the association between serpents

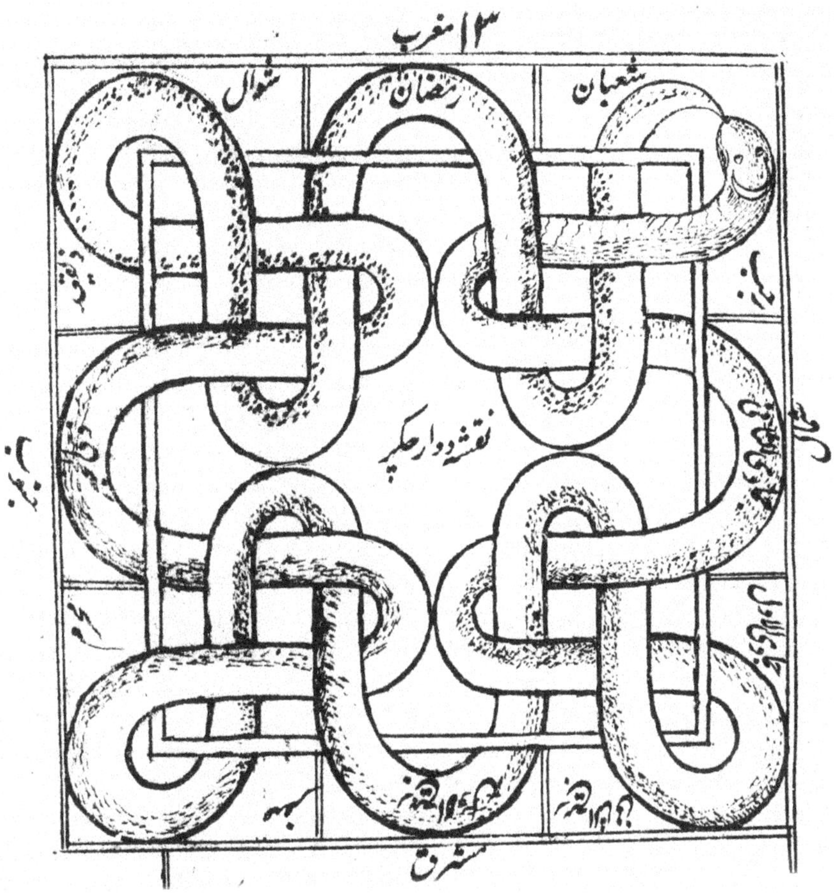

FIGURE 10. The ouroboros in Sarshar's *Tazkirah al-aiwān* (Fatehgarh: Dilkushā Press, 1875), labeled with the months of the year and the cardinal directions to demonstrate the auspicious order of construction. (© British Library Board VT 614, p. 13)

and *vastu*, Hindu traditions of building, and the *vastu naga* (snake), which in some traditions is worshipped as the serpent God of a building site.[46] Indeed, in the verses preceding the image, Sarshar identified the auspicious months for construction in the lunar months of the Hindu calendar as commonly used in North India.

He explained, for instance, that the months of Asādha and Bhādūṇ were particularly inauspicious for starting to build a structure, while beginning in the month of Phāgun would bring certain luck to the project.[47] He wrote, moreover, that he had calculated the cardinal directions associated with each of the Hijri months and suggested that knowing these associated directions would allow a reader to understand when it was auspicious to begin building. Sarshar's understanding of the relationship between Hindu traditions of *vastu* and pious Muslim construction remains somewhat ambiguous. Nonetheless, his use of the serpent to illustrate the order of auspicious construction is a signifier of what is often left out of many other Muslim artisan manuals: traditions that reflect the intersections of multiple Indian religious idioms. It sets his work apart from many of the other artisan manuals and histories analyzed in this book, as he embraced, rather than elided, evidence of knowledge exchange with non-Muslim communities.

Sharshar's work is distinct, therefore, both from many other artisan manuals and from the periodicals aimed at middle-class intermediaries trained by the colonial state. Unlike materials used by the consolidating middle class of technical intermediaries, Sarshar's book asserted that the technical training of masons was incomplete without pious practice. Texts aimed at middle-class technical intermediaries positioned lead masons and other master artisans as figures to be directed and controlled. Sarshar, conversely, positioned their labor, their authority, and their piety as central to construction, suggesting that structures were secure because masons were skilled with their hands and performed the correct prayers and supplications.

An equally important distinction between Sarshar's mode of writing and those that circulated among middle-class technical intermediaries lies in the way each conceptualized what made architecture Islamic. Periodicals like *Indian Architect* praised buildings that were understood as Islamic in the colonial schema discussed in the introduction to this chapter, and argued that these buildings might be models of education for Indians who hoped to "revive" regional architecture. To do so, the periodical suggested, they should apply new plasters, new tools, and new technologies to old schemas and styles in the model of the "Swiss."[48] But for Sarshar and the masons that he aimed to educate, a building was Islamic not just because of its style or its association with a Muslim past or Islamic religious practice. Certainly, a mason could accrue prestige and demonstrate piety by constructing a building that was used for worship or mourning, as Sarshar had done with the *imāmbāṛā* of Shamsabad. Architecture was also rendered Islamic through the practice and piety of the workers. This, Sarshar suggested, could apply to any building that they were recruited to work on if masons were sufficiently educated in the practice of pious construction and were permitted to carry out their work Islamically.

PATRONS AND PRAISE: CLAIMING TECHNOLOGY AND POWER

In addition to artisan lead masons and middle-class technical intermediaries, a third group circulated knowledge about stonemasonry and its relationship with Islam and the Muslim past. Patrons themselves—and the historians and poets they employed—also sometimes wrote about stonemasonry, albeit primarily to demonstrate their own religious, political, or technical authority. By the early twentieth century, consolidating technical hierarchies within the public works departments of princely states allowed patrons and members of the courtly elite to subsume the labor of stonemasons within the broader "technologizing power" of their states. Nonetheless, these patrons and courtly elites recognized the importance of masonry to the demonstration of their own political and religious authority.

Members of the Indian elite wrote about stonemasonry not only as a technical practice but also as a source of prestige, piety, and social influence to an extent greater than the other trades that I have examined so far—with the occasional exception of scribal work. As was the case with Sarshar's writing, patrons praised not just the structures that were popularly understood as sites of Muslim religious practice but sometimes also buildings more generally. But this praise, while ostensibly *about* stonemasons, was usually aimed at an elite audience and was used to assert the distinctiveness of the state as a site for the preservation of Muslim tradition and aesthetics, especially vis-à-vis British India.

For instance, in 1905 in Hyderabad State, the wealthy and prominent Muslim-led state in the South Indian Deccan region, a local courtly historian composed a ghazal praising the construction of a bazaar. Sponsored by a representative of the Hyderabadi state elite in the town of Beed, Maharashtra, the bazaar was constructed to represent courtly interest in the town's economy.[49] The ghazal, authored by a poet called Siddiqi, was written in Persian, as indeed was the entire text, even though Hyderabad had adopted Urdu as its official language in place of Persian in 1884.[50] The choice of Persian reflects the assumed elite or highly literate nature of the intended audience, highlighting the fact that verses in praise of masons were likely inaccessible and not intended to be read by the masons themselves.

Siddiqi praised the builder of the Mahbub Ganj bazaar through allusions to the classical story of Shireen and Farhad, in which Farhad was a sculptor ordered to carve through Mount Behistun as punishment for his love of the princess Shireen.[51] Simultaneously, the poet engaged with the imagery of God's creation and the narrative of the builder as a divinely influenced creator:

> Hail to you, chisel of the artisan
> Hail to you, Farhad-like craft
> Hail to you, plaything of the stonecutter
> Hail to you, mountain-cutting lover of Shireen
> Hail to you, who knows the pulse of hard stone
> Hail to you, layer of hardened brick
> Hail to you, builder of Mahbub Ganj
> Hail to you, sheikh of mud walls and glory
> Hail to you, stamped record of creation
> Hail to you, pen of Siddiqi, whose byword is truthfulness.[52]

In Rampur and Bahawalpur, state elites and patrons likewise occasionally praised both the projects that were completed by stonemasons and the stonemasons themselves. In doing so, they positioned these workers as the inheritors of an unbroken tradition of Islamic architecture, the laboring representatives of the state's claims on a prestigious Muslim past.

As was the case with the poem written in praise of the mason of the Mahbub Ganj bazaar, however, the intended audience of this praise was usually not the stonemasons themselves. Instead, the leaders of princely states such as Rampur positioned local stonemasons and other artisans as repositories of classical Indo-Islamic aesthetic traditions to demonstrate their own political, religious, and social authority. Rampur, for instance, held an annual *Jashn-i Baynaẕīr* (Unparalleled Festival), a fair meant to promote the state's products while also celebrating the state as a center of literary and cultural patronage. At the fair, attendees were often treated to tours of Rampur's architectural accomplishments. The 1879 fair featured the official opening of a shrine honoring a footprint of the Prophet Muhammad.[53] The footprint, reportedly brought from Arabia to the state a few years earlier, was installed under a decoratively carved shrine outside the state's *Baynaẕīr* palace. The opening of the shrine, according to Najmul Ghani Khan, an early twentieth-century historian of the state, led to a "great fervor" among the public, boosting attendance at the fair.[54]

Visitors to the *Jashn-i Baynaẕīr* were also encouraged to peer into erected model workshops meant to demonstrate the industriousness of the state's artisans. An 1894 report described these model workshops as "brightly lit and clean" and noted that the artisans—most of whom were woodworkers along with a few stone carvers—showed "all deference to the honored visitors."[55] Tours of both the state's religious architecture and its model workshops were meant to highlight the religious authority and technological capacity of its court. They did little, however, to directly address the interests and practices of artisans themselves. They reflected a broader trend in which princely patrons used Islamic histories of stonemasonry to assert regional religious authority but did not necessarily incorporate or consider artisan claims on the piety of their labor within these narratives.

STATE BUREAUCRACIES AND MATERIAL CHANGE IN STONEMASONRY

The late nineteenth century thus saw the intersection and interaction of three distinct narratives of stonemasonry. These were the technologizing narratives of middle-class technical intermediaries; the description and circulation of pious labor by Muslim lead masons; and the claims on religious authority asserted by elite patrons. These intersections played out in distinct ways at sites of Muslim architectural patronage across the subcontinent, but they are perhaps most clearly documented in Muslim-led princely states. In states such as Rampur and Bahawalpur, technical hierarchies were gradually reorganized in the late nineteenth and early twentieth centuries. This process placed lead masons more directly under the oversight of middle-class technical intermediaries, even in cases where they were employed to construct mosques, shrines, and tombs rather than state offices, railway stations, or other "secular" state projects. Pushed downward in technical hierarchies and facing a loss of social prestige and technical authority, these lead masons were increasingly aligned with the wider communities of artisans who labored under their supervision.

In both Rampur and Bahawalpur, new hierarchies of technical oversight emerged most clearly in the first two decades of the twentieth century. In Rampur, the state public works department was officially organized to mirror the public works department of the North-Western Provinces in 1888, and in 1899 Nawab Hamid 'Ali Khan appointed a retired British superintending engineer, W. C. Wright, as department head. Wright was responsible for the construction of a new city gate—still known as Wright's Gate—a new jail, a new canal system, and a new hospital, among many other notable local structures.[56] Most famously, he designed the Hamid Manzil, the central palace complex inside Rampur's old fort walls that has housed Rampur's renowned Raza Library since 1957. Wright designed and organized the construction of these structures, largely adhering to the Indo-Saracenic architectural style preferred by contemporary architects in British India.[57] However, the massive scale of Rampur's construction program in the post-1888 period meant the oversight of artisan labor was carried out by a growing cadre of technical intermediaries.

Before the 1910s, many of these intermediaries were Rampuri master artisans, contracted by the state to interpret the directives of Wright and his small cadre of engineers. For instance, beginning in 1905, a Rampur carpenter and contractor named 'Ali Muhammad led the construction of wooden terraces, roofs, and doors for Hamid Manzil and its main Darbar Hall. Working under Wright's direction, 'Ali Muhammad supervised and led both traditional wood carving and the use of plaster of paris to sculpt decorative exteriors.[58]

As suggested by 'Ali Muhammad's use of plaster of paris at Hamid Manzil, the public works departments and their engineers were especially influential in reshaping the materials used in state architecture. This included the materials that major courtly patrons identified as appropriate for religious architecture. Although at Hamid Manzil plaster of paris was used to sculpt decorative exteriors, other newly developed plasters were used to create a clean, finished look, especially on the domes of tombs, mosques, and shrines. Across South Asia, masons who worked completing this type of plastering were often the least prestigious and lowest paid within the hierarchy of masonry workshops.[59] The labor of plastering was sometimes assigned to new apprentices and in other cases carried out by laborers who were perceived by both employers and other masons as "low skill," employed by masonry workshops at low wages. Despite this dismissal of plasterers as unskilled, these workers were often expected to adapt most rapidly to public works department–influenced technological and material changes.

From the 1910s, Rampur increasingly recruited Indian overseers who had been educated at Roorkee to take on official supervising roles that had previously, unofficially, been undertaken by the state's lead masons and master artisans like 'Ali Muhammad. This new class of middle-class, state-educated overseers did not necessarily require that laborers use radically different materials and technologies than the displaced lead masons did, given that the lead mason class had also been responsive to material shifts. However, as lead masons were pushed downward in the hierarchies of technical oversight, social and religious distinctions emerged between artisan cadres and supervisors. Apprenticeship-trained lead masons were increasingly marginalized from state narratives and aligned with stoneworkers and other laborers, while the new class of technical intermediaries became the representatives of state ideologies.

Reports on the Bahawalpuri Public Works Department of the early twentieth century similarly highlight the formalization of its labor recruitment policies and labor practices in the early twentieth century and the gradual marginalization of the technical authority of apprenticeship-trained lead masons. A 1911 report notes, "Heretofore, works in the State were executed by daily labor or by granting advances to the contractors. This year, the schedule contracts were given, and payment was made to the contractor on a running account for the work done."[60] Moreover, the report explains, the public works department created new structures of oversight in 1910–11. The state was divided into three regions, and a public works department supervisor was assigned to each. In each region, the assigned supervisor was responsible for directing and inspecting the work of contracted lead masons or master artisans and their workshops.[61]

In the capital and the immediate surrounding region, the official public works department supervisor appointed in 1911 was Mirza Hamiduddin, with Munshi Abdul Hadi Khan appointed to the east and Umaruddin appointed to the west. In other princely states, including Rampur, educated locals sometimes complained that "outsiders" were preferred for official positions within the public works department.[62] In Bahawalpur, however, state records emphasize the commitment of the court to sending Bahawalpuris for education at centers of engineering training such as Lahore and Roorkee, and subsequently employing them in the state.[63] Whether that was the case with the three public works department supervisors appointed in 1911 is unclear, but it is possible that Bahawalpuri appointees had stronger social, linguistic, or economic ties to regional workshops than outsiders, allowing for clearer communication and circulation of shifting official preferences. However, regardless of whether the public works department supervisors were Bahawalpuri or recruited from elsewhere, they brought with them the models of building and preferences for building materials such as plasters that they had learned at British Indian engineering schools.

BUILDING THE MODERN MOSQUE IN RAMPUR AND BAHAWALPUR

In both states, the consolidation of models of technical oversight for stonemasonry that were preferred by the public works departments took place gradually. Monumental religious architecture commissioned in the late nineteenth and early twentieth centuries reflects the partial but not total influence of public works department technical preferences over the preferences of princely patrons. Likewise, mosques, tombs, and *imāmbāṛās* built in the period reveal the gradual and incomplete shift in authority from lead masons to middle-class technical intermediaries educated in British Indian engineering schools.

For instance, shortly after ascending to power in 1889, the ruling nawab of Rampur, Hamid ʿAli Khan, announced the construction of a new central mosque for the city.[64] The Rampur Jama Masjid was to be built with red sandstone imported to the state from Agra. This was an important marker of princely prestige, as the use of red sandstone during the height of the Mughal Empire had largely been restricted to the state's official projects and regional courts were unable to import it from Agra. The weekly state gazette printed to promote the actions of the state and its court pronounced on March 3, 1890, that "the façade of this mosque will be built of Rampur sugar and Agra stone," with "Rampur sugar" being a reference to the court's heavy investment in sugar cultivation as a crop intended to increase the state's wealth.[65]

The builder of this decadent facade, and indeed, of the mosque, was named Sheikh Kallu Mistrī, a local lead mason and master builder who had learned his trade from his father, who had likewise worked for the state in a similar position.[66] In constructing the new Rampur Jama Masjid, Sheikh Kallu Mistri and the laborers of his workshop likely engaged with narratives of artisan piety like those promulgated in Sarshar's *Tazkirah al-aiwān*. However, they also negotiated the fact that, in the late nineteenth century, architectural and technical authority in Rampur was increasingly directed through the state public works department, which was officially organized to mirror the public works department of the surrounding North-Western Provinces. Expectations about masonry training and practice increasingly flowed through the public works department, even for projects that members of the court patronized as individuals.

As a result, Sheikh Kallu Mistri and other members of his workshop likely encountered a wide variety of narratives and expectations about their trade as they labored at the Jama Masjid complex over the last decade of the nineteenth century. Sheikh Kallu Mistri himself was trained through an apprenticeship and likely learned to be a pious lead mason in the model of Sarshar from his father. However, the technical expectations of his patrons were almost certainly also influenced by an influx of engineers and overseers trained in British Indian institutions like Thomason College at Roorkee, even before Wright became the state's official chief engineer in

1899. New plasters and stucco mixes were especially important in the construction of the Jama Masjid, as the stucco moldings were meant to evoke the aesthetics of earlier regional dynasties and to suggest the state's application of the latest materials and technologies. Likewise, even the use of red sandstone in the state—largely a late nineteenth- and early twentieth-century phenomenon—required Rampuri lead masons like Sheikh Kalu Mistrī to adapt their material practices.

A mosque built roughly a decade later in Bahawalpur similarly reflected the circulation of materials, styles, and models of technical oversight from British India to Bahawalpur. The Nur Mahal (palace) Masjid was completed in 1903 and was located within Bahawalpur city's Nur Mahal complex. The Nur Mahal itself was a notable example of princely state interest in European architectural models. Commissioned by Nawab Muhammad Sadiq Khan IV, it was designed by an English engineer in the style of a neoclassical Italian palace in 1872.[67] But its accompanying mosque, built thirty years later through the patronage of Nawab Muhammad Bahawal Khan V—Sadiq Khan's son—differed markedly. It was a near-exact replica of the Aitchison College Mosque in Lahore, which Bahawal Khan had funded during his student days there.

Aitchison College aimed to provide a secondary education to the sons of "native chiefs" and regional princes, and school administrators, near the end of the nineteenth century, fretted that the campus did not include centers for the religious education of their charges. Consequently, funds and plans were sought for the construction of a masjid, a mandir, and a gurudwara on the campus. Bahawal Khan, then a student at the college, pledged his support to the mosque construction. The college itself had been designed by several of the leaders of the Mayo School of the Arts, including founder J. L. Kipling.[68] The mosque, likewise, was designed and overseen by Mayo School teachers and former students, at least one of whom was later recruited by the nawab to travel to Bahawalpur and oversee the construction of the Nur Mahal Mosque.[69]

The construction of the Aitchison College Mosque reflected the recruitment of technically trained middle-class Indians to a project of Muslim architectural revivalism, even as it required the participation of large cadres of apprenticeship-trained masons and other artisans. The exterior of the mosque was constructed in red sandstone—with its attendant evocations of the Mughal past—with a white marble dome.[70] The interior, elaborately decorated with moldings and brightly painted ceramic tiles, likewise reflected the late nineteenth-century reimagination of the Muslim past among both patrons and architects and technical intermediaries with prestigious training. Ceramic tilework had gained popularity in Europe, especially in Britain, in the mid-nineteenth century as part of a larger "Orientalist vogue."[71] By the 1890s, Indian elites had embraced this European interest in "Islamic tilework." A July 1894 article in the *Āyīnah-yi angrīzī saudāgarī* (Mirror of English manufactures), an Urdu journal that promoted British technical innovations, reflected the spread of interest in decorative ceramic tiles. The article explained that "several centuries ago India and Iran were the birthplaces of painted tiles. But because of the passage of time and revolutions of our era, today this art is no longer practiced in those regions, and the tiles can only be seen at ruins . . . but England has now brought a new perfection to this art."[72]

The Aitchison College Mosque—and its subsequent facsimile in Bahawalpur—thus reflected the efforts of both a consolidating technical intermediary class and patrons themselves to apply new technical practices to the revival of what they perceived as Islamic aesthetics. Moreover, in commissioning the construction of a copy of the mosque in Bahawalpur, Nawab Bahawal Khan V not only sought to evoke the prestige of an elite Indian Muslim past that he saw reflected in the red sandstone and decorative ceramic tiles. By building a near-exact replica of a modern Lahori mosque—one associated with a colonial educational institution—in Bahawalpur, he aimed to assert the technological and material parity of the state with British India. He brought overseers associated with the Mayo School to Bahawalpur to direct the labor of Bahawalpuri masons and other artisans. In doing so, he aimed to ensure that the Nur Mahal Masjid adhered to the technical and material properties of its Lahore predecessor. This was despite the fact that much of the work was done by artisans trained through apprenticeships in Bahawalpur, where they likely learned distinctive local practices, as opposed to the Mughal revivalist or "Indo-Saracenic" practices popular in Lahore.[73]

HIERARCHIES OF TECHNICAL AND RELIGIOUS KNOWLEDGE

The downward push of apprenticeship-trained lead masons and master builders within hierarchies of technical authority meant that these masons were increasingly alienated from state narratives about their work. Prior to the rise of middle-class cadres of overseers educated in British Indian engineering institutions, lead masons such as Sheikh Kallu Mistrī had been responsible for interpreting patron interests for cadres of laborers. But the rise of new classes of intermediaries placed an additional level of interpretation between the workers who built religious architecture and the patrons who funded these structures and made demands about their content. As they experienced a loss of authority within state hierarchies, some master builders and lead masons sought to reassert their authority within the workshop. They likely did so by strengthening their commitment to the distinctiveness of pious masonry, perhaps arguing, as Sarshar did, that the specific forms of piety and skill practiced in their workshops were necessary to the success of construction.[74]

In Bahawalpur, the post-1911 structure of contracting workshops likewise meant that stonemasons experienced more direct intervention from state overseers and engineers, and lead masons and master builders found their technical authority more constrained. The appointment of official public works department overseers to each region of the state meant that even comparatively remote projects received greater official intervention. Most notably, state policies toward the repair of some of its most notable tombs and shrines shifted. The state of Bahawalpur included the town of Uch Sharif, renowned for its array of shrines constructed between the twelfth and fifteenth centuries when Uch was an important religious center within the Delhi Sultanate.

Several of the monumental tombs in Uch had been damaged in the early nineteenth century by regional flooding.[75] Initially, any repairs to the shrines were commissioned by the *sajjāda nashīn*, or shrine custodian, of each, typically through waqf funds. However, with the creation of the British-led Architectural Survey of India (ASI) in 1861, the colonial regime placed increased emphasis on the preservation of what it called Indian monuments and pressured princely state elites to do the same. This was especially the case after 1904, when the British Indian government adopted the Ancient Monuments Preservation Act, which brought the "protection and acquisition of ancient monuments" formally under the jurisdiction of ASI.[76] As Michael Dodson has argued, the act aimed to "communicate to all levels of government the historical importance of ancient structures . . . and then also to direct local authorities to repair and preserve them with the appropriate practices of architectural conservation."[77] It marked attempted direct state control over restoration, often coordinated through local public works departments.

Although princely states did not formally fall under the remit of the ASI and the Ancient Monuments Preservation Act, British administrators and engineers in the states pushed state leaders to adopt similar approaches. As a result, in the late nineteenth century, the nawabs of Bahawalpur dedicated funds to the repair and restoration of the shrines and mosques of Uch, while in the early twentieth they assigned regional public works departments to oversee these repairs. The structures repaired included the mosque and shrine associated with Hazrat Jalaluddin Bokhari, the founder of the Jalali Sufi order, who died circa 1291–92 and whose tomb, constructed several centuries later, remains the site of a prominent *ʿurs* and annual mela. The mausoleum and mosque associated with his grandson, known as Jahaniyan Jahangasht (d. 1384), were likewise repaired through state funds.[78] When money was set aside for the restoration and repairs around 1870, under Nawab Muhammad Sadiq Khan, it seems to have been given directly to local masonry workshops to conduct the repairs according to their own methods, without significant state oversight. However, by the time the last nawab of Bahawalpur, Sadiq Muhammad Khan V, once again dedicated funds to the upkeep of the tombs and mosques, repairs were supervised by the regional public works department officer and his subordinates.[79]

As in Rampur, by the time Sadiq Muhammad Khan V dedicated funds to restore Uch Sharif in the 1910s, lead masons who contracted for state projects were no longer the primary intermediaries. In other words, they were no longer the primary translators between elite patron understandings of a project and the labor of larger cadres of workers. Instead, these lead masons themselves were directed and overseen by individuals with engineering training. These new intermediaries were appointed for their technical expertise derived from their training in Lahore or Roorkee, rather than from any specific attachment to Uch Sharif, and they sought to "modernize" the tools, techniques, and materials of restoration. As they worked, applying new mortars and plasters to the tombs and mosques, and even building new mud and brick walls, laborers were still directed by lead masons, but these lead masons themselves were subordinated to the demands of new PWD intermediaries.

• • •

As princely patrons reimagined their role in cultivating architectural symbols of a Muslim past, and members of the new technical intermediary class set to work applying "modernizing" technologies and materials to the tombs, what roles were left for stonemasons and other artisans? Did they simply adopt the technologies, materials, and ideologies of their new supervisors wholesale and, in doing so, reflect the idealized position that princely patrons had imagined for them? As I have suggested throughout this chapter, stonemasons' negotiation of the development of new hierarchies of technical oversight was often far more complex.

For princely patrons and many middle-class intermediaries, the technical practice of "modernity" was divorced from the Muslim heritage and authority represented by mosques, tombs, and *imāmbāṛās* but could nonetheless be used to improve their physical form. To this end, they participated in a physical manifestation of what Faisal Devji frames as the apologetics of Muslim debates on "modernity." The apologetics of Muslim modernity, in Devji's framing, made conceptual room for Muslims to "accommodate" modernizing discourses without necessitating systematic transformations of Islam.[80]

But stoneworker integration of the religious with the material and technological subverted this understanding, reflecting an alienation of many laborers and craftsmen from elite narratives of both religious authority and technical change. In the late nineteenth and early twentieth centuries, as public works bureaucracies expanded and exerted greater influence on masons' work, lead masons themselves turned to distinctive claims on Muslim piety to assert their authority at sites of labor. As we saw through Sarshar's writing, in contexts where stonemasons faced expanding influence of state bureaucracies—be they British or princely—lead masons often turned to the piety of their labor to assert influence and authority within their workshops and on projects of construction.

Ultimately, the experiences of stoneworkers responsible for constructing Islamic architecture suggest that laborers rapidly adapted to the technical demands of the state, while maintaining distinct understandings of the relationships between religion, work, and technology. Like many of the communities that I have discussed in this book, stonemasons necessarily worked within—and often embraced—technological and material change. But they interpreted this material change through their own lenses, often but not always reasserting the pious nature of their trade, reimagining and reclaiming their own social and technical roles within a shifting industry.

Conclusion

I opened this book with the words of Nazir, a blacksmith who lived, worked, and wrote poetry in Rampur in the mid-twentieth-century, postindependence, and post-Partition period. Nazir, in his verses, referenced the revelation of knowledge by God to the blacksmith, a theme we have returned to repeatedly throughout this book. He asserted, moreover, that such revelation and wisdom had forced the *sarmāyahdār*, or capitalist, to keep his "head bowed," suggesting a labor politics and class solidarity that centered the (God-given) power of workers.[1]

Artisans engaged with narratives of the Muslim past and claims on Islamic piety to navigate a bevy of social and technical challenges. One of the several contributions of artisan Islam that I have highlighted in this book was its impact on class-based solidarities. Writing in the mid-twentieth century, Nazir indicated the continuities in connections between Muslim claims on artisan traditions and class-based movements and identities. By way of epilogue and conclusion, I first draw together stories from across the chapters to ask how artisan Islam informed twentieth-century North Indian laboring class–based identities.

Second, I turn to the partition of artisan Islam and the post-Partition marginalization of Muslim artisans' technical knowledge by both India and Pakistan. Partition violently disrupted and reoriented Muslim artisans' networks of technical and religious knowledge exchange, just as it disrupted intellectual, material, and economic exchange across the subcontinent.[2] Rather than the gradual remaking of Muslim artisan communities and reimagining of artisan Islam through migration to urban centers, Partition represented a radical break from former localities and the rapid consolidation of new migrant communities. For those who migrated from regions such as the United Provinces—which remained entirely within India—to the newly established nation of Pakistan, the ability to maintain a pious connection with centers of worship and practice in their home regions was often made tenuous or broken. Conversely, those who remained in newly independent India, like Nazir, found themselves with more limited access to the translocal narratives and practices of artisan Islam that had characterized the previous century. These disruptions and reorientations are reflected in the archive of artisan Islam itself, and in its often piecemeal nature. The challenges of tying together writing produced in cities that were once part of tightly bound networks of knowledge exchange but are today divided between two (frequently oppositional) nation-states undoubtedly shaped the stories I was able to tell in this book.

In the final segment of this Conclusion, I return to the question of how *Pious Labor* might challenge our conception of the histories of South Asian Islam. Integrating the histories of labor and technology into our study of South Asian Islam suggests new potential paths within all three fields. Most notably, *Pious Labor* provides an opportunity to trouble persistent elisions in the study of South Asian Muslim communities. Placing laboring lives at the center of a study of South Asian Islam forces us to critically consider not only why they have so often been absent but also what forms of knowledge are lost by the insistence on a canon that privileges elite intellectual spaces.

RELIGION AND LABOR BEYOND COMMUNALISM AND CONFLICT?

Throughout this book, we have encountered early twentieth-century *kārīgar*s who engaged in or encouraged class solidarities and labor organization through narratives of artisan Islam. This was not the only way that *kārīgar*s asserted artisan Islam in contexts of wage labor and increased middle-class oversight, intervention, and ownership of their sites of work. But it was one prominent means by which artisan Islam not only retained but also broadened its social relevance in expanding, industrializing cities of urban North India.

Muslim claims on artisan traditions within Indian labor- and class-based movements in the early twentieth century suggest a potential nuancing of Dipesh Chakrabarty's depiction of the "inherent duality" of laborer politics. I do not dispute, as Chakrabarty argues, that in colonial India "act[s] of revolt against the authorities, such as . . . strike[s]," sometimes shifted, taking on "communal" characteristics that spurred religious conflict among workers.[3] But the examples analyzed in this book suggest that "revolts against the authorities" too were sometimes informed by narratives of piety and the religious past. Muslim experiences of pious labor informed worker solidarity, even shaping Muslim artisans' and laborers' willingness and ability to challenge the capitalist authority of workshop and factory owners or middle-class supervisors.

For instance, in the first chapter of this book, I analyzed the experiences of early twentieth-century lithographic laborers. For these workers, many of whom shared Muslim religious identities, popular understandings of social difference within the industrialized lithographic presses were often shaped by their labor, rather than along religious lines. Scribal workers sought to differentiate themselves from other lithographic workers by virtue of their claims on a distinctive engagement with a Muslim past and Muslim religious tradition for scribal practice. This was true even in a context like the Lahore lithographic presses, where a significant majority of laborers across most trades within presswork were Muslim.

In that context, the distinction that sometimes threatened to upend labor solidarities within the lithographic presses was not, in most instances, religious communalism. Instead, it was the varied social status and prestige ascribed to different technical and trade practices. Within individual trades such as scribal work, Muslim identity and narratives of the past operated as a force for cohesion and even solidarity. Islam, in the context of scribal labor at the lithographic presses, offered workers who had trained within the presses access to shared narratives of the Muslim past, even at times when they did not have access to prominent *ustād-murīd* lineages of scribal work. These narratives of trade-based social distinction, which often assumed shared Muslim identity, spurred the creation of a distinct union for scribal workers, though they did not, ultimately, prevent moments of workers' collaborative agitation against press owners and management.

Both at the presses and in other fields, Muslim owners and managers of factories and workshops sometimes sought to assert their shared religious identity with workers. In doing so, they aimed to reorient Muslim *kārīgar*s' forms of protest and resistance toward projects that held political resonance for elite and middle-class Muslims, and away from working-class agitation. In the first aim—securing mass participation in movements initially led by Muslim intellectuals and elites—they sometimes were successful, with urban laborers ultimately providing numerical strength for many of the major Muslim political movements and protests from the early twentieth century through to Partition in 1947.[4]

But this did not mean that *kārīgar*s' forms of protest were successfully oriented away from labor solidarities. On the contrary, in many of the trades studied in this book, Muslim workers remained committed to asserting their identities as both workers and Muslims. They drew on models and narratives from artisan Islam to demand improved wages and working conditions.[5] Commitment to identities and forms of solidarity were often rooted in a shared conception of physical labor as a distinguishing, pious practice. Even upwardly mobile and socially prominent master artisans such as the electroplater Mirza Ibrahim, the boilermaker Hakimuddin, and the lead mason Riyasat ʿAli Sarshar insisted on an artisan laboring identity that valorized physical work with one's hands as a pious practice, and one deserving of status and renumeration.

At the same time, engagement with labor politics was far from the only way that artisan Islam was reimagined in early twentieth-century contexts of technological and industrial change. As I show in chapter 3, artisan Islam was sometimes reasserted to meet a perceived challenge from emerging colonial and charitable educational institutions, with tailors insisting on the inherently masculine, heritable nature of the pious, Muslim, form of their labor. In other cases, such as through the Anjuman-i muṣlaḥ-i qaum-i āhangarān (Organization for the Uplift of the Community of Blacksmiths) explored in chapter 5, artisans sought to assert social status and prestige for their trades and laboring communities.

In their study of the adaptation of the Hindu tradition of Vishwakarma worship—often associated with artisans—in contexts of industrial labor, Kenneth George and Kiran Narayan note that there is "no intrinsic or immutable politics in Vishwakarma worship." Instead, it has the "capacity to lend itself for use as a public, political resource for mobilizations of different kinds."[6] The same might be said to be true of the traditions associated with artisan Islam that I have explored in this book; there are certainly no *intrinsic* politics to artisan assertions of Islam. But what has interested me, throughout this book, is the fact that so many artisans from across a wide range of trades sought to engage artisan Islam to improve the economic, social, and material well-being of their communities, be it through labor politics or other avenues. In Tirthankar Roy's framing, master artisans of the sort who wrote and circulated many of the texts examined in this book were often motivated by their efforts to distinguish themselves and improve their status as exceptionally innovative individuals.[7] But by claiming artisan traditions for their trades and asserting the pious nature of their materials and technologies, the artisans I have analyzed here sought to improve not just their own economic conditions and social status but also those of their communities. They sought to create new social spaces that privileged and valorized physical labor within a colonial economy that more often disciplined and marginalized members of their communities.

PARTITIONING ARTISAN ISLAM

Why has artisan Islam so often been overlooked, and how might we change our approach to the historical record to engage with traditions that circulated among Muslim workers? We have encountered several reasons for the marginalization of Muslim artisans and their pious labor in our understanding of the South Asian Muslim past, most notably persistent colonial-era claims that their Islam was "unorthodox" and even un-Islamic. Another reason that artisan Islam is often overlooked is rooted in the history of the partition of the subcontinent into the two new nation-states of India and Pakistan in 1947.

Partition marked a radical breaking point for many of the translocal and trans-urban networks of technical, material, and religious knowledge on which *kārīgar*s relied. It also contributed to the marginalization of the archive of artisan Islam, as the archival preservation practices of the two new states centered collections that highlighted the narratives and processes of their own creation. Tracing the mobility of the people, texts, and ideas central to artisan Islam thus becomes an exercise in reconstructing spaces and networks that were radically, often violently, disrupted.

As I have shown throughout the book, Muslim artisans exchanged understandings of pious labor across cities in colonial North India through the circulation of printed manuals and histories. These were, in turn, intended to be read aloud and interpreted within workshops and factories, with Muslim artisans likely adding notes and comments relevant to their localized communities. Likewise, regional migration within North India, often from small towns to larger cities within the same or neighboring provinces, brought localized inflections of artisan Islam into conversation with each other.

Partition spurred migration completely unlike the economic migration seen in previous decades on an unforeseen scale often remembered as "the largest mass migration in human history."[8] Partition migration often occurred during periods of extreme violence, with migrants moving because they feared for their lives and the lives of their families.[9] Artisans and laborers who migrated as a result of Partition violence often did return to their trades—or related trades—in the cities and regions where they settled, finding and organizing new laboring communities despite their displacement.[10] In an industrial neighborhood just outside the walled city of Lahore in summer 2022, I was introduced to several Muslim carpenters who told me of their pre-Partition familial origins in cities such as Amritsar, now in Indian Punjab, or in the towns of the United Provinces (now Uttar Pradesh). Nearly all these Pakistani carpenters boasted that their ancestors had been successful in woodworking or related fields in India before Partition.

Nonetheless, the scope and magnitude of Partition make it impossible to study these migrations through the same lens of exchange and adaptation as those analyzed in chapter 4. Although some artisans almost certainly reasserted and reimagined their traditions of pious labor in the wake of the mass migration of Partition, the translocal networks that allowed these traditions and practices to circulate and expand were violently unmade. The contemporary carpenters I spoke to in Lahore expressed intergenerational nostalgia for their ancestral cities and towns in India, and some also asserted a connection to a shrine or saintly lineage in India. But even among those who had family on the other side of the border, none had visited, and the possibility of meaningful material exchange seemed foreclosed.

Partition and the creation of two new nation-states (later three, with the creation of Bangladesh in 1971) also furthered processes of marginalizing artisan claims on technological expertise through the creation of national claims on science and technology. As Gyan Prakash notes, in the immediate pre-Partition and post-Partition periods Indian nationalists sought to claim an "indigenous science" or identify "indigenous cultural resources for science." In doing so, they "challenge[d] the dominant view that Western science's epistemology transcended its cultural location."[11] Simultaneously, in Pakistan, some of the state's new leaders took up narratives of the "compatibility" of Islam and science through reference to the scientific prowess of eighth- through thirteenth-century Muslims. They relocated and nationalized an understanding of the Muslim scientific past that had also circulated and been the subject of significant debate among Muslim reformists in colonial India.[12]

But there was little room for artisan Islam or Muslim artisan claims of technical expertise in either of these traditions. Prakash argues that even among Indian "secular nationalists" the indigeneity of scientific knowledge or resources was often rooted in an implicitly Hindu past.[13] And in Pakistan, claims for Muslim pasts of science and technology continued to draw on the elite Muslim narratives of decline from a supposed "golden age," one often emanating primarily from the supposed Arab and Persian ancestors of *sharīf* Muslims. Artisan Islam, in other words, had limited relevance to either of the new nationalizing ideologies of science and technology.

The national narratives of both new states, but especially of India, also conceptualized "craft traditions" as part of a postcolonial understanding of heritage and identity. In India, as Abigail McGowan notes, there was a concerted effort to frame "national life" around craft production.[14] Nationalizing narratives of craft sought to challenge colonial perceptions of the backwardness and inflexibility of Indian artisans, even as they also maintained the "timelessness" of Indian tradition. At the same time, they echoed colonial portrayals of the sharp distinction between "cottage" industries and urban, industrialized manufacturing. In this imagination of national crafts, there was little room for an urban Muslim *kārīgar* who moved between spaces of wage labor and familial workshops. Likewise, while not necessarily exclusively Hindu, nationalizing images of craftsmanship idealized a supposed timeless Indian village as the site of artisanship, often embodied by a rural Hindu woman.[15] The implicit Hindu social identity of the idealized Indian craftworker in the post-Partition period meant that the body of knowledge produced by Muslim artisans was seen as irrelevant to assertions of Indian national tradition.

As noted earlier, Partition—and the attendant violent displacements of the mid-twentieth century—did not just disrupt the translocal connections, patterns of migration and mobility, and community spaces of Muslim artisans. It also remade the ways that the histories and narratives of Muslim artisans were collected and preserved, while shaping the language that we, as historians, have available to us to describe the traditions of Muslim social and political practice on the modern subcontinent. On the most practical level, it has contributed to the loss and marginalization of materials on artisan Islam.

At the time of writing, India is a nation increasingly—and overwhelmingly—politically dominated by Hindutva ideology and the accompanying violent disavowal of Muslim pasts and futures. But even before the contemporary political turn, archival collections and regional histories perceived as Islamic were sometimes seen as beyond the remit of the secular Indian state, except when they demonstrated the state's understanding of an (often elite) aesthetic of Indian Islam. Many Indian public libraries devoted to the types of Urdu-language materials that may have circulated among artisans have been chronically underfunded. Collections that existed before Partition often lost their most significant benefactors and patrons after 1947. Conversely, in Pakistan, while there is state support for Urdu-language collections and Islamic histories, histories that receive the most funding and promotion are those that highlight an inexorable march toward Pakistani statehood. While alternative Muslim politics—including Muslim social movements and ideologies beyond the *ashrāf*—have attracted increased scholarly attention, they remain marginalized by state efforts to cultivate a specifically Pakistani history.[16]

Moreover, as Saloni Mathur has argued in the context of art historical approaches to Partition, the events of 1947 and their aftermath sometimes threaten to "overdetermine" our reading of modern South Asian histories. Mathur asks how Partition—and in some cases, our study of it—has limited "our ability to think against the status quo," in imagining both potential futures and past worlds.[17] In examining the connections and exchanges embedded in the manuals and community histories of artisan Islam, *Pious Labor* has centered alternative pasts of Indian Muslims. Within these pasts, debates over Muslim identity and practice were not just oriented—always and inexorably—toward debates over "nationhood" but instead encompassed a wide range of social projects that emphasized the role of Islam within Indian laboring lives.

ARTISAN ISLAM AS ISLAMIC HISTORY

Pious Labor has engaged in several projects of recovery. It has highlighted stories that have been marginalized by Partition, by the dominance of colonial archives over the vernacular, and by assumptions that laboring religious identities in South Asia are inherently communal or oppositional. It has sought to recover these stories because they are interesting but also because they suggest a potential reorientation of our understanding of the Muslim past in South Asia. Historiographically, this book has also argued for locating Islamic history with labor history and the history of technology and, conversely, for reading these fields as Islamic history. We can only understand the vastness of Muslim pasts when we consider not only the version of Islam produced in debates among religious scholars, or in histories popularly coded as Islamic, but also the versions of Islam embedded in a wide range of Muslim documents on their histories and practices.

Muslim artisans meaningfully engaged with the emergent elite-led religious movements of the late nineteenth and early twentieth centuries, and these movements had significant popular political and religious impacts. Indeed, Muslim intellectual addresses to the working classes and the popularization of religious movements that had originated within Muslim intellectual circles were common in early to mid-twentieth century South Asia.[18] But if we read colonial-era South Asian Islamic history through the technical manuals and community histories examined in this book, it becomes apparent that artisan engagement with Islam extended far beyond a popularization of elite reformist ideologies. We must therefore contend with Muslim experiences that differ radically from those reflected in the writings of Muslim intellectuals and the movements they create.

When we read Muslim religious, social, and material lives through the *Risālah-yi Idrīsiyah*, the *Tazkirah al-aiwān*, or the *Iksīr-i malmʿah*, we confront alternative narratives of the Muslim past. We are also exposed to the myriad ways that Muslims attempted to make sense of—and sometimes challenge—colonial economic and technical authority. The writings of master artisans such as Khwaja Muhammad, Riyasat ʿAli Sarshar, and Mirza Ibrahim center concerns about how to negotiate the economic and material marginalization of their communities under colonial authority. We should acknowledge that these concerns were themselves sometimes exclusionary or hierarchical, particularly given their erasure of women and nonmale artisans. Still, drawing on their engagement with Islam through artisanship, their manuals and histories offered visions for the futures of artisan and laboring communities that lay beyond the consolidating forms of exploitation engendered through the colonial economy.

Even in the contemporary Indian economic context, often dominated by the rise of multinational corporations and upper-caste Hindu technical authority, Muslim artisans continue to engage with Islam to negotiate their economic, social, and religious positionalities.[19] Despite the radical disruptions of Partition, artisan Islam seems to retain at least some personal and social relevance. And as in the past, artisan articulations of the Islamic nature of their work often seem to straddle divides between written and embodied knowledge.

For instance, in June 2022, in a scissor-making workshop in Meerut, I glimpsed a lithographed sheet of paper, hanging on the workshop wall in a silver frame. The page promised that "by hanging this page in the shop, it is protected from all evil and violence [*shar o fasād*]."[20] The same page provided numerical tables praising God, the Prophet Muhammad, and the early caliphs, emphasizing the number 786, which is often used to express "Bismillāh hir raḥmān nir raḥīm" through the *abjad* system where Arabic letters are assigned numerical value. And at the bottom was an *ayah* from the second *sūrah* of the Quran, *sūrah al-baqarah*, proclaiming: "God: There is no god but Him, the Ever Living, the Ever Watchful. Neither slumber nor sleep overtakes Him. All that is in the heavens and in the earth belongs to Him. Who is there that can intercede with Him except by His leave?"[21] This lithographed page on the wall of the scissor-making workshop—which also served as the proprietor's home—in contemporary Meerut suggests the continued relevance of Islamic knowledge and piety to spaces of artisan labor and production. Just as artisan Islam took on shifting social, political, and economic relevance in the context of colonial capitalism, we might speculate that contemporary Muslim artisans continue to remake the piety of their labor and religious practice today. That is, however, a subject for a different book, perhaps one that draws on methodologies beyond the archival. What I wish to highlight here is not the potential contours of artisan Islam in contemporary India but rather the persistence of artisanal forms, spaces, and texts of piety, despite the intensifying religious marginalization of Indian Muslims and the emergence of a neoliberal economy.

To that end, we might end where we began: with Nazir, who wrote in the post-Partition period but drew on ideals of Muslim artisanship that had circulated in the North Indian print economy over the previous century. Like so many of the materials examined in this book, his poetry reveals that Muslim artisans imagined worlds in which the God-given skill of the artisan was recognized not only as a source of status but also as a form of wisdom at the center of technical production. They did so despite, and in some cases because of, the rise of spaces of production that challenged or undermined their technical authority, and the rise of elite and middle-class narratives that belied artisanal piety. In articulating artisan Islam, Nazir and his predecessors pursued laboring and technological futures that celebrated the work and piety of Muslim artisan communities.

NOTES

Abbreviations used:

BL	British Library
IOR	India Office Records
NAI	National Archives of India

INTRODUCTION

1. Ibn Ḥasan Khurshīd, *Tażkirah-yi hunarmandān-i Rāmpūr* (Rampur: Raza Library Press, 2001), 44.

2. Khurshīd, *Tażkirah*, 43–44. Nazir's poetry was recorded in a poetic compendium that was printed in the nearby city of Moradabad, around the 1970s. See Muḥammad ʿAtīq, *Shamʿ-yi hidāyat* (Moradabad: Maktabah Jannat al-Nisān, n.d.), 6.

3. The literature on Indian urban industrialization, and the role of artisans and laborers within it, is vast. See Rajnarayan Chandavarkar, "Industrialization in India before 1947: Conventional Approaches and Alternative Perspectives," in *Imperial Power and Popular Politics* (Cambridge: Cambridge University Press, 1998), 30–73; William Glover, *Making Lahore Modern: Constructing and Imagining a Global City* (Minneapolis: University of Minnesota Press, 2008), 27–33; and Chitra Joshi, *Lost Worlds: Indian Labour and Its Forgotten Histories* (Delhi: Permanent Black, 2003), 38–45.

4. The region's pre-1902 name, the North-Western Provinces (NWP), should not be confused with the North West Frontier Province (NWFP), a province created in 1901 that included large portions of the territory now in Pakistan's Khyber Pakhtunkhwa.

5. Prasannan Parthasarathi, *Transition to a Colonial Economy: Weavers, Merchants, and Kings in South India, 1720–1800* (Cambridge: Cambridge University Press, 2001), 148.

6. Ajantha Subramanian, *The Caste of Merit: Engineering Education in India* (Cambridge, MA: Harvard University Press, 2019), 27; Arun Kumar, "Skilling and Its Histories: Labour

Market, Technical Knowledge, and the Making of Skilled Workers in Colonial India, 1880–1910," *Journal of South Asian Development* 13, no. 3 (2018): 255–57.

7. E.P. Thompson, *The Making of the English Working Class* (New York: Pantheon Books, 1966), 234.

8. Nita Kumar, *The Artisans of Banaras: Popular Culture and Identity, 1880–1986* (Princeton, NJ: Princeton University Press, 1988), 13–14.

9. Joshi, *Lost Worlds*, 8.

10. Dipesh Chakrabarty, *Rethinking Working-Class History: Bengal, 1890–1940* (Princeton, NJ: Princeton University Press, 1989), 217–18.

11. Chakrabarty, *Rethinking Working-Class History*, 187–90.

12. Nandini Gooptu, *The Politics of the Urban Poor in Early Twentieth-Century India* (Cambridge: Cambridge University Press, 2001), 278–81.

13. The most significant are Thomas Chambers, *Networks, Labour and Migration among Indian Muslim Artisans* (London: UCL Press, 2020), and Hussain Ahmad Khan, *Artisans, Sufis, Shrines: Colonial Architecture in Nineteenth-Century Punjab* (London: Bloomsbury, 2015).

14. This is not to dismiss the compelling nature of recent scholarship on these areas but rather to note a potential additional focus. On promising directions in the study of the *'ulama* and their role in modern South Asia, see Ali Altaf Mian, "Translating Scholars: Theorizing Modern South Asian 'Ulama' Studies," *Religion Compass* 16, no. 5 (2022): 1–11.

15. Shahzad Bashir, "Prospects for a New Idiom for Islamic History," in *What Is Islamic Studies: European and North American Approaches to a Contested Field*, ed. Leif Stenberg and Philip Wood (Edinburgh: Edinburgh University Press, 2022), 176–89.

16. Nile Green, *Bombay Islam: The Religious Economy of the West Indian Ocean, 1840–1915* (Cambridge: Cambridge University Press, 2011), 179–207.

17. Green, *Bombay Islam*, 182–83.

18. On shared religious spaces, see Anna Bigelow, *Sharing the Sacred: Practicing Pluralism in Muslim North India* (Oxford: Oxford University Press, 2010), 22–24, and Anand Vivek Taneja, *Jinnealogy: Time, Islam, and Ecological Thought in the Medieval Ruins of Delhi* (Stanford, CA: Stanford University Press, 2017), 139–40.

19. J.R.D. Smith, *Gazetteer of the Sialkot District, 1894–95* (Lahore: Civil and Military Gazetteer Press, 1895), 53.

20. SherAli Tareen, "Normativity, Heresy, and the Politics of Authenticity in South Asian Islam," *Muslim World* 99 (2009): 535–46.

21. Torsten Tschacher, "Rational Miracles, Cultural Rituals and the Fear of Syncretism: Defending Contentious Muslim Practice among Tamil-Speaking Muslims," *Asian Journal of Social Science* 37, no. 1 (2009): 56–59.

22. Margrit Pernau, *Ashraf into Middle Classes: Muslims in Nineteenth-Century Delhi* (Oxford: Oxford University Press, 2013): 57–65; M. Raisur Rahman, *Locale, Everyday Islam, and Modernity: Qasbah Towns and Muslim Life in Colonial India* (Delhi: Oxford University Press, 2015): 182–84; Shenila Khoja-Moolji, *Forging the Ideal Educated Girl: The Production of Desirable Subjects in Muslim South Asia* (Oakland: University of California Press, 2018), 23–59.

23. Imtiaz Ahmad, "The Ashraf and Ajlaf Categories in Indo-Muslim Society," *Economic and Political Weekly* 2, no. 19 (May 1967): 889–91. More recent studies have emphasized the

experiences of Dalit and other caste-marginalized Muslims, who often identify as *pasmānda* (marginalized) Muslims. See Joel Lee, "Who Is the True Halalkhor? Genealogy and Ethics in Dalit Muslim Oral Traditions," *Indian Sociology* 52, no. 1 (2018): 4–5, and Khalid Anis Ansari, "Rethinking the Pasmanda Movement," *Economic and Political Weekly* 44, no. 13 (2009): 8–10. On distinctions between "caste" and "caste-like practices" with reference to South Asian Muslims, see Safwan Amir, "Contempt and Labour: An Exploration through Muslim Barbers of South Asia," *Religions* 10, no. 11 (2019): 1–14. Like Amir, I use both terms, while emphasizing that "caste" is not experienced uniformly.

24. For an example of contestation within and across artisan castes among South Indian Hindu artisans, see Jan Brouwer, *The Makers of the World: Caste, Craft, and Mind of South Indian Artisans* (Delhi: Oxford University Press, 1995), 213–15.

25. Ashish Koul, "Making New Muslim Arians: Reform and Social Mobility in Colonial Punjab, 1890s–1910s," *South Asian History and Culture* 8, no. 1 (2017): 1–18; Lee, "Who Is the True Halalkhor?," 4–5.

26. David Gilmartin, "Environmental History, *Biradari*, and the Making of Pakistani Punjab," in *Punjab Reconsidered: History, Culture, and Practice*, ed. Anshu Malhotra and Farina Mir (Delhi: Oxford University Press, 2012), 290–93.

27. Lee, "Who Is the True Halalkhor?," 15.

28. Lee, "Who Is the True Halalkhor?," 20.

29. Sarah Qidwai, "Darwin or Design: Examining Sayyid Ahmad Khan's Views on Human Evolution," in *The Cambridge Companion to Sayyid Ahmad Khan*, ed. Yasmin Sakina and Raisur Rahman (Cambridge: Cambridge University Press, 2019), 214–32; S. Irfan Habib, *Jihad or Ijtihad: Religious Orthodoxy and Modern Science in Contemporary Islam* (Delhi: Harper Collins, 2012); Ali Altaf Mian, "Troubling Technology: The Deobandi Debate on the Loudspeaker and Ritual Prayer," *Islamic Law and Society* 24, no. 4 (2017): 355–83.

30. Kenneth M. George and Kiran Narayan, "Technophany and Its Publics: Artisans, Technicians, and the Rise of Vishwakarma Worship in India," *Journal of Asian Studies* 81, no. 1 (2022): 3–21; Shivani Kapoor, "The Search for 'Tanner's Blood': Caste and Technical Education in Colonial Uttar Pradesh," *Review of Development and Change* 23, no. 2 (2010): 118–38.

31. For a discussion of the conceptual limitations of "technology transfer," see David Arnold, *Everyday Technology: Machines and the Making of India's Modernity* (Chicago: University of Chicago Press, 2013), 40–42.

32. Projit Bihari Mukharji, *Doctoring Traditions: Ayurveda, Small Technologies, and Braided Technologies* (Chicago: University of Chicago Press, 2016), 169.

33. Mukharji, *Doctoring Traditions*, 80.

34. Arnold, *Everyday Technology*, 42.

35. Mirzā Ibrāhīm Dehlvī, *Iksīr-i malmʿah* (Delhi: Mayūr Press, 1893); Ḥākimuddīn, *Kalīd-i ṣanʿat* (Lahore: New Imperial Press, 1890).

36. Projit Bihari Mukharji, "Vernacularizing the Body: Informational Egalitarianism, Hindu Divine Design, and Race in Physiology Schoolbooks, Bengal, 1859–1877," *Bulletin of the History of Medicine* 91, no. 3 (2017): 579–80.

37. Charu Singh, "Science in the Vernacular? Translation, Terminology and Lexicography in the Hindi Scientific Glossary (1906)," *South Asian History and Culture* 13, no. 1 (2022): 63–86.

38. Thompson, *Making of the English Working Class*, 234.

39. Tirthankar Roy, "Out of Tradition: Master Artisans and Economic Change in Colonial India," *Journal of Asian Studies* 66, no. 4 (2007): 964–65.

40. Michael Dodson, "Translating Science, Translating Empire: The Power of Language in Colonial North India," *Society for Comparative Study of Society and History* 47, no. 4 (2005): 819–21.

41. Sheikh Khwājah Muḥammad, *Risālah-yi Idrīsiyah* (Allahabad: Anwār Aḥmadi Press, 1907), 14.

42. Riyāsat ʿAlī Sarshār, *Taẕkirah al-aiwān* (Fatehgarh: Dilkushā Press, 1875).

43. Mahmood Kooria, "Texts as Objects of Value and Veneration: Islamic Law Books in the Indian Ocean Littoral," *Sociology of Islam* 6, no. 1 (2018): 60–83.

44. For an analysis of the interplay between embodied and textual knowledge among artisans in early modern Europe, see Pamela Smith, *From Lived Experience to the Written Word: Reconstructing Practical Knowledge in the Early Modern World* (Chicago: University of Chicago Press, 2022).

45. See also Kooria's effort to understand how religious texts "operate among their possessors, disseminators, teachers, students, producers and consumers" ("Texts as Objects," 62).

46. Jorell A. Meléndez-Badillo, *The Lettered Barriada: Workers, Archival Power, and the Politics of Knowledge in Puerto Rico* (Durham, NC: Duke University Press, 2021), 2 and 53.

47. Tobias Higbie, *Labor's Mind: A History of Working-Class Intellectual Life* (Urbana: University of Illinois Press, 2019), 15.

48. I understand "Hindustani" as a broad language continuum encompassing both modern Urdu and Hindi, which themselves contain multiple registers and dialects that are often but not always highly mutually intelligible. For the histories of these terms, see David Lunn, "Hindustani," in *Encyclopaedia of Islam, Three*, ed. Kate Fleet, Gudrun Krämer, Denis Matringe, John Nawas, and Everett Rowson, online ed. (Leiden: Brill, 2019), https://referenceworks.brillonline.com/browse/encyclopaedia-of-islam-3.

49. On colonial support for publishing in Urdu over Punjabi, see Farina Mir, *The Social Space of Language: Vernacular Culture in British Colonial Punjab* (Berkeley: University of California Press, 2010), 12–14.

50. On Urdu as a means to connect readers across South Asia, see Kavita Datla, *The Language of Secular Islam: Urdu Nationalism and Colonial India* (Honolulu: University of Hawaiʻi Press, 2013), 8–11.

51. Douglas E. Haynes, *Small Town Capitalism in Western India: Artisans, Merchants, and the Making of the Informal Economy, 1870–1960* (New York: Cambridge University Press, 2012), 23.

52. Recent reevaluations of deindustrialization include Prasannan Parthasarathi's argument, in "Indian Labor History," *International Labor and Working Class History* 82 (2012): 127–35, that the rise of the British East India Company subjected weavers to "immense disciplinary pressures" that forced wages down and sparked their loss of economic and political power (5–6). Conversely, Tirthankar Roy's (2010) study of eighteenth-century Bengal, "Economic Conditions in Early Modern Bengal: A Contribution to the Divergence Debate." *Journal of Economic History* 70, no. 1 (2010): 179–94, found that laborers maintained relatively stable incomes, suggesting that "natural production conditions," rather than imperial power, changed employment patterns (188–90).

53. Christopher A. Bayly, *Rulers, Townsmen and Bazaars: North Indian Society in the Age of British Expansion 1770–1870*, 3rd ed. (Delhi: Oxford University Press, 2012), 520–23.

54. Gooptu, *Politics of the Urban Poor*, 277–79. On the intersection of the local and transregional in claims on orthodoxy, see Chiara Formichi, *Islam and Asia: A History* (Cambridge: Cambridge University Press, 2020), 7.

55. Green, *Bombay Islam*, 20–21.

56. Michael Dodson, *Bureaucracy, Belonging, and the City in North India, 1870–1930* (New York: Routledge, 2020), 11.

57. N. Kumar, *Artisans of Banaras*, 15–16 and 36.

58. Khwājah Muḥammad, *Risālah-yi Idrīsiyah*, 2–4.

59. Abigail McGowan, "Mothers and Godmothers of Crafts: Female Leadership and the Imagination of India as a Crafts Nation, 1947–67," *South Asia* 44, no. 2 (2021): 289.

60. Samita Sen, *Women and Labour in Late Colonial India: The Bengal Jute Industry* (Cambridge: Cambridge University Press, 1999), 7.

61. Pernau, *Ashraf into Middle Classes*, 226–35; Tanika Sarkar, *Hindu Wife, Hindu Nation: Community, Religion, and Cultural Nationalism* (Bloomington: Indiana University Press, 2010), 122–25.

1. LITHOGRAPHIC LABOR: LOCATING MUSLIM ARTISANS IN THE PRINT ECONOMY

1. Karīmullah Khān, *Daftar-i khaṭṭāṭ*, 1885 (Pers., no. 2454, Raza Library, Rampur, Uttar Pradesh).

2. K. Khān, *Daftar-i khaṭṭāṭ*, 132.

3. K. Khān, *Daftar-i khaṭṭāṭ*, 135.

4. K. Khān, *Daftar-i khaṭṭāṭ*, 135–36. Mirror writing directly on stones was reportedly sometimes also used to compose entire texts by the most skilled and well-paid scribes and calligraphers, though this is not mentioned in Karīmullah Khān's work. See Ulrike Stark, *An Empire of Books: The Naval Kishore Press and the Diffusion of the Printed Word in Colonial India* (Delhi: Orient Blackswan, 2007), 172–73.

5. Home, Political, no. 7/5 (1936), 6–8, NAI.

6. Home, Political, no. 7/5 (1936), 56, NAI. On these issues in the presses of Lahore more generally, see Ahmad Mukhtar, *Factory Labour in the Punjab* (Madras: Huxley Press, 1929), 7–8 and 45–47.

7. Home, Political, no. 7/5 (1936), 56–57, NAI.

8. Ram Chandra, *History of the Naujawan Bharat Sabha* (Chandigarh: Unistar Books, 1997), 34.

9. On the transregional circulation of printing cultures, see Nile Green, "Journeymen, Middlemen: Travel, Transculture, and the Origins of Muslim Printing," *International Journal of Middle East Studies*, 41, no. 2 (2009): 203–24.

10. I have previously developed portions of this argument in Amanda Lanzillo, "Translating the Scribe: Lithographic Print and Vernacularization in Colonial India, 1857–1915," *Comparative Critical Studies* 16, nos. 2–3 (2019): 281–300. Edited sections of this article are reproduced here with permission from Edinburgh University Press through PLSclear.

11. Important interventions in the North Indian context, especially for Urdu, include those by Stark, *Empire of Books*, and Megan Robb, *Print and the Urdu Public: Muslims, Newspapers, and Urban Life in Colonial North India* (New York: Oxford University Press, 2020). Beyond this North Indian context, see also Anindita Ghosh, *Power in Print:*

Popular Publishing and the Politics of Language and Culture in a Colonial Society, 1778–1905 (New York: Oxford University Press, 2006), Rochelle Pinto, *Between Empires: Print and Politics in Goa* (Oxford: Oxford University Press, 2007), and Stuart H. Blackburn, *Print, Folklore, and Nationalism in South India* (Delhi: Permanent Black, 2006).

12. Robb, *Print and the Urdu Public*, 92.

13. Ahmed El Shamsy, *Rediscovering the Islamic Classics: How Editors and Print Culture Transformed an Intellectual Tradition* (Princeton, NJ: Princeton University Press, 2020), 127–28 and 155–56.

14. Rajeev Kinra, *Writing Self, Writing Empire: Chandar Bhan Brahman and the Cultural World of the Indo-Persian State Secretary* (Berkeley: University of California Press, 2015), 29; Sunil Sharma, *Mughal Arcadia: Persian Literature in an Indian Court* (Cambridge, MA: Harvard University Press, 2017), 59.

15. Yves Porter, *Painters, Paintings and Books: An Essay on Indo-Persian Technical Literature, 12–19th Centuries* (New York: Routledge, 2020), 154–55.

16. Irfan Habib, "Persian Book Writing and Book Use in the Pre-printing Age," *Proceedings of the Indian History Congress* 66 (2005–6): 529.

17. Bhavani Raman, *Document Raj: Writing and Scribes in Early Colonial South India* (Chicago: University of Chicago Press, 2012); Miles Ogborn, *Indian Ink: Script and Print in the Making of the English East India Company* (Chicago: University of Chicago Press, 2007), 237–45.

18. Raman, *Document Raj*, 54.

19. For comparative experiments in Perso-Arabic script print, see Hala Auji, *Printing Arab Modernity: Book Culture and the American Press in Nineteenth-Century Beirut* (Leiden: Brill, 2016), 69–70, and Orlin Sabev, *Waiting for Müteferrika: Glimpses of Ottoman Print Culture* (Boston: Academic Studies Press, 2018).

20. Andrew Amstutz, "The Lead Letters of *Nasta'līq:* Print Technologies and Technoscientific Modernity in the Hyderabad State," paper presented at the virtual annual meeting of the Society for the History of Technology, November 2021, 2–3.

21. Ian Proudfoot, "Mass Producing Houri's Moles, or Aesthetics and Choice of Technology in Early Muslim Book Printing," in *Islam: Essays on Scripture, Thought, and Society*, ed. Tony Street and Peter Riddel (Leiden: Brill, 1997), 163–64.

22. Green, *Bombay Islam*, 99–103.

23. Evidence of this export is reflected in a recent British Library Endangered Archives projects to digitize collections held in former Soviet Central Asia, which included an array of books printed in Lahore, Lucknow, and Kanpur; see "(Re)Collecting the Heritage of the Silk Road: Tajikistan's Pre-Russian Past in Documents (EAP910)," accessed February 2023, https://eap.bl.uk/project/EAP910, BL.

24. Several of the printed texts discussed later in this book identify the scribe and provide a colophon including a chronogram identifying the date of production. See, for instance, Ḥāfiẓ Anwār ʿAlī, *Tuḥfah-yi talmīʿ bah-kharbāyī* (Meerut: Hāshmī Press, 1872), 59, and Sarshār, *Taẕkirah al-aiwān*, 16.

25. *Reports on Publications Issued and Registered in the Several Provinces of India during the Year 1887* (Calcutta: Superintendent of Government Printing, 1878), 118.

26. W.C. Abel, *Gazetteer of the Rampur State, 1911* (Allahabad: Government Press, 1911), 52.

27. For the Deccani-South Indian rise of Persian, which differs from the North Indian context, see Emma J. Flatt, *The Courts of the Deccan Sultanates: Living Well in the Persian Cosmopolis* (Cambridge: Cambridge University Press, 2019), 167–209.

28. Muzaffar Alam, Françoise Delvoye, and Marc Gaborieau, *The Making of Indo-Persian Culture: Indian and French Studies* (Delhi: Manohar, 2000), 24–25.

29. Annemarie Schimmel, *Calligraphy and Islamic Culture* (New York: New York University Press, 1990), 92–94.

30. See, for instance, Ghulām Muḥammad Dehlvī, *Tazkirah-yi khūshnavīsān* (Calcutta: Asiatic Society of Bengal, 1910), 72–73 and 83.

31. K. Khān, *Daftar-i khaṯṯāṯ*, 5.

32. Muhammad ʿAbdul Raḥman, *Raīl khushnavīsī* (Kanpur: Niẓāmī Press, 1872), 5.

33. ʿAbdul Raḥman, *Raīl khushnavīsī*, 9.

34. ʿAbdul Raḥman, *Raīl khushnavīsī*, 15.

35. ʿAbdul Raḥman, *Raīl khushnavīsī*, 8.

36. ʿAbdul Raḥman, *Raīl khushnavīsī*, 9.

37. ʿAbdul Raḥman, *Raīl khushnavīsī*, 8.

38. Amīr Ḥasan Nūrānī, *Munshī Naval Kishūr aur unke khaṯṯāṯ aur khūshnavīsān* (Delhi: Taraqqi Urdu Board), 71–74.

39. G. Dehlvī, *Tazkirah-yi khūshnavīsān*. I am drawing primarily on the published edition of this work, referenced above, but have also consulted a manuscript copy, BL, Or. 471 (1824), the copying of which is ascribed to Dehlvī himself, and which differs slightly from the printed edition in its ordering of chapters.

40. G. Dehlvī, *Tazkirah-yi khūshnavīsān*, 71 and 82.

41. G. Dehlvī, *Tazkirah-yi khūshnavīsān*, 2.

42. ʿAbdul Raḥman, *Raīl khushnavīsī*, 2. Quranic translation from M. A. S. Abdel-Haleem, *The Qur'an: A New Translation* (Oxford: Oxford University Press, 2004), 36:41, 175.

43. ʿAbdul Raḥman, *Raīl khushnavīsī*, 7.

44. G. Dehlvī, *Tazkirah-yi khūshnavīsān*, 2.

45. ʿAbdul Raḥman, *Raīl khushnavīsī*, 3.

46. Stark, *Empire of Books*, 173.

47. Stark, *Empire of Books*, 66.

48. Stark, *Empire of Books*, 183.

49. Nūrānī, *Munshī Naval Kishūr*, 55–58.

50. Robb, *Print and the Urdu Public*, 59; Rahman, *Locale, Everyday Islam, and Modernity*, 14.

51. Home, Political B, no. 68–69 (1911), 23, NAI.

52. Home, Political B, no. 68–69 (1911), 23, NAI.

53. United Provinces, Labor Department (1901–9), 1903 forms III-IV and 1907 form V, IOR, BL.

54. *Royal Commission on Labour in India: Evidence*, vol. 3, pt. 1 (London: H. M. Stationery Office, 1931), 219.

55. *Royal Commission on Labour*, 219–21; and Stark, *Empire of Books*, 183.

56. *Royal Commission on Labour*, 241.

57. See, for example, Home, Political B, no. 68–69 (July 1911), 65, NAI; and "Breach of the Press Act," *The Tribune* (Lahore), December 9, 1909, 6.

58. *Royal Commission on Labour*, 241.

59. Sayyid Yusuf Ḥussain, *Risālah-yi jild sāzī*, ed. Iraj Afshar (Tehran: Miras Maktūb, 2011), 2–3.

60. S. Y. Ḥussain, *Risālah-yi jild sāzī*. See also Y. Porter, *Painters, Paintings, and Books*, 117–25.

61. William Hoey, *A Monograph on the Trades and Manufactures of Northern India* (Lucknow: American Methodist Mission Press, 1880), 122–23.

62. Legislative Reports, Libraries, no. 14 (1930), 2, NAI.

63. Stark, *Empire of Books*, 207.

64. *Report of the Committee Appointed to Consider the Grievances of Pieceworkers in the Government of India Presses* (Shimla: GM Press, 1922), 15–19.

65. Home, Jails, prog. no. 6–7 (August 1907), 3, NAI.

66. *The Punjab Record, or Reference Book for Civil Offices*, vol. 32 (Lahore: Civil and Military Gazette Press, 1897), 11.

67. Home, Report of the Prison Conference (1892), 40, IOR, BL.

68. E. A. Scott, *Annual Report on the Working of the Indian Factories Act (1911), for the Year 1924* (Lahore: Government Press, 1925), 8.

69. Home, Political B, no. 189 (April 1920), 2 and 5, NAI; Home, Political B, no. 281 (November 1920), 3, NAI.

70. Home, Political B, proceedings no. 3 (October 1912), 2, NAI.

71. Munshī Mahbūb ʿAlām, *Safarnāmah-yi eūrūp* (Lahore: Khādim al-Ṭaʿlīm Press, 1909), 2–4.

72. For examples, see Michael Laffan, *The Makings of Indonesian Islam: Orientalism and the Narration of a Sufi Past* (Princeton, NJ: Princeton University Press, 2011), 60–62, and Ilham Khuri-Makdisi, *The Eastern Mediterranean and the Making of Global Radicalism, 1860–1914* (Berkeley: University of California Press, 2010), 47–58.

73. Mahbūb ʿAlām, *Safarnāmah-yi eūrūp*, 734–47 and 923–29.

74. Mahbūb ʿAlām, *Safarnāmah-yi eūrūp*, 923–25.

75. Proudfoot, "Mass Producing Houri's Moles," 161–84; Kathryn A. Schwartz, "Did Ottoman Sultans Ban Print?," *Book History* 20 (2017): 1–39.

76. Schimmel, *Calligraphy and Islamic Culture*, 27–29.

77. Mahbūb ʿAlām, *Safarnāmah-yi eūrūp*, 926–27.

78. Mahbūb ʿAlām, *Safarnāmah-yi eūrūp*, 735 and 924.

79. Āftāb Aḥmad, *Al Inḍīā muḥmadān anglū-aurīnṭal ijūkīshanal kānfarans* (Aligarh, 1914), 7.

80. Āftāb Aḥmad, *Al Inḍīā muḥmadān*, 18.

81. Home, Political B, no. 189 (April 1920), 3, NAI; *Report of the Committee on Industrial Unrest in Bengal* (Calcutta: Secretariat Press, 1921), 2 and ii-iii.

82. Home, Political, no. 89 (March 1920), 7–9, NAI.

83. Home, Political, no. 89 (March 1920), 7, NAI.

84. W. E. J. Dobbs, *A Monograph on Iron and Steel Work in the United Provinces of Agra and Oudh* (Allahabad: United Provinces Government Press, 1907), 21–22.

85. Khurshīd, *Taẕkirah-yi hunarmandān-i Rāmpūr*, 44. See also H. A. Rose, A *Glossary of the Tribes and Castes of the Punjab and North-West Frontier Province, Based on the Census Report for the Punjab, 1883*, vol. 3 (Lahore: Civil and Military Gazette, 1914), 36–37; Haleem, *Qur'an*, 34:21, 273.

86. Home, Political, "Confidential Report of the Indian Owned Newspapers in the Punjab" (1937), 9, NAI.

87. Home, Political, no. 21 (April 1921), 2–5, NAI.

88. Kishwar Sultana, "Maulana Zafar Ali Khan, Majlis-e Ittihad-e Millat, and the All India Muslim League," *Journal of the Research Society of Pakistan* 53, no. 1 (2016): 115–23; Akhtarunnisā, *ʿAllāmah Iqbāl aur roznāmah zamīndār* (Lahore: Bazm-i Iqbāl, 2011).

89. Ahmad Azhar, "The Rowlatt Satyagraha and the Railway Strike of 1920," in *Working Lives and Worker Militancy: The Politics of Labour in Colonial India*, ed. Ravi Ahuja (Delhi: Tulika Books, 2013), 159.

90. *Zamīndār*, June 5, 2020, quoted in Azhar, "Rowlatt Satyagraha," 160.

91. "The Zemindar Confiscation," *The Leader* (Allahabad), January 24, 1913, 8.

92. Home, Political, no. 52/1 (1935), 291–93, NAI.

93. Home, Political, no. 7/5 (1936), xi and 6–8, NAI.

94. Home, Political, no. 7/5 (1936), 56–57, NAI.

95. Chakrabarty, *Rethinking Working-Class History*, 123.

96. Barbara Crossette, "Calling Strike, Urdu Scribes Sheathe Pens," *New York Times*, June 4, 1989, 6.

97. Muḥammad Hidayat Ḥusain, "Dar biyān ḥadis-i rasm-i ḥaṭṭ-i ʿarabī," in G. Dehlvī, *Taẕkirah-yi khūshnavīsān*, 11–12.

98. Ḥusain, "Dar biyān ḥadis-i rasm-i ḥaṭṭ-i ʿarabī," 14.

2. ELECTROPLATING AS ALCHEMY: LABOR AND TECHNOLOGY AMONG MUSLIM METALSMITHS

1. Anwār ʿAlī, *Tuḥfah-yi talmīʿ*, 59.

2. Anwār ʿAlī, *Tuḥfah-yi talmīʿ*, 1–2.

3. Anwār ʿAlī, *Tuḥfah-yi talmīʿ*, 3–8, 49–50, and 52–54.

4. In addition to the texts explored in this chapter, see others noted in D. Maclagan, *Monograph on the Gold and Silver Works of the Punjab* (Lahore: Government Press, 1890), 29.

5. Dobbs, *Monograph on Iron*, 21–22; Ganga Narian Bhargava, *Industrial Survey of the United Provinces* (Allahabad: Superintendent of the Government Press, 1923), v and 10.

6. A. P. Charles, *Monograph on Gold and Silverware Produced in the United Provinces* (Allahabad: Government Press, 1905), 22–23; Home, Education, no. 26–27 (1873), 5, NAI.

7. Baden Henry Baden-Powell, *Handbook of Manufactures and Arts of the Punjab* (Lahore: Punjab Printing, 1872), 172.

8. For comparative Hindi-language projects, see C. Singh, "Science in the Vernacular?," 66.

9. For instance, M. Dehlvī, *Iksīr-i malmʿah*.

10. Dhruv Raina and S. Irfan Habib, *Domesticating Modern Science: A Social History of Science and Culture in Colonial India* (Delhi: Tulika Books, 2004), 83–84.

11. H. Khan, *Artisans, Sufis, Shrines*, 57–59; Alain Lefebvre, *Kinship, Honour and Money in Rural Pakistan: Subsistence Economy and the Effects of International Migration* (Richmond, UK: Curzon, 1999), 149–51.

12. Iwan Rhys Morus, *Frankenstein's Children: Electricity, Exhibition, and Experiment in Early-Nineteenth-Century London* (Princeton, NJ: Princeton University Press, 1998), 167–68.

13. Morus, *Frankenstein's Children*, 170–71.

14. "Electro-Plating and Gilding," *Scientific American*, 21, no. 10 (September 1869), 153–54.

15. Morus, *Frankenstein's Children*, 171.

16. Private Secretary's Office: Correspondence, Mss. Eur F699/2/5/11, file no. 21 (October 1856), IOR, BL.

17. Baden-Powell, *Handbook of Manufactures*, 172.

18. Baden-Powell, *Handbook of Manufactures*, 269.

19. H. A. Rose, *Census of India, 1901*, vol. 17, *The Punjab, Its Feudatories, and the North-West Frontier Province* (Lahore: Government Press, 1902) 76; *The Fifth Indian Industrial Conference, Held at Lahore, 30 December 1909* (Amraoti: Indian Industrial Conference, 1910), 376–77.

20. Baden-Powell, *Handbook of Manufactures*, 172.

21. Hoey, *Monograph on the Trades*, 162.

22. Hoey, *Monograph on the Trades*, 162–63.

23. William Crooke, *The Tribes and Castes of the North-Western Provinces and Oudh* (Calcutta: Superintendent of Government Printing, 1896), 184; G. Worsley, *Monograph on Iron and Steel Industries in the Punjab* (Lahore: Civil and Military Gazette, 1908), 6.

24. Joel Lee, *Deceptive Majority: Dalits, Hinduism, and Underground Religion* (Cambridge: Cambridge University Press, 2021), 25.

25. J. Smith, *Gazetteer of the Sialkot District*, 53.

26. William Crooke, *The Popular Religion and Folklore of Northern India*, vol. 1 (London: Archibald Constable, 1889), 203, and Abdel-Haleem, *Qur'an*, 34:21, 273.

27. H. Khan, *Artisans, Sufis, Shrines*, 21.

28. Toqeer Ahmad Warraich, Samia Tahir, and Saira Ramzan, "Tomb of Musa Ahangar: An Analysis of Its Architecture and Decoration," *Pakistan Heritage* 11 (2019): 83–84.

29. H. Khan, *Artisans, Sufis, Shrines*, 57–59.

30. Lefebvre, *Kinship, Honour and Money*, 149.

31. Lefebvre, *Kinship, Honour and Money*, 149–51.

32. Anwār ʿAlī, *Tuḥfah-yi talmīʿ*, 2–3.

33. Ramẓān ʿAlī and Qamaruddīn Khān, *Risālah-yi fan-i talmīʿ* (Gujranwala: Gyan Press, 1870), cover page–2.

34. Ramẓān ʿAlī and Q. Khān, *Risālah-yi fan-i talmīʿ*, 7.

35. Pernau, *Ashraf into Middle Classes*, 262.

36. Pernau, *Ashraf into Middle Classes*, 259–61.

37. Ramẓān ʿAlī and Q. Khān, *Risālah-yi fan-i talmīʿ*, cover page.

38. Ramẓān ʿAlī and Q. Khān, *Risālah-yi fan-i talmīʿ*, 1.

39. Mukharji, *Doctoring Traditions:*, 13.

40. Anwār ʿAlī, *Tuḥfah-yi talmīʿ*, 2.

41. Anwār ʿAlī, *Tuḥfah-yi talmīʿ*, 49–50.

42. Anwār ʿAlī, *Tuḥfah-yi talmīʿ*, 59.

43. Jawārhalāl Shaidā, *Jāmaʿ-yi tarākīb-i talmīʿ* (Lucknow: Naval Kishore Press, 1880), 8.

44. Shaidā, *Jāmaʿ-yi tarākīb-i talmīʿ*, 8–15.

45. Dobbs, *Monograph on Iron*, 20–21; Atul Chandra Chatterjee, *Notes on the Industries of the United Provinces* (Allahabad: Government Press, 1908), 124–26.

46. Shaidā, *Jāmaʿ-yi tarākīb-i talmīʿ*, 5.

47. Shaidā, *Jāmaʿ-yi tarākīb-i talmīʿ*, cover page and 1.

48. Kinra, *Writing Self, Writing Empire*.

49. Shaidā, *Jāmaʿ-yi tarākīb-i talmīʿ*, 6.

50. Shaidā, *Jāmaʿ-yi tarākīb-i talmīʿ*, 5.

51. Nāgindās Dayaldās, *Gilīṭ nī Copḍī* (Surat: Victoria Press, 1899), 2. I am grateful to Vinit Vayas for this translation.

52. Dayaldās, *Gilīṭ nī Copḍī*, 3–5 and 16.

53. M. Dehlvī, *Iksīr-i malmʿah*, 4–6.

54. M. Dehlvī, *Iksīr-i malmʿah*, 9.

55. M. Dehlvī, *Iksīr-i malmʿah*, 34–36. On the manufacture of trunks, see Worsley, *Monograph on Iron*, 3–4.

56. M. Dehlvī, *Iksīr-i malmʿah*, 21–23.

57. M. Dehlvī, *Iksīr-i malmʿah*, 21–22.

58. M. Dehlvī, *Iksīr-i malmʿah*, 17–20.

59. M. Dehlvī, *Iksīr-i malmʿah*, cover page.

60. M. Dehlvī, *Iksīr-i malmʿah*, 2.

61. M. Dehlvī, *Iksīr-i malmʿah*, 1–2.

62. M. Dehlvī, *Iksīr-i malmʿah*, 2.

63. M. Dehlvī, *Iksīr-i malmʿah*, cover page and 2.

64. Anwār ʿAlī, *Tuḥfah-yi talmīʿ*, 59.

65. Bruce T. Moran, "Art and Artisanship in Early Modern Alchemy," *Getty Research Journal* no. 5 (2013): 1–4.

66. Moran, "Art and Artisanship," 1–2.

67. *Majmūʿat al-ṣanāiʿ*, copied 1780, Islamic 2363, 21–23 and 176–79, IOR, BL.

68. *Majmūʿat al-ṣanāiʿ* (Calcutta: Aftāb-i ʿalāmtāb Press, 1847), cover page.

69. "A Short Tract on Quicksilver," Islamic 2788, no. 4, 6–8, IOR, BL.

70. For example, Allāma Shiblī Nuʿmānī, "Mīkāniks aur musulmān," *Risāil-i Shiblī* (Amritsar: Roz Bāzār Press, 1898), 106–12.

71. Indian Muslim claims on the history of European science and alchemy were sometimes contested by Hindus, who sought to locate the history of European science in a Vedic or Tantic past. Pratik Chakrabarti, *Western Science in Modern India: Metropolitan Methods, Colonial Practices* (Delhi: Permanent Black, 2004), 222–39.

72. M. Dehlvī, *Iksīr-i malmʿah*, 14–16.

73. M. Dehlvī, *Iksīr-i malmʿah*, 17.

74. G.R. Dampier, *A Monograph on the Brass and Copper Wares of the North-Western Provinces and Oudh* (Allahabad: North-Western Provinces and Oudh Government Press, 1899), 18–19; H. Rose, *A Glossary of the Tribes and Castes of the Punjab and North-West Frontier Province, Based on the Census Report for the Punjab, 1883*, vol. 3 (Lahore: Civil and Military Gazette, 1914), 373–76.

75. Worsley, *Monograph on Iron*, 2. See also Dobbs, *Monograph on Iron*, 21–22.

76. Abigail McGowan, *Crafting the Nation in Colonial India* (New York: Palgrave Macmillan, 2009), 80.

77. On nonproletarianized forms of production, see Parthasarathi, "Indian Labor History," 129.

78. M. Dehlvī, *Iksīr-i malmʿah*, 2–3.

79. M. Dehlvī, *Iksīr-i malmʿah*, 3.

80. Khalid Nadvi, "Shifting Ties: Social Networks in the Surgical Instrument Cluster of Sialkot, Pakistan," *Development and Change* 30 (1999): 141–75; Louise Tickle, "Why Does So Much of the NHS's Surgical Equipment Start Life in the Sweatshops of Pakistan?," *The Independent*, January 19, 2015.

81. William Wilson Hunter, *The Imperial Gazetteer of India*, vol. 12 (London: Trubner, 1885), 445.

82. Ghulām Sarwar Lāhori, *Tārīkh-i makhzan-i punjāb* (Lahore: Naval Kishore Press, 1877), 258.

83. Worsley, *Monograph on Iron*, 6.

84. United Provinces, Home Department, "Indian Arms Act, United Provinces Rules" (1909), 4, IOR, BL.

85. N. Kumar, *Artisans of Banaras*, 12.

86. Baden-Powell, *Handbook of Manufactures*, 172.

87. J. Smith, *Gazetteer of the Sialkot District*, 34.

88. Thomas Holbein Hendley, "Indian Jewelry," *Journal of Indian Art* 12 (1909): 54–60.

89. *Punjab District Gazetteers*, vol. 23 A, *Sialkot District* (Lahore: Government Printing Press, 1921), 113. See also Ilyas Chattha, *Partition and Locality: Violence, Migration and Development in Gujranwala and Sialkot, 1947–1961* (Karachi: Oxford University Press, 2011), 47–54.

90. *Punjab District Gazetteers*, vol. 23 A, *Sialkot District*, 125.

91. Chattha, *Partition and Locality*, 59–61.

92. Nadvi, "Shifting Ties," 160.

93. *Punjab District Gazetteers*, vol. 23 A, *Sialkot District*, 125.

94. W. H. Abel, *Annual Report on the Working of the Indian Factories Act (1911) in the Punjab for 1920* (Lahore: Government Press, 1921).

95. Nadvi, "Shifting Ties," 159–61.

96. Nadvi, "Shifting Ties," 147; Lāhori, *Tārīkh-i makhzan-i punjāb*, 258.

97. On embodied skill and machines, see Simon Penny and Tom Fisher, "Twist-Hands and Shuttle-Kissing: Understanding Industrial Craft Skills via Embodied and Distributed Cognition," *Form Akademisk* 14, no. 2 (2021): 1–13.

98. Raina and Habib, *Domesticating Modern Science*, 83–84.

3. SEWING WITH IDRIS: ARTISAN KNOWLEDGE AND COMMUNITY HISTORY

1. Khwājah Muḥammad, *Risālah-yi Idrīsiyah*, cover page.

2. Idrīs as the first to sew clothes is referenced in hadith, and this narrative also circulated widely from the eighth century in Arabic-language religious genealogies of Enoch/Idris that also sometimes identified the prophet with Hermes. See Kevin Van Bladel, *The Arabic Hermes: From Pagan Sage to Prophet of Science* (Oxford: Oxford University Press, 2009), 164–70.

3. Khwājah Muḥammad, *Risālah-yi Idrīsiyah*, 2–3.

4. Khwājah Muḥammad, *Risālah-yi Idrīsiyah*, 3.

5. Khwājah Muḥammad, *Risālah-yi Idrīsiyah*, 3–4.

6. Khwājah Muḥammad, *Risālah-yi Idrīsiyah*, 5. The Quranic verses referenced are 22:74 and 36:60. See Abedl-Haleem, *Qur'an*, 214 and 283.

7. The Urdu word *muft* translates to "free," as in "free of cost," but does not contain the connotations of liberty contained in the English translation.

8. Shabīhunnisā, *Muft kā darzī* (Lucknow: Isnā ʿAsharī Press, 1907), 3.

9. Shabīhunnisā, *Muft kā darzī*, 2, 24, 28, 31, 57–59.

10. Shabīhunnisā, *Muft kā darzī*, 2 and 59.

11. I have developed similar arguments in my recent article on a trade history for butchers; see Amanda Lanzillo, "Butchers between Archives: Community History in Early Twentieth-Century Delhi," *South Asian History and Culture* 12, no. 4 (2021): 357–70.

12. C. J. Fuller, "Anthropologists and Viceroys: Colonial Knowledge and Policy Making in India, 1871–1911," *Modern Asian Studies* 50, no. 1 (2015): 217–58.

13. Bernard Cohn, *An Anthropologist among the Historians and Other Essays* (Delhi: Oxford University Press, 1987), 157–62.

14. Shahid Amin, *Conquest and Community: The Afterlife of Warrior Saint Ghazi Miyan* (Chicago: University of Chicago Press, 2013), 118.

15. Crooke, *Tribes and Castes*, 2:254–56.

16. Crooke, *Tribes and Castes*, 2:254.

17. Cohn, *Anthropologist among the Historians*, 154.

18. Rose, *Glossary of the Tribes*, 223.

19. Rose, *Glossary of the Tribes*, 223.

20. Defense B, no. 1735–1741 (April 1901), 1, NAI; H. H. Risley, *Census of India, 1901*, vol. 1, *Ethnographic Appendices* (Calcutta: Superintendent of Government Printing, 1903), 51.

21. K. Ansari, "Rethinking the Pasmanda Movement," 8.

22. Kate Imy, *Faithful Fighters: Identity and Power in the British Indian Army* (Stanford, CA: Stanford University Press, 2019), 54–55.

23. Defense B, no. 1735–1741 (April 1901), 1, NAI.

24. Pierre Bourdieu, *Distinction: A Social Critique of the Judgment of Taste* (London: Routledge, 1984), 374–75.

25. On *ashrāf* narratives of descent, see Pernau, *Ashraf into Middle Classes*, 57–65, and Soheb Niazi, "Sayyids and the Social Stratification of Muslims in Colonial India: Genealogy and Narration of the Past in Amroha," *Journal of the Royal Asiatic Society* 30, no. 3 (2020): 267–87.

26. Rose, *Glossary of the Tribes*, 399.

27. See also Niazi, "Sayyids and Social Stratification," 485.

28. Home, Political A, no. 63 (1921), 5, NAI.

29. Home, Political A, no. 63 (1921), 5, NAI.

30. Arnold, *Everyday Technology*, 36.

31. Nira Wickramasinghe, *Metallic Modern: Everyday Machines in Colonial Sri Lanka* (New York: Berghahn Books, 2014), 29 and 122–23.

32. Home, Education, no. 15 (1880), 4, NAI.

33. Home, Education (1905), 26–28, NAI.

34. Home, Education (1905), 26–28, NAI; Industries Department, sl. 29, no. 226 (1909), 2, Uttar Pradesh State Archives; Matthew Kempson, *Report on the Progress of Education in the North-Western Provinces, 1869–70* (Allahabad: Government Press, 1870), 62 and 56.

35. Home, Education, Proceedings (1879), 450, NAI.

36. H. Sharp, *Progress of Education in India, 1912–17* (Calcutta: Superintendent of Government Printing, 1918), 167–70; *Education Commission Report by the Central Provinces Provincial Committee* (Calcutta: Superintendent of Government Printing, 1884), 76–79.

37. Chatterjee, *Notes on the Industries*, 34.

38. Soni, "Learning to Labour: 'Native' Orphans in Colonial India, 1840s–1920s," *International Review of Social History* 65, no. 1 (2020): 16–17.

39. Methodist Episcopal Church (United States of America), *Annual Report of Missionary Work in Bareilly City and District: American Methodist Episcopal Church Mission* (Lucknow: American Methodist Missionary Press, 1870), 5–6.

40. Charu Gupta, "Intimate Desires: Dalit Women and Religious Conversions in Colonial India," *Journal of Asian Studies*, 73, no. 3 (2014): 669.

41. Soni, "Learning to Labour," 16–17; Arun Kumar, "The 'Untouchable School': American Missionaries, Hindu Social Reformers and the Educational Dreams of Labouring Dalits in Colonial North India," *South Asia* 42, no. 5 (2019): 823–44.

42. For elite Muslim women's writing on appropriate labor for Muslim girls, see Khoja-Moolji, *Forging the Ideal Educated Girl*, 46–48.

43. Miyān 'Abdul Ghafūr, *Risālah-yi dovum al-yatāmá* (Kanpur: Intiẓāmī Press, 1918), 18.

44. Miyān 'Abdul Ghafūr, *Risālah-yi dovum al-yatāmá*, 19.

45. Miyān 'Abdul Ghafūr, *Risālah-yi dovum al-yatāmá*, 9.

46. Khoja-Moolji, *Forging the Ideal Educated Girl*, 23–25.

47. Shabīhunnisā, *Muft kā darzī*, 58.

48. Shabīhunnisā, *Muft kā darzī*, 58.

49. Shabīhunnisā, *Muft kā darzī*, 59.

50. Shabīhunnisā, *Muft kā darzī*, 5.

51. Shabīhunnisā, *Muft kā darzī*, 3.

52. Shabīhunnisā, *Muft kā darzī*, 56.

53. Shabīhunnisā, *Muft kā darzī*, 32.

54. R. R. Bakhale, *First Report of the United Provinces Labour Enquiry Committee, 1946–48*, vol. 1 (Allahabad: Printing and Stationery, United Provinces, 1948), 111–13 and 406–10.

55. Hoey, *Monograph on Trade*, 100.

56. Home, Education A, no. 109 (June 1914), 5–7, NAI.

57. Anjuman Islāmiya Bareilly, *Fasānah-yi yatīm khānah, 1314 hijri* (Lucknow: Anvār Muḥammadī Press, 1895), 3–4 and 72.

58. Julia Stephens, *Governing Islam: Law, Empire, and Secularism in Modern South Asia* (Cambridge: Cambridge University Press, 2018), 105 and 124–25.

59. Stephens, *Governing Islam*, 106.

60. Tschacher, "Rational Miracles," 54–62.

61. Christopher A. Bayly, *The Local Roots of Indian Politics: Allahabad, 1880–1920* (Oxford: Clarendon Press, 1975), 80–82 and 254–56; Gooptu, *Politics of the Urban Poor*, 244–65.

62. Gooptu, *Politics of the Urban Poor*, 247–48.

63. Bayly, *Local Roots*, 81.

64. On debates about "ecstatic" mass worship usually associated with popular Sufi practice, see Tareen, "Normativity, Heresy," 544–45. Tareen maintains that even Muslim scholars who abjured these forms of worship allowed room for "enchantment" in their understanding of correct Islamic practice.

65. Gooptu, *Politics of the Urban Poor*, 247–49.

66. Bayly, *Local Roots*, 80–81 and 171–72.

67. Khwājah Muḥammad, *Risālah-yi Idrīsiyah*, 4.

68. Khwājah Muḥammad, *Risālah-yi Idrīsiyah*, 2.

69. Khwājah Muḥammad, *Risālah-yi Idrīsiyah*, 2.

70. On the assertion of Persianate literary pasts in Indian modernity and the claiming of Persianate pasts as Muslim pasts, see Alexander Jabbari, "The Making of Modernity in Persianate Literary History," *Comparative Studies of South Asia, Africa and the Middle East* 3, no. 3 (2016): 418–34.

71. Khwājah Muḥammad, *Risālah-yi Idrīsiyah*, 5.

72. Khwājah Muḥammad, *Risālah-yi Idrīsiyah*, 4.

73. Farhad Daftary, "Ahl al-Kisāʾ," in *Encyclopaedia of Islam, Three*, ed. Kate Fleet, Gudrun Krämer, Denis Matringe, John Nawas, and Devin J. Stewart, online ed. (Leiden: Brill, 2022), https://referenceworks.brillonline.com/browse/encyclopaedia-of-islam-3.

74. Gooptu, *Politics of the Urban Poor*, 245–52.

75. Hoey, *Monograph on Trade*, 28, 89, and 103.

76. Khwājah Muḥammad, *Risālah-yi Idrīsiyah*, 6.

77. Badri Narayan, *Women Heroes and Dalit Assertion in North India: Culture, Identity, and Politics* (Delhi: Sage Publications, 2006), 50–58 and 70–71.

78. Santosh Kumar Rai, "Forms of Organization and Practices of Mobilization: Julaha Weavers in Early Twentieth-Century North India," in *The Vernacularization of Labour politics*, ed. Sabyasachi Bhattacharya and Rana Behal (Delhi: Tulika, 2016), 84–85.

79. Muḥammad Badruddīn Sheikh Qureshī Naqshbandī, *Risālah-yi banī Quṣṣá* (Delhi: Mustanṣir Press, 1925), 7–8.

80. Qureshī Naqshbandī, *Risālah-yi banī Quṣṣá*, 11–13.

81. On elite Muslim genealogical projects in colonial North India, see Niazi, "Sayyids and Social Stratification," 267–87.

82. Qureshī Naqshbandī, *Risālah-yi banī Quṣṣa*, 43–44.

83. Latika Chaudhary and Manuj Garg, "Does History Matter? Colonial Education Investments in India," *Economic History Review* 68, no. 3 (2015): 938–41; N. Kumar, *Artisans of Banaras*, 44–61.

84. Khwājah Muḥammad, *Risālah-yi Idrīsiyah*, 7.

85. Qureshī Naqshbandī, *Risālah-yi banī Quṣṣá*, 1–2 and 18–25.

86. Khwājah Muḥammad, *Risālah-yi Idrīsiyah*, 1 and 8.

87. Khwājah Muḥammad, *Risālah-yi Idrīsiyah*, 1–2.

88. Amin, *Conquest and Community*, 159.

4. MIGRANT CARPENTERS, MIGRANT MUSLIMS: RELIGIOUS AND TECHNICAL KNOWLEDGE IN MOTION

1. *Lakṛī kā kām sikhānewālī kitāb* (Kanpur: Islāmī Press, n.d., 1910s), 1.

2. *Lakṛī kā kām*, 1–19.

3. *Lakṛī kā kām*, 13 and 16.

4. H.R. Nevill, *Cawnpore: A Gazetteer, Being Volume XIX of the District Gazetteers of the United Provinces of Agra and Oudh* (Allahabad: Government Press, 1909), 77 and 125.

5. Joshi, *Lost Worlds*, 28–33.

6. United Provinces, Labour Department, "Annual Report on the Working of the Indian Factories Act in the United Provinces" (1897), 8, IOR, BL; "UP Labour Supply: Unequal to the Demand," *Times of India*, July 6, 1906, 7.

7. "UP Labour Supply," *Times of India*, July 6, 1906, 7; Nevill, *Cawnpore*, 77–78.

8. *Lakṛī kā kām*, 21–23.

9. *Lakṛī kā kām*, cover page.

10. Sayyid Muḥammad ʻAbdullah, *Guldastah-yi tahzīb* (Kanpur: Islāmī Press, n.d., ca. 1910s), 9–11 and 14.

11. S.H. Fremantle, *Report on the Supply of Labour in the United Provinces and Bengal* (Lucknow: London Printing Press, 1906), 2–3; *Report on the First Regular Wages Survey of the Punjab Taken in December 1912* (Lahore: Government Press, 1913), table A.

12. M.F. O'Dwyer, *Monograph on Wood Manufactures in the Punjab, 1887–88* (Lahore: Civil and Military Gazette Press, 1889), 19–20; Jagdish Sahay Vatal, *Report on the Industrial Survey of the United Provinces: Cawnpore District* (Allahabad: Government Press, 1923).

13. Green, *Bombay Islam*, 180.

14. Green, *Bombay Islam*, 182–83.

15. *Gazetteer of the Lahore District, 1883–4* (Calcutta: Central Press, 1884), 98–99; *Punjab District Gazetteers*, vol. 30 B (Lahore: Superintendent of Government Printing, 1916); Nevill, *Cawnpore*, 125.

16. Baden-Powell, *Handbook of Manufactures*, 204–5.

17. United Provinces, Labour Department, "Annual Report on the Working of the Indian Factories Act in the United Provinces, 1901," Form III, 8, BL; Alma Latifi, *The Industrial Punjab: A Survey of Facts, Conditions, and Possibilities* (Calcutta: Longmans, Green, 1911), 210–22.

18. Douglas E. Haynes and Nikhil Rao, "Beyond the Colonial City: Re-evaluating the Urban History of India, ca. 1920–1970," *South Asia* 36, no. 3 (2013): 317–35.

19. Fremantle, *Report on the Supply*, 3.

20. Fremantle, *Report on the Supply*, 3.

21. Fremantle, *Report on the Supply*, 3–4.

22. Bayly, *Rulers, Townsmen and Bazaars*, 531.

23. Maulvi Hamid Raza Jaffery, *Report of the Industrial Survey of the United Provinces: Etah District* (Allahabad: Government Press, 1923), 18.

24. E.R. Neave, *Etah: A Gazetteer, Being Volume XII of the District Gazetteers of the United Provinces of Agra and Oudh* (Allahabad: Government Press, 1911), 187–90.

25. Jaffery, *Report of the Industrial Survey*, 18.

26. Joshi, *Lost Worlds*, 70–71.

27. Fremantle, *Report on the Supply*, 4.

28. Chatterjee, *Notes on the Industries*, 138.

29. H.R. Nevill, *Saharanpur: A Gazetteer* (Allahabad: Government Press, 1909), 84.

30. J.L. Maffey, *A Monograph on Wood Carving in the United Provinces of Agra and Oudh* (Allahabad: Government Press, 1903), 7.

31. Nevill, *Saharanpur*, 78. On woodworking in Saharanpur, see also Chambers, *Networks, Labour and Migration*, 22–48.

32. Chatterjee, *Notes on the Industries*, 143.

33. Chatterjee, *Notes on the Industries*, 143.

34. Denzil Ibbetson, *Report of the Census of the Punjab, Taken on 17th February 1881*, vol. 3 (Lahore: Central Gaol Press, 1883), table X.

35. Latifi, *Industrial Punjab*, 217.

36. O'Dwyer, *Monograph on Wood Manufacture*, 14.

37. Ibbetson, *Gazetteer of the Gujrat District, 1892–93* (Lahore: Punjab Government, 1893), 32–33.

38. T.W. Holderness, *Report on the Famine in the Punjab, 1896–97* (Lahore: Punjab Government Press, 1898), 6–7 and xviii.

39. O'Dwyer, *Monograph on Wood Manufactures*, 12–18.

40. Chatterjee, *Notes on the Industries*, 137–46; Latifi, *Industrial Punjab*, 209–28.

41. Chatterjee, *Notes on the Industries*, 138–44.

42. O'Dwyer, *Monograph on Wood Manufactures*, iii–xiii; Sardar Bahadur Ramsing, "Wood Carving in the Punjab," in *Fifth Indian Industrial Conference*, 341.

43. Taneja, *Jinnealogy*, 62.

44. See also Tschacher, "Rational Miracles," 56–59.

45. Rose, *Glossary of the Tribes*, 398.

46. Bahādur Singh, *Yādgar-i bahāduri*, 1652, f. 266b, IOR, BL.

47. ʿAlīmuddīn Nairang Hashmī, *Asrār al-ṣanʿat* (Agra: 'Azīzī Press, 1927), 175.

48. Pernau. *Ashraf into Middle Classes*, 250–52.

49. H. Khan. *Artisans, Sufis, Shrines*, 24.

50. Brannon Ingram, *Revival from Below: The Deoband Movement and Global Islam* (Oakland: University of California Press, 2018), 94.

51. Ingram, *Revival from Below*, 93–94.

52. Jaffery, *Report of the Industrial Survey*, 11–12 and 18.

53. H. R. Nevill, *Bijnor: A Gazetteer Being Volume XIV of the District Gazetteers of the United Provinces of Agra and Oudh* (Allahabad: Government Press, 1908), 76.

54. Ḥāfiẓ Muḥammad Raḥmatullah Naginvī, *Islāmi akhāṛā* (Bijnor: Raḥmānī Press, 1904), 2.

55. Naginvī, *Islāmi akhāṛā*, 33–36.

56. *Lakṛī kā kām*, 2.

57. Maffey, *Monograph on Wood Carving*, 21; Chatterjee, *Notes on the Industries*, 142–43.

58. Maffey, *Monograph on Wood Carving*, 21.

59. *Lakṛī kā kām*, 2–3.

60. Eugenia Lean, *Vernacular Industrialism in China: Local Innovation and Translated Technologies in the Making of a Cosmetics Empire, 1900–1940* (New York: Columbia University Press, 2020), 114.

61. Maffey, *Monograph on Wood Carving*, 21–22; Nevill, *Bijnor*, 76–77.

62. *Lakṛī kā kām*, 2–13.

63. *Lakṛī kā kām*, 4–7.

64. John Hurd II and Ian J. Kerr, *India's Railway History: A Research Handbook* (Leiden: Brill, 2012), 10.

65. *Report on the Administration of the Punjab and Its Dependencies, 1913–14* (Lahore: Government Press, 1915), viii and 48.

66. A. C. Badenoch, *Punjab Industries: 1911–1917* (Lahore: Government Printing, Punjab, 1917), 31.

67. John G. Beazley, *Annual Report on the Working of the Indian Factories Act, 1911, in the Punjab, for the Year 1922* (Lahore: Government Press, 1923), 5.

68. Beazley, *Annual Report*, 6.

69. Laura Bear, *Lines of the Nation: Indian Railway Workers, Bureaucracy, and the Intimate Historical Self* (New York: Columbia University Press, 2007), 80–83.

70. Ilyas Chattha, "Economic Change and Community Relations in Lahore before Partition," *Journal of Pakistan Studies* 19, no. 2 (2014): 194. See also *Punjab District Gazetteers*, vol. 30 B, xxiii.

71. Railways, Railway Construction, "Design of Marshalling Yard," file no. 45–51 (September 1909), 3, NAI.

72. Naveeda Khan, *Muslim Becoming: Aspiration and Skepticism in Pakistan* (Durham, NC: Duke University Press, 2012), 7.

73. Naveeda Khan, *Muslim Becoming*, 28–29.

74. Naveeda Khan, *Muslim Becoming*, 28–29.

75. Tirthankar Roy, "Apprenticeship and Industrialization in India, 1600–1930," in *Technology, Skills, and the Premodern Economy in the East and West*, ed. Maarten Prak and Jan Luiten van Zanden (Leiden: Brill, 2013), 77–80.

76. The extensive body of scholarship on Kipling and the Mayo School includes Nadhra Shahbaz Khan, "Industrial Art Education in Colonial Punjab: Kipling's Pedagogy and Hereditary Craftsmen," in *John Lockwood Kipling: Arts and Crafts in the Punjab and London*, ed. Julius Bryant and Susan Weber (New Haven, CT: Yale University Press, 2017), 469–88, Glover, *Making Lahore Modern*, 72–90, and Nadeem Omar Tarar, "From 'Primitive' Artisans to 'Modern' Craftsmen: Colonialism, Culture, and Art Education in the Late Nineteenth-Century Punjab," *South Asian Studies* 27, no. 2 (2011): 199–219.

77. Glover, *Making Lahore Modern*, 82.

78. J. Sime, *Report on Public Instruction in the Punjab and Its Dependencies for the Year 1900–1901* (Lahore: Civil and Military Gazette Press, 1901), 23–24.

79. Sime, *Report on Public Instruction* [1901], 24.

80. J. Sime, *Report on Public Instruction in the Punjab and Its Dependencies for the Year 1899–1900* (Lahore: Civil and Military Gazette Press, 1900), 68.

81. E.H. Atkinson and T.S. Dawson, *An Enquiry to Bring Technical Institutions into Closer Touch and More Practical Relations with the Employers of Labour in India* (Calcutta: Government Printing, 1912), 83–85.

82. Atkinson and Dawson, *Enquiry*, 84.

83. Higbie, *Labor's Mind*, 10.

84. Hashmī, *Asrār al-ṣan ʿat*, 175.

85. Hashmī, *Asrār al-ṣan ʿat*, 2 and 176.

86. Pernau, *Ashraf into Middle Classes*, 250–52.

87. Niazi, "Sayyids and Social Stratification," 471.

88. *Tuḥfah-yi Muḥammadiyah* (Kanpur: Ahmadi Press), November 1892, 3–6 and 14–16.

89. C. Ryan Perkins, "A New *Pablik*: Abdul Halim Sharar, Volunteerism, and the Anjuman-e Dar-us-Salam in Late Nineteenth-Century India," *Modern Asian Studies* 49, no. 4 (2015): 1049.

90. *Lakṛī kā kām*, cover page.

91. Muhammad Nazir Ahmad Khan, *Lecture at the Eighth Annual Meeting of the Anjuman-i Himayat-i Islam* (Lahore: Islamiya Press, 1893), 17.

92. Abdul Ghafūr, *Risālah-yi aval*, 6.

93. Anjuman-i ḥimāyat-i Islām (Lahore), *Māhvārī risālah*, October 1915, 32–33.

94. Robert Ivermee, *Secularism, Islam and Education in India, 1830–1910* (New York: Routledge, 2015), 104.

95. For comparisons with Christian and Hindu orphanages, see A. Kumar, "'Untouchable School,'" 823–44.

96. Council of Governor General of India Proceedings, "Resolutions Regarding Promotion of Industries: Appendix B" (1914), 309–10, IOR, BL.

97. Anjuman-i ḥimāyat-i Islām (Lahore), *Māhvārī risālah*, October 1915, 33.

98. *Report of the Industrial Reorganization Committee, United Provinces* (Allahabad: Government Printing, 1934), 54A.

99. Abdul Ghafūr, *Maryam Muslim yatīmkhāna*, 15.

100. Abdul Ghafūr, *Maryam Muslim yatīmkhāna*, 1–2.

101. Abdul Ghafūr, *Maryam Muslim yatīmkhāna*, 16.

102. Hashmī, *Asrār al-ṣan ʿat*, 2–3.

103. Joshi, *Lost Worlds*, 101–3.

104. Stephens, *Governing Islam*, 101–3.

105. AHI, *Māhvārī risālah*, October 1915, 10–15. See also Gail Minault, "Women's Magazines in Urdu as Sources for Muslim Social History," *Indian Journal of Gender Studies* 5, no. 2 (1998): 208; Khoja-Moolji, *Forging the Ideal Educated Girl*, 56–58.

106. AHI, *Māhvārī risālah*, October 1915, 12.

107. AHI, *Māhvārī risālah*, October 1915, 14.

108. Chambers, *Networks, Labour and Migration*, 192–94.

109. Gooptu, *Politics of the Urban Poor*, 270–71; Sana Haroon, *The Mosques of Colonial South Asia: A Social and Legal History of Muslim Worship* (London: I. B. Tauris, 2021), 80–83.

110. Joshi, *Lost Worlds*, 259–60.

111. Joshi, *Lost Worlds*, 260–61; Gooptu, *Politics of the Urban Poor*, 270–71; Haroon, *Mosques of Colonial South Asia*, 82.

112. Haroon, *Mosques of Colonial South Asia*, 83–85.

113. Home, Political A, "Riot at Cawnpore in Connection with the Demolition of a Mosque in Machli Bazaar" (October 1913), 128–34, NAI.

114. Azhar, "Rowlatt Satyagraha," 162.

115. Azhar, "Rowlatt Satyagraha," 160.

5. THE STEAM ENGINE AS A MUSLIM TECHNOLOGY: BOILERMAKING AND ARTISAN ISLAM

1. Ḥākimuddīn, *Kalīd-i ṣan ʿat* (Lahore: New Imperial Press, 1890), 2–4, 9–12, and 97–98. Note that his name is Ḥākimuddīn, rather than the more common Ḥakīmuddīn, both rendered Hakimuddin without diacritics.

2. References here are to the first edition, published in 1890, unless otherwise noted. I have also consulted two subsequent editions, Ḥākimuddīn, *Kalīd-i ṣan ʿat* (Lahore: Khādim al-Ṭa ʿlīm Press, 1899 and 1921).

3. Ḥākimuddīn, *Kalīd-i ṣan ʿat*, 3.

4. Ḥākimuddīn, *Kalīd-i ṣan ʿat*, 1.

5. Ḥākimuddīn, *Kalīd-i ṣan ʿat*, 1.

6. Ḥākimuddīn, *Kalīd-i ṣan ʿat*, 7.

7. Ḥākimuddīn, *Kalīd-i ṣan ʿat*, 79.

8. Ḥākimuddīn, *Kalīd-i ṣan ʿat*, 79–80.

9. Ḥākimuddīn, *Kalīd-i ṣan ʿat*, 2.

10. Ḥākimuddīn, *Kalīd-i ṣan ʿat*, 4.

11. Subramanian, *Caste of Merit*, 27.

12. George and Narayan, "Technophany and Its Publics," 4.

13. Ian J. Kerr, *Building the Railways of the Raj* (Delhi: Oxford University Press, 1995), 138–39 and 149–50.

14. *Report from the Select Committee on East India (Railways)* (London: House of Commons, 1858), 98–102 and 237–39. For a later, but comprehensive, account of the

positions open to Indians, see J.H. Whitley, *Memorandum by the Railway Board for the Royal Commission on Labour* (Lahore: North Western Railway Press, 1930), 9–11.

15. For a parallel in eighteenth- and nineteenth-century Britain, see Thompson, *Making of the English Working Class*, 245.

16. V.L. Raven, *Report of the State Railways Committee* (Calcutta: Government of India Publications Branch, 1926), 115–16 and 158.

17. Sudhanshu Shekhar and Vidyanand Jha, "Emergence of the Small-Scale Iron Foundry Industry in Howrah (India), 1833–1913," *Business History* 63, no. 2 (2011): 249–70; N. Benjamin, "Steam Boilers and Industrialization of Bombay, c. 1850–1900: A Techno-Economic History," *Proceedings of the Indian History Congress* 69 (2008): 612–24.

18. Kerr, *Building the Railways*, 17.

19. Home, Education A, no. 15–17 (1875), xxvi, NAI.

20. Aparajita Mukhopadhyay, *Imperial Technology and "Native" Agency: A Social History of Railways in Colonial India, 1850–1920* (London: Routledge, 2018), 11.

21. Mehdi Abilash, "Infrastructural Contingencies and Contingent Sovereignties on the Indo-Afghan Frontier," *Modern Asian Studies* 54, no. 6 (2020): 1949–86.

22. Raven, *Report of the State Railways Committee*, 39–41.

23. Ḥākimuddīn, *Kalīd-i ṣan ʿat*, 1–3.

24. F. Lehmann, "Railway Workshops, Technology Transfer, and Skilled Labour Recruitment in Colonial India," *Journal of Historical Research* 20, no. 1 (1977): 49–61. See also Kerr, *Building the Railways*, 2.

25. On racial hierarchies and colonial technical work, see Aparajith Ramnath, *The Birth of an Indian Profession: Engineers, Industry, and the State, 1900–1947* (Oxford: Oxford University Press, 2017), 11.

26. Waller Buchler, "Boiler Work in British India," *Boiler Maker and Plate Fabricator* 35, no. 11 (1935): 320–21.

27. *Report of the Boiler Laws Committee* (Delhi: Superintendent of Government Printing, 1921), 4–5.

28. *Report of the Boiler Laws Committee*, 6.

29. R.A. Sergeaunt, *Administration Report on the Railways in India for 1892–3, Part II* (Calcutta: Office of the Superintendent of Government Printing, 1893), xxiv. See also Raven, *Report of the State Railways Workshops Committee*, 119.

30. Sime, *Report on Public Instruction* [1901], 23–24.

31. *Report of the Boiler Laws Committee*, 29–30 and 149; Raven, *Report of the State Railways Committee*, 8–16.

32. "Locomotive Cadre, N.W. Railway," *Indian Engineering* 42 (October 26, 1907): 268.

33. Joshua Grace, *African Motors: Technology, Gender, and the History of Development* (Durham, NC: Duke University Press, 2021), 85–86.

34. Whitley, *Memorandum*, 71 and 116–19. For an early twentieth-century description of the sometimes mortal dangers of this work in a North American context, see Henry T. Harris, "The Occupation Hazard of Locomotive Firemen," *Publications of the American Statistical Association* 14, no. 107 (1914): 177–202.

35. Lajpat Jagga notes that "native" firemen often saw their efforts to move upward in railway hierarchies stymied by racial discrimination. See Lajpat Jagga, "Colonial Railwaymen and British Rule: A Probe into Railway Agitation in India, 1919–1922," *Studies in History* 3, nos. 1 and 2 (1981): 102–3.

36. Ḥākimuddīn, *Kalīd-i ṣan ʿat*, 97.

37. Ḥākimuddīn, *Kalīd-i ṣan'at*, 90–91.

38. Ḥākimuddīn, *Kalīd-i ṣan'at*, 98.

39. Ḥākimuddīn, *Kalīd-i ṣan'at*, 99.

40. Ramnath, *Birth of an Indian Profession*, 11.

41. David Arnold, *Science, Technology, and Medicine in Colonial India* (Cambridge: Cambridge University Press, 2000), 14.

42. Arun Kumar has analyzed the social hierarchies of labor education in colonial Lucknow. See A. Kumar, "Skilling and Its Histories," 250–69.

43. Ḥākimuddīn, *Kalīd-i ṣan'at*, 2 and 10.

44. "Locomotive Cadre, N.W. Railway," 268.

45. Ḥākimuddīn, *Kalīd-i ṣan'at*, cover page and 3.

46. Ḥākimuddīn, *Kalīd-i ṣan'at*, 4.

47. Ḥākimuddīn, *Kalīd-i ṣan'at*, 3.

48. Meléndez-Badillo, *Lettered Barriada*, 26–29.

49. Ḥākimuddīn, *Kalīd-i ṣan'at* (1899), cover page.

50. Ḥākimuddīn, *Kalīd-i ṣan'at* (1921), cover page.

51. Khurshīd, *Tazkirah-yi hunarmandān*, 5 and 14.

52. On icehouses, see David G. Dickason, "The Nineteenth-Century Indo-American Ice Trade: A Hyperborean Epic," *Modern Asian Studies* 25, no. 1 (1991): 53–89. On Rampur's icehouse, see Muḥammad Najmul Ghani Khān, *Akhbār al-ṣanādīd, jild-i dovum* (Lucknow: Naval Kishore Press, 1918), 27.

53. Khurshīd, *Tazkirah-yi hunarmandān*, 5.

54. *Firhrist-i mulāzmīn riyāsat-i Rāmpūr* (Rampur: Government Press, 1904), 84.

55. Khurshīd, *Tazkirah-yi hunarmandān*, 14–15.

56. For employment records from the Rampur Public Works Department in the 1910s and 1920s, see *Firhrist-i mulāzmīn riyāsat-i Rāmpūr* (Rampur: Government Press, 1916), 20–25, and *Sivil list riyāsat-i Rāmpūr* (Rampur: Government Press, 1926), 59–63.

57. Ḥākimuddīn, *Kalīd-i ṣan'at*, 2–3.

58. Ḥākimuddīn, *Kalīd-i ṣan'at*, 4 and 7.

59. Ḥākimuddīn, *Kalīd-i ṣan'at*, 8.

60. Paul Losensky, *Welcoming Fighānī: Imitation and Poetic Individuality in the Safavid-Mughal Ghazal* (Costa Mesa, CA: Mazda, 1998), 197.

61. Ḥākimuddīn, *Kalīd-i ṣan'at*, 8–9.

62. George and Narayan, "Technophany and Its Publics," 11.

63. On official preferences for Anglo-Indians in certain railway positions, see Bear, *Lines of the Nation*, 95.

64. Ḥākimuddīn, *Kalīd-i ṣan'at*, 6–7.

65. The name of the institution was changed to Thomason College of Civil Engineering in 1854. It later became the University of Roorkee in 1949, and today it is the Indian Institute of Technology Roorkee.

66. Ramnath, *Birth of an Indian Profession*, 124.

67. *Thomason Civil Engineering College Calendar, 1871* (Roorkee: Thomason Civil Engineering Press, 1871), 66.

68. Mushirul Hasan, "Maulawi Zaka Ullah: Sharif Culture and Colonial Rule," in *The Delhi College: Traditional Elites, the Colonial State, and Education before 1857*, ed. Margrit Pernau (Delhi: Oxford University Press, 2006), 263.

69. *Indian Arkitīkt* (Lahore) 11, no. 7 (July 1895): 112.

70. *Indian Arkitīkt* 11, no. 7 (July 185): 112.

71. Maffey, *Monograph on Wood Carving*, 31. See also Glover, *Making Lahore Modern*, 89.

72. See "Report of the Committee on Technical Education, Punjab," in *Papers Relating to Technical Education in India, 1886–1904* (Calcutta: Government Printing, 1906), 136–41.

73. Glover, *Making Lahore Modern*, 82.

74. Sayyid Taṣdiq Ḥussain, *Injinīring buk* (Shahjahanpur: Nāmī Press, 1913), 2–12.

75. S. T. Ḥussain, *Injinīring buk*, 59.

76. David Lelyveld, *Aligarh's First Generation: Muslim Solidarity in British India* (Princeton, NJ: Princeton University Press, 1978), 79.

77. *Aligarh Institute Gazette* 2, no. 9 (February 1902): 5; *Aligarh Institute Gazette* 2, no. 2 (January 1897): 9.

78. Lelyveld, *Aligarh's First Generation*, 79–80.

79. See Barbara Metcalf, *Islamic Revival in British India: Deoband, 1860–1900* (Princeton, NJ: Princeton University Press, 1982), 333–43.

80. Nuʿmānī, "Mīkāniks aur musulmān," 107.

81. Nuʿmānī, "Mīkāniks aur musulmān," 107.

82. Nuʿmānī, "Mīkāniks aur musulmān," 109.

83. Chakrabarti, *Western Science*, 6–8.

84. *Taraqqī* (Lahore: Mufīd-i ʿām Press), January 1906, 60–66.

85. *Taraqqī*, January 1906, 42–44.

86. Francis Robinson, "Islamic Reform and Modernities in South Asia," *Modern Asian Studies* 42, nos. 2–3 (2008): 262.

87. Robinson, "Islamic Reform," 262–67.

88. Ḥākimuddīn, *Kalīd-i ṣanʿat*, 4.

89. Aashish Velkar, "*Swadeshi* Capitalism in Colonial Bombay," *History Journal* 64, no. 4 (2021): 1071.

90. Ḥākimuddīn, *Kalīd-i ṣanʿat*, 3 and 5.

91. Ḥākimuddīn, *Kalīd-i ṣanʿat*, 5–9.

92. Home, Political B, "Report on Newspapers and Periodicals Published in the Punjab and North-West Fronter Provinces for the Year 1911" (October 1912), 60–61, NAI.

93. "Report on Newspapers" (1912), 60–61, NAI.

94. "Report on Newspapers" (1912), 60–61, NAI; Home, Political B, "Report on the Press in the Punjab and North West Frontier Provinces for the Year 1910" (October 1911), 61–62, NAI.

95. "Report on Newspapers" (1912), 61, NAI.

96. "Report on Newspapers" (1912), 60–61, NAI; "Report on Newspapers" (1911), 61–62, NAI.

97. Railway, Establishment, no. 278 (June 1908), 2–5, NAI.

98. Radhika Singha, *The Coolie's Great War: Indian Labor in a Global Conflict* (New York: Oxford University Press, 2020), 32–38.

99. Singha, *Coolie's Great War*, 313–16.

100. Home, Political B, "Statement Showing Details of Labour Strikes Which Have Recently Taken Place in India" (April 1920), 1–2, NAI.

101. Nitin Sinha, "The World of Workers' Politics: Some Issues of Railway Workers in Colonial India, 1918–1922," *Modern Asian Studies* 42, no. 5 (2008): 1032.

102. Ali Raza, *Revolutionary Pasts: Communist Internationalism in Colonial India* (Cambridge: Cambridge University Press, 2020), 53 and 105.

103. Subramanian, *Caste of Merit*, 2.

6. BUILDING THE MODERN MOSQUE: STONEMASONRY AS RELIGION AND LABOR

1. Sarshār, *Taẕkirah al-aiwān*, cover page.

2. Sarshār, *Taẕkirah al-aiwān*, 7–10.

3. Sarshār, *Taẕkirah al-aiwān*, cover page and 4.

4. Haroon, *Mosques of Colonial South Asia*, 17.

5. Sarshār, *Taẕkirah al-aiwān*, 4.

6. Sarshār, *Taẕkirah al-aiwān*, 5.

7. Sarshār, *Taẕkirah al-aiwān*, 5–6.

8. Sarshār, *Taẕkirah al-aiwān*, 8–11.

9. Sarshār, *Taẕkirah al-aiwān*, 11–12.

10. Sarshār, *Taẕkirah al-aiwān*, 11–14.

11. Kāli Prasāna Mukherjī and Sayyid ʿAlī, *Notes on Engineering in Urdu: Building Materials* (Patna: Bhignapaharee Lithographic Press, 1874), translated from John Millington, *Elements of Civil Engineering* (Philadelphia: J. Dobson, 1839); Lāla Bihārī Laʿal, *Taʿamīr-I ʾimārat* (Roorkee: Thomason Civil Engineering College Press, 1877), translated from "Section VI: Buildings," in *The Roorkee Treatise on Civil Engineering*, vol. 2, 2nd ed. (Roorkee: Thomason College of Civil Engineering, 1873).

12. I have developed portions of this argument in Amanda Lanzillo, "Between Industry and Islam: Stonework and Tomb-Construction in Colonial-Era India," *Modern Asian Studies* 55, no. 5 (2021): 1510–43, published by Cambridge University Press. Edited portions of this article have been reproduced with permission of Cambridge University Press. © The Author(s), 2021.

13. Anna Bigelow, introduction to *Islam through Objects*, ed. Anna Bigelow (London: Bloomsbury, 2022), 12.

14. Gyan Prakash, *Another Reason: Science and the Imagination of Modern India* (Princeton, NJ: Princeton University Press, 1999), 169–70.

15. Prakash, *Another Reason*, 170.

16. See, for instance, Sugata Ray, "Colonial Frames, 'Native' Claims: The Jaipur Economic and Industrial Museum," *Art Bulletin* 96, no. 2 (2014): 196–212, and Jessica Ratcliff, "Travancore's Magnetic Crusade: Geomagnetism and the Geography of Scientific Production in a Princely State," *British Journal for the History of Science* 49, no. 3 (2016): 325–52.

17. Gordon Sanderson, *Types of Modern Indian Buildings at Delhi, Agra, Allahabad, Lucknow, Ajmer, Bhopal, Bikaner, Gwalior, Jaipur, Jodhpur and Udaipur* (Allahabad: Government Press, 1913), 11.

18. Nasser Rabbat, "What Is Islamic Architecture Anyway?," *Journal of Art Historiography* 6 (2012): 1–2.

19. Rabbat, "What Is Islamic Architecture Anyway?," 2–4.

20. Rabbat, "What Is Islamic Architecture Anyway?," 3.

21. J. Begg, introduction to Sanderson, *Types of Modern Indian Buildings*, 2.

22. Hannah L. Archambault, "Becoming Mughal in the Nineteenth Century: The Case of the Bhopal Princely State," *South Asia* 36, no. 4 (2013): 479–95; Vandana Bawjea, "Messy Modernisms: Otto Koenigsberger's Early Work in Princely Mysore, 1939–41," *South Asian Studies* 13, no. 1 (2015): 1–26; Jyoti Pandey Sharma, "From Marrakesh to India: A Colonial Maharaja's Pursuit of Architectural Glory in Kapurthala," *International Journal of Islamic Architecture* 1, no. 2 (2012): 269–300.

23. Haroon, *Mosques of Colonial South Asia*, 7.

24. Barbara N. Ramusack, *Indian Princes and Their States* (New York: Cambridge University Press, 2003), 57–62; Robin Jeffrey, *People, Princes, and Paramount Power: Society and Politics in Indian Princely States* (Delhi: Oxford University Press, 1978), 11.

25. Malik Muhammad Din, *Bahawalpur State with Map, 1904* (repr., Lahore: Sang-e-Meel Publications, 2001), 53–55.

26. Muhammad Din, *Bahawalpur State with Map*, 68–74.

27. Muḥammad Najmul Ghani Khān, *Akhbār al-ṣanādīd, jild-i dovum*, 694–700.

28. *The Annual Administrative Report of the Bahawalpur State for the Year 1910–1911* (Lahore: News Press, 1911), 5–6 and 45–47; Muḥammad Najmul Ghanī Khān, *Akhbār al-ṣanādīd, jild-i aval* (Rampur: Raza Library Press, 1997), 173–78.

29. Mirza Mehdi Khan, *Imperial Gazetteer of India, Provincial Series: Hyderabad State* (Calcutta: Government Printing Press, 1909), 20.

30. Muhammad Din, *Bahawalpur State with Map*, 89–95; and W. C. Abel, *Gazetteer of the Rampur State*, 41–43.

31. Jeffrey, *People, Princes*, 7–9.

32. Government of the North-Western Provinces, Revenue Department, "Administrative Reports: Rampur State" (December 1872), 2–3, IOR, BL.

33. Government of the North-Western Provinces, Revenue Department, "Administrative Reports: Rampur State" (December 1877), 5, IOR, BL.

34. Sarshār, *Tazkirah al-aiwān*, 10–11.

35. Ramnath, *Birth of an Indian Profession*, 38–41.

36. Biharī La'l, *Ta'mīr-i 'imārat*, i.

37. Biharī La'l, *Ta'mīr-i 'imārat*, 40–42, 57–60, and 72–78.

38. *Instructions on Building: A Translation of "Instructions for Buildings for Meerut, Agra, Bareilly, and Malwa"* (Meerut: United Provinces Public Works, 1877).

39. *Inḍiyan Arkitīkt* 2, no. 1 (January 1890): cover page.

40. Minault, "Women's Magazines in Urdu," 201.

41. *Inḍiyan Arkitīkt* 11, no. 5 (July 1895): 110–12.

42. *Inḍiyan Arkitīkt* 10, no. 1 (January 1894): 5–6.

43. Sarshār, *Tazkirah al-aiwān*, 15.

44. Sarshār, *Tazkirah al-aiwān*, 16.

45. Sarshār, *Tazkirah al-aiwān*, 13.

46. Stella Kramrisch, *The Hindu Temple*, vol. 1 (Delhi: Motilal Banarsidass, 1976), 85.

47. Sarshār, *Tazkirah al-aiwān*, 12.

48. *Inḍiyan Arkitīkt* 10, no. 1 (January 1894): 5–6.

49. *Waqāya'-i Mahbūb Ganj* (Hyderabad: Shafīq Press, 1906), cover page and 1–3.

50. Datla, *Language of Secular Islam*, 12.

51. *Waqāya'-i Mahbūb Ganj*, 9.

52. *Waqāya'-i Mahbūb Ganj*, 9. See appendix for original.

53. Muḥammad Najmul Ghani Khān, *Akhbār al-ṣanādīd, jild-i dovum*, 139.

54. Muḥammad Najmul Ghani Khān, *Akhbār al-ṣanādīd, jild-i dovum*, 139–40.

55. Muḥammad Fayrūz Shāh, *Rāmpūr kī namāyish: Taqrīb bīnaẓīr* (Agra: Mufīd-i ʿAām Press, 1894), 12.

56. Razak Khan, "Local Histories: Space, Emotions and Identities in Vernacular Histories of Princely Rampur," *Journal of the Economic and Social History of the Orient* 58, no. 5 (2015): 693–731.

57. Thomas Metcalf, *An Imperial Vision: Indian Architecture and Britain's Raj* (Oxford: Oxford University Press, 1989), 9–13.

58. Khurshīd, *Taẕkirah-yi hunarmandān*, 27–28; 'Alī Asghār Āzād Chistī, *Waqāya' dilpaẕīr* (Lucknow: Nārāyān Press, 1906), 120.

59. Sanderson, *Types of Modern Indian Buildings*, 9–10.

60. *Annual Administrative Report of the Bahawalpur State*, 47–48.

61. *Annual Administrative Report of the Bahawalpur State*, 48.

62. Government of the United Provinces, Revenue Department, "Administrative Reports: Rampur State" (1936), 28–29, IOR, BL.

63. Muhammad Din, *Bahawalpur State with Map*, 331–34; R. M. Crofton, *Report on the Administration of the Bahawalpur State for the Year 1944–45* (Lahore: Civil and Military Gazette, 1946), 13–14.

64. Muhammad Najmul Ghani Khān, *Akhbār al-sanādīd, jild-i dovum*, 267.

65. *Gazit Riyāsat-i rāmpūr*, no. 9 (March 3, 1890): 2.

66. *Gazit Riyāsat-i rāmpūr*, no. 9 (March 3, 1890): 2–3.

67. Muhammad Din, *Bahawalpur State with Map*, 357. See also Shujaat Zamir Dar, *Sights in the Sands of Cholistan: Bahawalpur's History and Architecture* (Karachi: Oxford University Press, 2007), 62.

68. Julius Bryant, "Colonial Architecture in Lahore: J. L. Kipling and the 'Indo-Saracenic' Styles," *South Asian Studies* 36, no. 1 (2020): 63–64.

69. Muhammad Din, *Bahawalpur State with Map*, 62.

70. H. S. Crosthwaite, *A Monograph on Stone Carving in the United Provinces* (Allahabad: Government Press, 1906), 19.

71. Venetia Porter, "William De Morgan and the Islamic Tiles of Leighton House," *Journal of the Decorative Arts Society* 16 (1992): 76.

72. Āyīnah-yi angrīzī saudāgarī (London), July 1894, 21.

73. On Indo-Saracenic architecture and Mughal aesthetic revivalism, see T. Metcalf, *Imperial Vision*, 48–50.

74. Sarshār, *Taẕkirah al-aiwān*, 2–4 and 15–16.

75. Muhammad Din, *Bahawalpur State with Map*, 389–90.

76. Dodson, *Bureaucracy, Belonging*, 149.

77. Dodson, *Bureaucracy, Belonging*, 149–50.

78. Dar, *Sights in the Sands*, 66–67. On Jahaniyan Jahangasht, see also Manan Ahmed Asif, *A Book of Conquest: The* Chachnama *and Muslim Origins in South Asia* (Cambridge, MA: Harvard University Press, 2016), 23–24.

79. Crofton, *Report on the Administration*, 21–22.

80. Faisal Devji, "Apologetic Modernity," *Modern Intellectual History* 4, no. 1 (2007): 70–72.

CONCLUSION

1. Khurshīd, *Taẕkirah-yi hunarmandān-i Rāmpūr* (Rampur: Raza Library Press, 2001), 44.

2. David Gilmartin, "Partition, Pakistan, and South Asian History: In Search of a Narrative," *Journal of Asian Studies* 57, no. 4 (1998): 1090–91; Saloni Mathur, "Partition and the Visual Arts: Reflections on Method," *Third Text* 31, nos. 2–3 (2017): 205–12.

3. Chakrabarty, *Rethinking Working-Class History*, 198.

4. Gooptu, *Politics of the Urban Poor*, 244–321; Venkat Dhulipala, *Creating a New Medina: State Power, Islam, and the Quest for Pakistan in Late Colonial North India* (Cambridge: Cambridge University Press, 2015), 50–61.

5. Azhar, "Rowlatt Satyagraha," 159–62.

6. George and Narayan, "Technophany and Its Publics," 19–20.

7. Roy, "Out of Tradition," 965.

8. Sarah Ansari, "Thinking about . . . the Partition of British India in August 1947," *Teaching History* 167 (2017): 5.

9. Yasmin Khan, *The Great Partition: The Making of India and Pakistan* (New Haven, CT: Yale University Press, 2017), 128–42.

10. Chattha, *Partition and Locality*, 181–85.

11. Prakash, *Another Reason*, 230.

12. On debates surrounding Islam and science in South Asia and their relevance to early Pakistani nationalism, see S. Irfan Habib, *Jihad or Ijtihad: Religious Orthodoxy and Modern Science in Contemporary Islam* (Delhi: Harper Collins, 2012), 84–88, and Dhulipala, *Creating a New Medina*, 19 and 111–12.

13. Prakash, *Another Reason*, 231.

14. McGowan, "Mothers and Godmothers," 290.

15. McGowan, "Mothers and Godmothers," 291.

16. Ali Usman Qasmi and Megan Robb, *Muslims against the Muslim League: Critiques of the Idea of Pakistan* (Cambridge: Cambridge University Press, 2017), 4–12.

17. Mathur, "Partition and the Visual Arts," 208.

18. Ingram, *Revival from Below*, 17–26; Chambers, *Networks, Labour and Migration*, 145–47.

19. On forms of upper-caste Hindu technical authority in contemporary India, see Subramanian, *Caste of Merit*, 155–61.

20. Lithographed single page on wall of scissor-making workshop, photographed in Meerut, June 2022.

21. Lithographed single page on wall of scissor-making workshop; Abdel-Haleem, *Qur'an*, 29.

BIBLIOGRAPHY

PRIMARY SOURCES: PRINTED BOOKS

ʿAbdul Ghafūr, Miyan. *Risālah-yi aval al-yatāmá: Maryam Muslim yatīmkhāna*. Kanpur: Intiẕāmī Press, 1918.

———. *Risālah-yi dovum al-yatāmá*. Kanpur: Intiẕāmī Press, 1918.

ʿAbdul Raḥman, Muhammad. *Raīl khushnavīsī*. Kanpur: Niẓāmī Press, 1872.

ʿAbdullah, Sayyid Muḥammad. *Guldastah-yi tahzīb*. Kanpur: Islāmī Press, n.d., ca. 1910s.

Abel, W. C. *Gazetteer of the Rampur State, 1911*. Allahabad: Government Press, 1911.

Abel, W. H. *Annual Report on the Working of the Indian Factories Act (1911) in the Punjab for 1920*. Lahore: Government Press, 1921.

Aḥmad, Āftāb. *Al inḍīā muḥmadān anglū-aurīnṭal ijūkīshanal kānfarans*. Aligarh, 1914.

ʿAlām, Munshī Mahbūb. *Safarnāmah-yi eūrūp*. Lahore: Khādim al-Ṭaʿlīm Press, 1909.

Anjuman Islāmiya Bareilly. *Fasānah-yi yatīm khānah, 1314 hijri*. Lucknow: Anvār Muḥammadī Press, 1895.

The Annual Administrative Report of the Bahawalpur State for the Year 1910–1911. Lahore: News Press, 1911.

Anwār ʿAli, Ḥāfiẓ. *Tuḥfah-yi talmīʿ bah-kharbāyī*. Meerut: Hāshmī Press, 1872.

ʿAtīq, Muḥammad. *Shamʿ-yi hidāyat*. Moradabad: Maktabah Jannat al-Nisān, n.d.

Atkinson, E. H., and T. S. Dawson. *An Enquiry to Bring Technical Institutions into Closer Touch and More Practical Relations with the Employers of Labour in India*. Calcutta: Government Printing, 1912.

Badenoch, A. C. *Punjab Industries: 1911–1917*. Lahore: Government Printing, Punjab, 1917.

Baden-Powell, Baden Henry. *Handbook of Manufactures and Arts of the Punjab*. Lahore: Punjab Printing, 1872.

Bakhale, R. R. *First Report of the United Provinces Labour Enquiry Committee, 1946–48*. Vol. 1. Allahabad: Printing and Stationery, United Provinces, 1948.

Barabanki: A Gazetteer, Volume XLVIII of the District Gazetteers of the United Provinces of Agra and Oudh. Allahabad: Government Press of the United Provinces, 1901.

Beazley, John G. *Annual Report on the Working of the Indian Factories Act, 1911, in the Punjab, for the Year 1922*. Lahore: Government Press, 1923.

———. *Annual Report on the Working of the Indian Factories Act, 1911, in the Punjab, for the Year 1923*. Lahore: Government Press, 1924.

Bhargava, Ganga Narian. *Industrial Survey of the United Provinces*. Allahabad: Superintendent of the Government Press, 1923.

Biharī La'l, Lāla. *Ta'mīr-i 'imārat*. Roorkee: Thomason Civil Engineering College Press, 1877.

Charles, A. P. *Monograph on Gold and Silverware Produced in the United Provinces*. Allahabad: Government Press, 1905.

Chatterjee, Atul Chandra. *Notes on the Industries of the United Provinces*. Allahabad: Government Press, 1908.

Chistī, 'Alī Asghār Āzād. *Waqāya' dilpazīr*. Lucknow: Nārāyān Press, 1906.

Crofton, R. M. *Report on the Administration of the Bahawalpur State for the Year 1944–45*. Lahore: Civil and Military Gazette, 1946.

Crooke, William. *The Popular Religion and Folklore of Northern India*. Vol. 1. London: Archibald Constable, 1889.

———. *The Tribes and Castes of the North-Western Provinces and Oudh*. Calcutta: Superintendent of Government Printing, 1896

Crosthwaite, H. S. *A Monograph on Stone Carving in the United Provinces*. Allahabad: Government Press, 1906.

Dampier, G. R. *A Monograph on the Brass and Copper Wares of the North-Western Provinces and Oudh*. Allahabad: North-Western Provinces and Oudh Government Press, 1899.

Dayaldās, Nāgindās. *Gilīṭ nī Copḍī*. Surat: Victoria Press, 1899.

Dehlvī, Ghulām Muḥammad. *Tazkirah-yi khūshnavīsān*. Calcutta: Asiatic Society of Bengal, 1910.

Dehlvī, Mirzā Ibrāhīm. *Iksīr-i malm'ah*. Delhi: Mayūr Press, 1893.

Dobbs, W. E. J. *A Monograph on Iron and Steel Work in the United Provinces of Agra and Oudh*. Allahabad: United Provinces Government Press, 1907.

Education Commission Report by the Central Provinces Provincial Committee. Calcutta: Superintendent of Government Printing, 1884.

The Fifth Indian Industrial Conference, Held at Lahore, 30 December 1909. Amraoti: Indian Industrial Conference, 1910.

Firhrist-i mulāzmīn riyāsat-i Rāmpūr. Rampur: Government Press, 1904.

Firhrist-i mulāzmīn riyāsat-i Rāmpūr. Rampur: Government Press, 1916.

Fremantle, S. H. *Report on the Supply of Labour in the United Provinces and Bengal*. Lucknow: London Printing Press, 1906.

Gazetteer of the Lahore District, 1883–4. Calcutta: Central Press, 1884.

Ḥākimuddīn. *Kalīd-i ṣan'at*. Lahore: New Imperial Press, 1890.

———. *Kalīd-i ṣan'at*. Lahore: Khādim al-Ṭa'līm Press, 1899 and 1921.

Hashmī, 'Alīmuddīn Nairang. *Asrār al-ṣan'*at. Agra: 'Azīzī Press, 1927.

Hoey, William. *A Monograph on the Trades and Manufactures of Northern India*. Lucknow: American Methodist Mission Press, 1880.

Holderness, T. W. *Report on the Famine in the Punjab, 1896–97*. Lahore: Punjab Government Press, 1898.

Hunter, William Wilson. *The Imperial Gazetteer of India*. Vol. 12. London: Trubner, 1885.

Ḥussain, Sayyid Taṣdiq. *Injinīring buk*. Shahjahanpur: Nāmī Press, 1913.

Ḥussain, Sayyid Yusuf. *Risālah-yi jild sāzī*. Edited by Iraj Afshar. Tehran: Miras Maktūb, 2011.

Ibbetson, Denzil. *Gazetteer of the Gujrat District, 1892–93*. Lahore: Punjab Government, 1893.

———. *Report of the Census of the Punjab, Taken on 17th February 1881*. Vol. 3. Lahore: Central Gaol Press, 1883.

Instructions on Building: A Translation of "Instructions for Buildings for Meerut, Agra, Bareilly, and Malwa." Meerut: United Provinces Public Works, 1877.

Jaffery, Maulvi Hamid Raza. *Report of the Industrial Survey of the United Provinces: Etah District*. Allahabad: Government Press, 1923.

Kempson, Matthew. *Report on the Progress of Education in the North-Western Provinces, 1869–70*. Allahabad: Government Press, 1870.

Khan, Mirza Mehdi. *Imperial Gazetteer of India, Provincial Series: Hyderabad State*. Calcutta: Government Printing Press, 1909.

Khān, Muḥammad Najmul Ghani. *Akhbār al-ṣanādīd, jild-i aval*. Rampur: Raza Library Press, 1997.

———. *Akhbār al-ṣanādīd, jild-i dovum*. Lucknow: Naval Kishore Press, 1918.

Khan, Muhammad Nazir Ahmad. *Lecture at the Eighth Annual Meeting of the Anjuman-i Himayat-i Islam*. Lahore: Islamiya Press, 1893.

Khwājah Muḥammad, Sheikh. *Risālah-yi Idrīsiyah*. Allahabad: Anwār Aḥmadi Press, 1907.

Lāhori, Ghulām Sarwar. *Tārīkh-i makhzan-i punjāb*. Lahore: Naval Kishore Press, 1877.

Lakṛī kā kām sikhānewālī kitab. Kanpur: Islāmī Press, n.d., ca. 1910.

Latifi, Alma. *The Industrial Punjab: A Survey of Facts, Conditions, and Possibilities*. Calcutta: Longmans, Green, 1911.

Maclagan, E. D. *Monograph on the Gold and Silver Works of the Punjab*. Lahore: Government Press, 1890.

Maffey, J. L. *A Monograph on Wood Carving in the United Provinces of Agra and Oudh*. Allahabad: Government Press, 1903.

Majmuʿat al-sanaiʿ. Calcutta: Aftāb-i ʿalāmtāb Press, 1847.

Methodist Episcopal Church (United States of America). *Annual Report of Missionary Work in Bareilly City and District for 1869: American Methodist Episcopal Church Mission*. Lucknow: American Methodist Missionary Press, 1870.

Millington, John. *Elements of Civil Engineering*. Philadelphia: J. Dobson, 1839.

Muhammad Din, Malik. *Bahawalpur State with Map, 1904*. Reprint, Lahore: Sang-e-Meel Publications, 2001.

Mukherjī, Kāli Prasāna, and Sayyid ʿAlī. *Notes on Engineering in Urdu: Building Materials*. Patna: Bhignapaharee Lithographic Press, 1874.

Mukhtar, Ahmad. *Factory Labour in the Punjab*. Madras: Huxley Press, 1929.

Naginvī, Ḥāfiẓ Muḥammad Raḥmatullah. *Islāmi akhāṛā*. Bijnor: Raḥmānī Press, 1904.

Neave, E. R. *Etah: A Gazetteer, Being Volume XII of the District Gazetteers of the United Provinces of Agra and Oudh*. Allahabad: Government Press, 1911.

Nevill, H. R. *Bijnor: A Gazetteer*. Allahabad: Government Press, 1908.

———. *Cawnpore: A Gazetteer, Being Volume XIX of the District Gazetteers of the United Provinces of Agra and Oudh*. Allahabad: Government Press, 1909.

———. *Saharanpur: A Gazetteer*. Allahabad: Government Press, 1909.

Nuʿmānī, Allāma Shiblī. "Mīkāniks aur musulmān." In *Risāil-i Shiblī*, edited by Allāma Shiblī Nuʿmānī, 106–12. Amritsar: Roz Bāzār Press, 1898.

O'Dwyer, M. F. *Monograph on Wood Manufactures in the Punjab, 1887–88*. Lahore: Civil and Military Gazette Press, 1889.

Papers Relating to Technical Education in India, 1886–1904. Calcutta: Government Printing, 1906.

Punjab District Gazetteers. Vol. 23 A, *Sialkot District*. Lahore: Government Printing Press, 1921.

Punjab District Gazetteers. Vol. 30 B. Lahore: Superintendent of Government Printing, 1916.

The Punjab Record, or Reference Book for Civil Offices. Vol. 32. Lahore: Civil and Military Gazette Press, 1897.

Qureshī Naqshbandī, Muḥammad Badruddīn Sheikh. *Risālah-yi banī Quṣṣá*. Delhi: Mustanṣir Press, 1925.

Ramẓān ʿAlī and Qamaruddīn Khān. *Risālah-yi fan-I talmīʿ*. Gujranwala: Gyan Press, 1870.

Raven, V. L. *Report of the State Railways Committee*. Calcutta: Government of India Publications Branch, 1926.

Report from the Select Committee on East India (Railways). London: House of Commons, 1858.

Report of the Boiler Laws Committee. Delhi: Superintendent of Government Printing, 1921.

Report of the Committee Appointed to Consider the Grievances of Pieceworkers in the Government of India Presses. Shimla: GM Press, 1922.

Report of the Committee on Industrial Unrest in Bengal. Calcutta: Secretariat Press, 1921.

Report of the Industrial Reorganization Committee, United Provinces. Allahabad: Government Printing, 1934.

Report on the Administration of the Punjab and Its Dependencies, 1913–14. Lahore: Government Press, 1915.

Report on the First Regular Wages Survey of the Punjab Taken in December 1912. Lahore: Government Press, 1913.

Reports on Publications Issued and Registered in the Several Provinces of India during the Year 1887. Calcutta: Superintendent of Government Printing, 1878.

Risley, H. H. *Census of India, 1901*. Vol. 1, *Ethnographic Appendices*. Calcutta: Superintendent of Government Printing, 1903.

Riẓvī, Muḥammad Rafīʿ. *Makhzan al-fawāyid*. Moradabad: Maṭbaʿ al-ʿulūm, 1909.

The Roorkee Treatise on Civil Engineering. Vol. 2. 2nd ed. Roorkee: Thomason College of Civil Engineering, 1873.

Rose, H. A. *Census of India, 1901*. Vol. 17, *The Punjab, Its Feudatories, and the North-West Frontier Province*. Lahore: Government Press, 1902.

———. *A Glossary of the Tribes and Castes of the Punjab and North-West Frontier Province, 1883*. Vols. 2–3. Lahore: Civil and Military Gazette Press, 1914.

Royal Commission on Labour in India: Evidence. Vol. 3, Pt. 1. London: H.M. Stationery Office, 1931.

Sanderson, Gordon. *Types of Modern Indian Buildings at Delhi, Agra, Allahabad, Lucknow, Ajmer, Bhopal, Bikaner, Gwalior, Jaipur, Jodhpur and Udaipur*. Allahabad: Government Press, 1913.

Sarshār, Riyasat ʿAlī. *Taẕkirah al-aiwān*. Fatehgarh: Dilkushā Press, 1875.

Scott, E. A. *Annual Report on the Working of the Indian Factories Act (1911), for the Year 1924*. Lahore: Government Press, 1925.

Sergeaunt, R. A. *Administration Report on the Railways in India for 1892–3, Part II*. Calcutta: Office of the Superintendent of Government Printing, 1893.

Shabīhunnisā. *Muft kā darzī*. Lucknow: Isnā ʿAsharī Press, 1907.

Shāh, Muḥammad Fayrūz. *Rāmpūr kī namāyish: Taqrīb bīnaẓīr*. Agra: Mufīd-I ʿAām Press, 1894.

Shaidā, Jawārhalāl. *Jāmaʿ-yi tarākīb-I talmīʿ*. Lucknow: Naval Kishore Press, 1880.

Sharp, H. *Progress of Education in India, 1912–17*. Calcutta: Superintendent of Government Printing, 1918.

Sime, J. *Report on Public Instruction in the Punjab and Its Dependencies for the Year 1899–1900*. Lahore: Civil and Military Gazette Press, 1900.

———. *Report on Public Instruction in the Punjab and Its Dependencies for the Year 1900–1901*. Lahore: Civil and Military Gazette Press, 1901.

Sivil list riyāsat-I Rāmpūr. Rampur: Government Press, 1926.

Smith, J. R. D. *Gazetteer of the Sialkot District, 1894–95*. Lahore: Civil and Military Gazetteer Press, 1895.

Thomason Civil Engineering College Calendar, 1871. Roorkee: Thomason Civil Engineering Press, 1871.

Vatal, Jagdish Sahay. *Report on the Industrial Survey of the United Provinces: Cawnpore District*. Allahabad: Government Press, 1923.

Waqāyaʿ-i Mahbūb Ganj. Hyderabad: Shafiq Press, 1906.

Whitley, J. H. *Memorandum by the Railway Board for the Royal Commission on Labour*. Lahore: North Western Railway Press, 1930.

Worsley, G. *Monograph on Iron and Steel Industries in the Punjab*. Lahore: Civil and Military Gazette, 1908.

PRIMARY SOURCES: MANUSCRIPTS

Dehlvī, Ghulām Muhammad. *Tazkirah-yi khūshnavīsān*. 1824. Or. 471, British Library, UK.

Khān, Karīmullah. *Daftar-i khaṭṭāṭ*. 1885. Pers., no. 2454, Raza Library, Rampur, Uttar Pradesh.

Majmuʿat al-sanaiʿ. 1780, Islamic 2363, India Office Records, British Library, UK.

"A Short Tract on Quicksilver." Islamic 2788, no. 4, India Office Records, British Library, UK.

Singh, Bahādur. *Yādgar-i bahāduri*. Or. 1652, British Library, UK.

PRIMARY SOURCES: RECORDS

National Archives of India (NAI)

Government of India. Department of Defense.

Government of India. Home Department: Education Office.

Government of India. Home Department: Jails Office.
Government of India. Home Department: Political Office.
Government of India. Legislative Reports: Libraries Office.
Government of India. Railways Department.

British Library (BL), India Office Records (IOR)

Government of India. Council of Governor General of India Proceedings.
Government of India. Home Department: Reports of the Prison Conference.
Government of India. Private Secretary's Office Papers: Correspondence.
Government of the North-Western Provinces: Revenue Department.
Government of the United Provinces. Home Department.
Government of the United Provinces. Labor Department Proceedings.
Government of the United Provinces. Revenue Department.

Uttar Pradesh State Archives

Government of the United Provinces. Industries Department.

PRIMARY SOURCES: PERIODICALS

Aligarh Institute Gazette (Aligarh)
Anjuman-i ḥimāyat-i Islām, *Māhvārī risālah* (Lahore)
Āyīnah-yi angrīzī saudāgarī (London)
Boiler Maker and Plate Fabricator (New York)
Gazit Riyāsat-i rāmpūr (Rampur)
The Independent (London)
Indian Engineering (Calcutta)
Inḍiyan Arkitīkt (Lahore)
Journal of Indian Art (London)
New York Times (New York)
Publications of the American Statistical Association (New York)
Scientific American (New York)
Taraqqī (Lahore)
Times of India (Bombay)
The Tribune (Lahore)
Tuḥfah-yi Muḥammadiyah (Kanpur)

SECONDARY LITERATURE

Abdel-Haleem, M. A. S., trans. *The Qur'an: A New Translation*. Oxford: Oxford University Press, 2004.
Abilash, Mehdi. "Infrastructural Contingencies and Contingent Sovereignties on the Indo–Afghan Frontier." *Modern Asian Studies* 54, no. 6 (2020): 1949–86.
Ahmad, Imtiaz. "The Ashraf and Ajlaf Categories in Indo-Muslim Society." *Economic and Political Weekly* 2, no. 19 (May 1967): 889–91.
Ahmed Asif, Manan. *A Book of Conquest: The* Chachnama *and Muslim Origins in South Asia*. Cambridge, MA: Harvard University Press, 2016.

Akhtarunnisā. ʿAllāmah Iqbāl aur roznāmah zamindar. Lahore: Bazm-i Iqbāl, 2011.
Alam, Muzaffar, Françoise Delvoye, and Marc Gaborieau. *The Making of Indo-Persian Culture: Indian and French Studies*. Delhi: Manohar, 2000.
Amin, Shahid. *Conquest and Community: The Afterlife of Warrior Saint Ghazi Miyan*. Chicago: University of Chicago Press, 2013.
Amir, Safwan. "Contempt and Labour: An Exploration through Muslim Barbers of South Asia." *Religions* 10, no. 11 (2019): 1–14.
Amstutz, Andrew. "The Lead Letters of *Nasta'līq*: Print Technologies and Technoscientific Modernity in the Hyderabad State." Paper presented at the virtual annual meeting of the Society for the History of Technology, November 2021.
Ansari, Khalid Anis. "Rethinking the Pasmanda Movement." *Economic and Political Weekly* 44, no. 13 (2009): 8–10.
Ansari, Sarah. "Thinking about . . . the Partition of British India in August 1947." *Teaching History* 167 (2017): 4–8.
Archambault, Hannah L. "Becoming Mughal in the Nineteenth Century: The Case of the Bhopal Princely State." *South Asia* 36, no. 4 (2013): 479–95.
Arnold, David. *Everyday Technology: Machines and the Making of India's Modernity*. Chicago: University of Chicago Press, 2013.
———. *Science, Technology, and Medicine in Colonial India*. Cambridge: Cambridge University Press, 2000.
Auji, Hala. *Printing Arab Modernity: Book Culture and the American Press in Nineteenth-Century Beirut*. Leiden: Brill, 2016.
Azhar, Ahmad. "The Rowlatt Satyagraha and the Railway Strike of 1920." In *Working Lives and Worker Militancy: The Politics of Labour in Colonial India*, edited by Ravi Ahuja, 134–73. Delhi: Tulika Books, 2013.
Bashir, Shahzad. "Prospects for a New Idiom for Islamic History." In *What Is Islamic Studies: European and North American Approaches to a Contested Field*, edited by Leif Stenberg and Philip Wood, 176–89. Edinburgh: Edinburgh University Press, 2022.
Bawjea, Vandana. "Messy Modernisms: Otto Koenigsberger's Early Work in Princely Mysore, 1939–41." *South Asian Studies* 13, no. 1 (2015): 1–26.
Bayly, Christopher A. *The Local Roots of Indian Politics: Allahabad, 1880–1920*. Oxford: Clarendon Press, 1975.
———. *Rulers, Townsmen and Bazaars: North Indian Society in the Age of British Expansion, 1770–1870*. 3rd ed. Delhi: Oxford University Press, 2012.
Bear, Laura. *Lines of the Nation: Indian Railway Workers, Bureaucracy, and the Intimate Historical Self*. New York: Columbia University Press, 2007.
Benjamin, N. "Steam Boilers and Industrialization of Bombay, c. 1850–1900: A Techno-Economic History." *Proceedings of the Indian History Congress* 69 (2008): 612–24.
Bigelow, Anna, ed. *Islam through Objects*. London: Bloomsbury, 2022.
———. *Sharing the Sacred: Practicing Pluralism in Muslim North India*. Oxford: Oxford University Press, 2010.
Blackburn, Stuart H. *Print, Folklore, and Nationalism in South India*. Delhi: Permanent Black, 2006.
Bourdieu, Pierre. *Distinction: A Social Critique of the Judgment of Taste*. London: Routledge, 1984.

Brouwer, Jan. *The Makers of the World: Caste, Craft, and Mind of South Indian Artisans*. Delhi: Oxford University Press, 1995.

Bryant, Julius. "Colonial Architecture in Lahore: J. L. Kipling and the 'Indo-Saracenic' Styles." *South Asian Studies* 36, no. 1 (2020): 61–71.

Chakrabarti, Pratik. *Western Science in Modern India: Metropolitan Methods, Colonial Practices*. Delhi: Permanent Black, 2004.

Chakrabarty, Dipesh. *Rethinking Working-Class History: Bengal, 1890–1940*. Princeton, NJ: Princeton University Press, 1989.

Chambers, Thomas. *Networks, Labour and Migration among Indian Muslim Artisans*. London: UCL Press, 2020.

Chandavarkar, Rajnarayan. "Industrialization in India before 1947: Conventional Approaches and Alternative Perspectives." In *Imperial Power and Popular Politics*, 30–73. Cambridge: Cambridge University Press, 1998.

Chandra, Ram. *History of the Naujawan Bharat Sabha*. Chandigarh: Unistar Books, 1997.

Chattha, Ilyas. "Economic Change and Community Relations in Lahore before Partition." *Journal of Pakistan Studies* 19, no. 2 (2014): 193–214.

———. *Partition and Locality: Violence, Migration and Development in Gujranwala and Sialkot, 1947–1961*. Karachi: Oxford University Press, 2011.

Chaudhary, Latika, and Manuj Garg. "Does History Matter? Colonial Education Investments in India." *Economic History Review* 68, no. 3 (2015): 937–61.

Cohn, Bernard. *An Anthropologist among the Historians and Other Essays*. New York: Oxford University Press, 1987.

Daftary, Farhad. "Ahl al-Kisāʾ." In *Encyclopaedia of Islam, Three*, edited by Kate Fleet, Gudrun Krämer, Denis Matringe, John Nawas, Devin J. Stewart, online ed. Leiden: Brill, 2022. https://referenceworks.brillonline.com/browse/encyclopaedia-of-islam-3.

Dar, Shujaat Zamir. *Sights in the Sands of Cholistan: Bahawalpur's History and Architecture*. Karachi: Oxford University Press, 2007.

Datla, Kavita. *The Language of Secular Islam: Urdu Nationalism and Colonial India*. Honolulu: University of Hawaiʻi Press, 2013.

Devji, Faisal. "Apologetic Modernity." *Modern Intellectual History* 4, no. 1 (2007): 61–76.

Dhulipala, Venkat. *Creating a New Medina: State Power, Islam, and the Quest for Pakistan in Late Colonial North India*. Cambridge: Cambridge University Press, 2015.

Dickason, David G. "The Nineteenth-Century Indo-American Ice Trade: A Hyperborean Epic." *Modern Asian Studies* 25, no. 1 (1991): 53–89.

Dodson, Michael. *Bureaucracy, Belonging, and the City in North India, 1870–1930*. New York: Routledge, 2020.

———. "Translating Science, Translating Empire: The Power of Language in Colonial North India." *Comparative Studies in Society and History* 47, no. 4 (2005): 809–35.

El Shamsy, Ahmed. *Rediscovering the Islamic Classics: How Editors and Print Culture Transformed an Intellectual Tradition*. Princeton, NJ: Princeton University Press, 2020.

Flatt, Emma J. *The Courts of the Deccan Sultanates: Living Well in the Persian Cosmopolis*. Cambridge: Cambridge University Press, 2019.

Formichi, Chiara. *Islam and Asia: A History*. Cambridge: Cambridge University Press, 2020.

Fuller, C. J. "Anthropologists and Viceroys: Colonial Knowledge and Policy Making in India, 1871–1911." *Modern Asian Studies* 50, no. 1 (2015): 217–58.

George, Kenneth M., and Kiran Narayan. "Technophany and Its Publics: Artisans, Technicians, and the Rise of Vishwakarma Worship in India." *Journal of Asian Studies* 81, no. 1 (2022): 3–21.

Ghosh, Anindita. *Power in Print: Popular Publishing and the Politics of Language and Culture in a Colonial Society, 1778–1905*. New York: Oxford University Press, 2006.

Gilmartin, David. "Environmental History, *Biradari*, and the Making of Pakistani Punjab." In *Punjab Reconsidered: History, Culture, and Practice*, edited by Anshu Malhotra and Farina Mir, 289–319. Delhi: Oxford University Press, 2012.

———. "Partition, Pakistan, and South Asian History: In Search of a Narrative." *Journal of Asian Studies* 57, no. 4 (1998): 1068–95.

Glover, William. *Making Lahore Modern: Constructing and Imagining a Global City*. Minneapolis: University of Minnesota Press, 2008.

Gooptu, Nandini. *The Politics of the Urban Poor in Early Twentieth-Century India*. Cambridge: Cambridge University Press, 2001.

Grace, Joshua. *African Motors: Technology, Gender, and the History of Development*. Durham, NC: Duke University Press, 2021.

Green, Nile. *Bombay Islam: The Religious Economy of the West Indian Ocean, 1840–1915*. Cambridge: Cambridge University Press, 2011.

———. "Journeymen, Middlemen: Travel, Transculture, and Technology in the Origins of Muslim Printing." *International Journal of Middle East Studies* 41, no. 2 (2009): 203–24.

Gupta, Charu. "Intimate Desires: Dalit Women and Religious Conversions in Colonial India." *Journal of Asian Studies* 73, no. 3 (2014): 661–87.

Habib, Irfan. "Persian Book Writing and Book Use in the Pre-printing Age." *Proceedings of the Indian History Congress* 66 (2005–6): 514–37.

Habib, S. Irfan. *Jihad or Ijtihad: Religious Orthodoxy and Modern Science in Contemporary Islam*. Delhi: Harper Collins, 2012.

Haroon, Sana. *The Mosques of Colonial South Asia: A Social and Legal History of Muslim Worship*. London: I. B. Tauris, 2021.

Hasan, Mushirul. "Maulawi Zaka Ullah: Sharif Culture and Colonial Rule." In *The Delhi College: Traditional Elites, the Colonial State, and Education before 1857*, edited by Margrit Pernau, 261–99. Delhi: Oxford University Press, 2006.

Haynes, Douglas E. *Small Town Capitalism in Western India: Artisans, Merchants, and the Making of the Informal Economy, 1870–1960*. New York: Cambridge University Press, 2012.

Haynes, Douglas E., and Nikhil Rao. "Beyond the Colonial City: Re-evaluating the Urban History of India, ca. 1920–1970." *South Asia* 36, no. 3 (2013): 317–35.

Higbie, Tobais. *Labor's Mind: A History of Working-Class Intellectual Life*. Urbana: University of Illinois Press, 2019.

Hurd, John, II, and Ian J. Kerr. *India's Railway History: A Research Handbook*. Leiden: Brill, 2012.

Imy, Kate. *Faithful Fighters: Identity and Power in the British Indian Army*. Stanford, CA: Stanford University Press, 2019.

Ingram, Brannon. *Revival from Below: The Deoband Movement and Global Islam*. Oakland: University of California Press, 2018.

Ivermee, Robert. *Secularism, Islam and Education in India, 1830–1910*. New York: Routledge, 2015.
Jabbari, Alexander. "The Making of Modernity in Persianate Literary History." *Comparative Studies of South Asia, Africa and the Middle East* 3, no. 3 (2016): 418–34.
Jagga, Lajpat. "Colonial Railwaymen and British Rule: A Probe into Railway Agitation in India, 1919–1922." *Studies in History* 3, nos. 1–2 (1981): 102–3.
Jeffrey, Robin. *People, Princes, and Paramount Power: Society and Politics in Indian Princely States*. Delhi: Oxford University Press, 1978.
Joshi, Chitra. *Lost Worlds: Indian Labour and Its Forgotten Histories*. Delhi: Permanent Black, 2003.
Kapoor, Shivani. "The Search for 'Tanner's Blood': Caste and Technical Education in Colonial Uttar Pradesh." *Review of Development and Change* 23, no. 2 (2010): 118–38.
Kerr, Ian J. *Building the Railways of the Raj*. Delhi: Oxford University Press, 1995.
Khan, Hussain Ahmad. *Artisans, Sufis, Shrines: Colonial Architecture in Nineteenth Century Punjab*. London: Bloomsbury, 2015.
Khan, Nadhra Shahbaz. "Industrial Art Education in Colonial Punjab: Kipling's Pedagogy and Hereditary Craftsmen." In *John Lockwood Kipling: Arts and Crafts in the Punjab and London*, edited by Julius Bryant and Susan Weber, 469–88. New Haven, CT: Yale University Press, 2017.
Khan, Naveeda. *Muslim Becoming: Aspiration and Skepticism in Pakistan*. Durham, NC: Duke University Press, 2012.
Khan, Razak. "Local Histories: Space, Emotions and Identities in Vernacular Histories of Princely Rampur." *Journal of the Economic and Social History of the Orient* 58, no. 5 (2015): 693–731.
Khan, Yasmin. *The Great Partition: The Making of India and Pakistan*. New Haven, CT: Yale University Press, 2017.
Khoja-Moolji, Shenila. *Forging the Ideal Educated Girl: The Production of Desirable Subjects in Muslim South Asia*. Oakland: University of California Press, 2018.
Khuri-Makdisi, Ilham. *The Eastern Mediterranean and the Making of Global Radicalism, 1860–1914*. Berkeley: University of California Press, 2010.
Khurshīd, Ibn Ḥasan. *Taẕkirah-yi hunarmandān-I Rāmpūr*. Rampur: Raza Library Press, 2001.
Kinra, Rajeev. *Writing Self, Writing Empire: Chandar Bhan Brahman and the Cultural World of the Indo-Persian State Secretary*. Berkeley: University of California Press, 2015.
Kooria, Mahmood. "Texts as Objects of Value and Veneration: Islamic Law Books in the Indian Ocean Littoral." *Sociology of Islam* 6, no. 1 (2018): 60–83.
Koul, Ashish. "Making New Muslim Arians: Reform and Social Mobility in Colonial Punjab, 1890s–1910s." *South Asian History and Culture* 8, no. 1 (2017): 1–18.
Kramrisch, Stella. *The Hindu Temple*. Vol. 1. Delhi: Motilal Banarsidass, 1976.
Kumar, Arun. "Skilling and Its Histories: Labour Market, Technical Knowledge and the Making of Skilled Workers in Colonial India (1880–1910)." *Journal of South Asian Development* 13, no. 3 (2018): 249–71.
———. "The 'Untouchable School': American Missionaries, Hindu Social Reformers and the Educational Dreams of Labouring Dalits in Colonial North India." *South Asia* 42, no. 5 (2019): 823–44.

Kumar, Nita. *The Artisans of Banaras: Popular Culture and Identity, 1880–1986*. Princeton, NJ: Princeton University Press, 1988.

Laffan, Michael. *The Makings of Indonesian Islam: Orientalism and the Narration of a Sufi Past*. Princeton, NJ: Princeton University Press, 2011.

Lanzillo, Amanda. "Between Industry and Islam: Stonework and Tomb Construction in Colonial-Era India." *Modern Asian Studies* 55, no. 5 (2021): 1510–43.

———. "Butchers between Archives: Community History in Early Twentieth-Century Delhi." *South Asian History and Culture* 12, no. 4 (2021): 357–70.

———. "Translating the Scribe: Lithographic Print and Vernacularization in Colonial India, 1857–1915." *Comparative Critical Studies* 16, nos. 2–3 (2019): 281–300.

Lean, Eugenia. *Vernacular Industrialism in China: Local Innovation and Translated Technologies in the Making of a Cosmetics Empire, 1900–1940*. New York: Columbia University Press, 2020.

Lee, Joel. *Deceptive Majority: Dalits, Hinduism, and Underground Religion*. Cambridge: Cambridge University Press, 2021.

———. "Who Is the True Halalkhor? Genealogy and Ethics in Dalit Muslim Oral Traditions." *Indian Sociology* 52, no. 1 (2018): 1–27.

Lefebvre, Alain. *Kinship, Honour and Money in Rural Pakistan: Subsistence Economy and the Effects of International Migration*. Richmond, UK: Curzon, 1999.

Lehmann, F. "Railway Workshops, Technology Transfer, and Skilled Labour Recruitment in Colonial India." *Journal of Historical Research* 20, no. 1 (1977): 49–61.

Lelyveld, David. *Aligarh's First Generation: Muslim Solidarity in British India*. Princeton, NJ: Princeton University Press, 1978.

Losensky, Paul. *Welcoming Fighānī: Imitation and Poetic Individuality in the Safavid-Mughal Ghazal*. Costa Mesa, CA: Mazda, 1998.

Lunn, David. "Hindustani." In *Encyclopaedia of Islam, Three*, edited by Kate Fleet, Gudrun Krämer, Denis Matringe, John Nawas, and Everett Rowson, online ed. Leiden: Brill 2019. https://referenceworks.brillonline.com/browse/encyclopaedia-of-islam-3.

Mathur, Saloni. "Partition and the Visual Arts: Reflections on Method." *Third Text* 31, nos. 2–3 (2017): 205–12.

McGowan, Abigail. *Crafting the Nation in Colonial India*. New York: Palgrave Macmillan, 2009.

———. "Mothers and Godmothers of Crafts: Female Leadership and the Imagination of India as a Crafts Nation, 1947–67." *South Asia* 44, no. 2 (2021): 282–97.

Meléndez-Badillo, Jorell A. *The Lettered Barriada: Workers, Archival Power, and the Politics of Knowledge in Puerto Rico*. Durham, NC: Duke University Press, 2021.

Metcalf, Barbara. *Islamic Revival in British India: Deoband, 1860–1900*. Princeton, NJ: Princeton University Press, 1982.

Metcalf, Thomas. *An Imperial Vision: Indian Architecture and Britain's Raj*. Oxford: Oxford University Press, 1989.

Mian, Ali Altaf. "Translating Scholars: Theorizing Modern South Asian 'Ulama' Studies." *Religion Compass* 16, no. 5 (2022): 1–11.

———. "Troubling Technology: The Deobandi Debate on the Loudspeaker and Ritual Prayer." *Islamic Law and Society* 24, no. 4 (2017): 355–83.

Minault, Gail. "Women's Magazines in Urdu as Sources for Muslim Social History." *Indian Journal of Gender Studies* 5, no. 2 (1998): 201–14.

Mir, Farina. *The Social Space of Language: Vernacular Culture in British Colonial Punjab*. Berkeley: University of California Press, 2010.

Moran, Bruce T. "Art and Artisanship in Early Modern Alchemy." *Getty Research Journal* 5, no. 5 (2013): 1–14.

Morus, Iwan Rhys. *Frankenstein's Children: Electricity, Exhibition, and Experiment in Early-Nineteenth-Century London*. Princeton, NJ: Princeton University Press, 1998.

Mukharji, Projit Bihari. *Doctoring Traditions: Ayurveda, Small Technologies, and Braided Technologies*. Chicago: University of Chicago Press, 2016.

———. "Vernacularizing the Body: Informational Egalitarianism, Hindu Divine Design, and Race in Physiology Schoolbooks, Bengal, 1859–1877." *Bulletin of the History of Medicine* 91, no. 3 (2017): 554–85.

Mukhopadhyay, Aparajita. *Imperial Technology and "Native" Agency: A Social History of Railways in Colonial India, 1850–1920*. London: Routledge, 2018.

Nadvi, Khalid. "Shifting Ties: Social Networks in the Surgical Instrument Cluster of Sialkot, Pakistan." *Development and Change* 30 (1999): 141–75.

Narayan, Badri. *Women Heroes and Dalit Assertion in North India: Culture, Identity, and Politics*. Delhi: Sage Publications, 2006.

Niazi, Soheb. "Sayyids and Social Stratification of Muslims in Colonial India: Genealogy and Narration of the Past in Amroha." *Journal of the Royal Asiatic Society* 30, no. 3 (2020): 267–87.

Nūrāni, Amīr Ḥasan. *Munshī Naval Kishūr aur unke khaṭṭāṭ aur khūshnavīs*. Delhi: Taraqqi Urdu Board, 1994.

Ogborn, Miles. *Indian Ink: Script and Print in the Making of the English East India Company*. Chicago: University of Chicago Press, 2007.

Parthasarathi, Prasannan. "Indian Labor History." *International Labor and Working Class History* 82 (2012): 127–35.

———. *Transition to a Colonial Economy: Weavers, Merchants, and Kings in South India, 1720–1800*. Cambridge: Cambridge University Press, 2001.

Penny, Simon, and Tom Fisher. "Twist-Hands and Shuttle-Kissing: Understanding Industrial Craft Skills via Embodied and Distributed Cognition." *Form Akademisk* 14, no. 2 (2021): 1–13.

Perkins, C. Ryan. "A New *Pablik:* Abdul Halim Sharar, Volunteerism, and the Anjuman-e Dar-us-Salam in Late Nineteenth-Century India." *Modern Asian Studies* 49, no. 4 (2015): 1049–90.

Pernau, Margrit. *Ashraf into Middle Classes: Muslims in Nineteenth-Century Delhi*. Oxford: Oxford University Press, 2013.

Pinto, Rochelle. *Between Empires: Print and Politics in Goa*. Oxford: Oxford University Press, 2007.

Porter, Venetia. "William De Morgan and the Islamic Tiles of Leighton House." *Journal of the Decorative Arts Society* 16 (1992): 76–79.

Porter, Yves. *Painters, Paintings and Books: An Essay on Indo-Persian Technical Literature, 12–19th Centuries*. New York: Routledge, 2020.

Prakash, Gyan. *Another Reason: Science and the Imagination of Modern India*. Princeton, NJ: Princeton University Press, 1999.

Proudfoot, Ian. "Mass Producing Houri's Moles, or Aesthetics and Choice of Technology in Early Muslim Book Printing." In *Islam: Essays on Scripture, Thought, and Society*, edited by Tony Street and Peter Riddell, 161–84. Leiden: Brill, 1997.

Qasmi, Ali Usman, and Megan Robb. *Muslims against the Muslim League: Critiques of the Idea of Pakistan*. Cambridge: Cambridge University Press, 2017.

Qidwai, Sarah. "Darwin or Design: Examining Sayyid Ahmad Khan's Views on Human Evolution." In *The Cambridge Companion to Sayyid Ahmad Khan*, edited by Yasmin Sakina and Raisur Rahman, 214–32. Cambridge: Cambridge University Press, 2019.

Rabbat, Nasser. "What Is Islamic Architecture Anyway?" *Journal of Art Historiography* 6 (2012): 1–15.

Rahman, M. Raisur. *Locale, Everyday Islam, and Modernity: Qasbah Towns and Muslim Life in Colonial India*. Delhi: Oxford University Press, 2015.

Rai, Santosh Kumar. "Forms of Organization and Practices of Mobilization: Julaha Weavers in Early Twentieth-Century North India." In *The Vernacularization of Labour Politics*, edited by Sabyasachi Bhattacharya and Rana Behal, 83–101. Delhi: Tulika, 2016.

Raina, Dhruv, and S. Irfan Habib. *Domesticating Modern Science: A Social History of Science and Culture in Colonial India*. Delhi: Tulika Books, 2004.

Raman, Bhavani. *Document Raj: Writing and Scribes in Early Colonial South India*. Chicago: University of Chicago Press, 2012.

Ramnath, Aparajith. *The Birth of an Indian Profession: Engineers, Industry, and the State, 1900–1947*. Oxford: Oxford University Press, 2017.

Ramusack, Barbara N. *Indian Princes and Their States*. New York: Cambridge University Press, 2003.

Ratcliff, Jessica. "Travancore's Magnetic Crusade: Geomagnetism and the Geography of Scientific Production in a Princely State." *British Journal for the History of Science* 49, no. 3 (2016): 325–52.

Ray, Sugata. "Colonial Frames, 'Native' Claims: The Jaipur Economic and Industrial Museum." *Art Bulletin* 96, no. 2 (2014): 196–212.

Raza, Ali. *Revolutionary Pasts: Communist Internationalism in Colonial India*. Cambridge: Cambridge University Press, 2020.

Robb, Megan. *Print and the Urdu Public: Muslims, Newspapers, and Urban Life in Colonial North India*. New York: Oxford University Press, 2020.

Robinson, Francis. "Islamic Reform and Modernities in South Asia." *Modern Asian Studies* 42, nos. 2–3 (2008): 259–81.

Roy, Tirthankar. "Apprenticeship and Industrialization in India, 1600–1930." In *Technology, Skills, and the Premodern Economy in the East and West*, edited by Maarten Prak and Jan Luiten van Zanden, 69–92. Leiden: Brill, 2013.

———. "Economic Conditions in Early Modern Bengal: A Contribution to the Divergence Debate." *Journal of Economic History* 70, no. 1 (2010): 179–94.

———. "Out of Tradition: Master Artisans and Economic Change in Colonial India." *Journal of Asian Studies* 66, no. 4 (2007): 963–91.

Sabev, Orlin. *Waiting for Müteferrika: Glimpses of Ottoman Print Culture*. Boston: Academic Studies Press, 2018.

Sarkar, Tanika. *Hindu Wife, Hindu Nation: Community, Religion, and Cultural Nationalism*. Bloomington: Indiana University Press, 2010.

Schimmel, Annemarie. *Calligraphy and Islamic Culture*. New York: New York University Press, 1990.

Schwartz, Kathryn A. "Did the Ottoman Sultans Ban Print?" *Book History* 20 (2017): 1–39.

Sen, Samita. *Women and Labour in Late Colonial India: The Bengal Jute Industry*. Cambridge: Cambridge University Press, 1999.

Sharma, Jyoti Pandey. "From Marrakesh to India: A Colonial Maharaja's Pursuit of Architectural Glory in Kapurthala." *International Journal of Islamic Architecture* 1, no. 2 (2012): 269–300.

Sharma, Sunil. *Mughal Arcadia: Persian Literature in an Indian Court*. Cambridge, MA: Harvard University Press, 2017.

Shekhar, Sudhanshu, and Vidyanand Jha. "Emergence of the Small-Scale Iron Foundry Industry in Howrah (India), 1833–1913." *Business History* 63, no. 2 (2011): 249–70.

Singh, Charu. "Science in the Vernacular? Translation, Terminology and Lexicography in the Hindi Scientific Glossary (1906)." *South Asian History and Culture* 13, no. 1 (2022): 63–86.

Singha, Radhika. *The Coolies' Great War: Indian Labor in a Global Conflict*. New York: Oxford University Press, 2020.

Sinha, Nitin. "The World of Workers' Politics: Some Issues of Railway Workers in Colonial India, 1918–1922." *Modern Asian Studies* 42, no. 5 (2008): 999–1033.

Smith, Pamela. *From Lived Experience to the Written Word: Reconstructing Practical Knowledge in the Early Modern World*. Chicago: University of Chicago Press, 2022.

Soni. "Learning to Labour: 'Native' Orphans in Colonial India, 1840s–1920s." *International Review of Social History* 65, no. 1 (2020): 15–42.

Stark, Ulrike. *An Empire of Books: The Naval Kishore Press and the Diffusion of the Printed Word in Colonial India*. Delhi: Orient Blackswan, 2007.

Stephens, Julia. *Governing Islam: Law, Empire, and Secularism in Modern South Asia*. Cambridge: Cambridge University Press, 2018.

Subramanian, Ajantha. *The Caste of Merit: Engineering Education in India*. Cambridge, MA: Harvard University Press, 2019.

Sultana, Kishwar. "Maulana Zafar Ali Khan, Majlis-e Ittihad-e Millat, and the All India Muslim League." *Journal of the Research Society of Pakistan* 53, no. 1 (2016): 115–23.

Taneja, Anand Vivek. *Jinnealogy: Time, Islam, and Ecological Thought in the Medieval Ruins of Delhi*. Stanford, CA: Stanford University Press, 2017.

Tarar, Nadeem Omar. "From 'Primitive' Artisans to 'Modern' Craftsmen: Colonialism, Culture, and Art Education in the Late Nineteenth-Century Punjab." *South Asian Studies* 27, no. 2 (2011): 199–219.

Tareen, SherAli. "Normativity, Heresy, and the Politics of Authenticity in South Asian Islam." *Muslim World* 99 (2009): 535–46.

Thompson, E. P. *The Making of the English Working Class*. New York: Pantheon Books, 1966.

Tschacher, Torsten. "Rational Miracles, Cultural Rituals and the Fear of Syncretism: Defending Contentious Muslim Practice among Tamil-Speaking Muslims." *Asian Journal of Social Science* 37, no. 1 (2009): 55–82.

Van Bladel, Kevin. *The Arabic Hermes: From Pagan Sage to Prophet of Science*. Oxford: Oxford University Press, 2009.

Velkar, Aashish. "*Swadeshi* Capitalism in Colonial Bombay." *History Journal* 64, no. 4 (2021): 1009–34.

Warraich, Toqeer Ahmad, Samia Tahir, and Saira Ramzan. "Tomb of Musa Ahangar: An Analysis of Its Architecture and Decoration." *Pakistan Heritage* 11 (2019): 83–92.

Wickramasinghe, Nira. *Metallic Modern: Everyday Machines in Colonial Sri Lanka*. New York: Berghahn Books, 2014.

INDEX

Abbasid Caliphate, 143
Abdul Hadi Khan, Munshi, 164
ʿAbdul Rahman, Muhammad, 29–31
Adam, Prophet, 31, 43, 114, 150
Afghanistan, 28, 147
Agra, red sandstone from, 165
Ahmad, A. F., 65
Ahmad Khan, Sayyid, 142
Aitchison College Mosque (Lahore), 166, 167
ajlāf, 6, 7, 78, 119
Akbar (Mughal emperor), 51
alchemists (*kīmiyāgars*), 46, 47, 48, 59, 62. See also *kīmiyā* (alchemy, chemistry)
ʿAli, Ramzan, 52, 53
ʿAli, 31
ʿAli Khan, Zafar, 40, 41, 43
ʿAli Malihabadi, ʿEwwaz, 28
ʿAli Muhammad, 163, 164
Aligarh Institute Gazette, 142
Aligarh Muhammadan Anglo-Oriental College (later Aligarh Muslim University), 143
Aligarh Scientific Society, 142
Allahabad, city of, 34, 73, 88–89, 101
All-India Muslim Education Conference, 38
Amin, Shahid, 77, 95
Amritsar, city and district of, 42, 46, 50, 63, 125, 131, 175
Ancient Monuments Preservation Act (1904), 168
Anglo-Afghan War (1839–42), 154
Anglo-Indians, 130, 133, 140
Anglo-Sikh war, first (1846), 155
Anglo-Sikh war, second (1848–49), 64, 155
Anjuman-i ḥimāyat-i Islām [AHI] (Association for the Defense of Islam), 116, 117, 118, 119
Anjuman-i Islāmiyah (Islamic Association), 87, 90, 116, 117
Anjuman-i muṣlaḥ-i qaum-i āhangarān [AMQA] (Organization for the Uplift of the Community of Blacksmiths), 145–47, 174
Anjuman-i muʿayyid al-ṣanʿ at [AMS] (Organization for the Strengthening of Industry), 146
anjumans (civic organizations), 86, 116–19, 152–53, 156
Anwar ʿAli, Hafiz, 45–46, 53, 56
apprenticeship, 81, 112, 150; metalsmiths and, 61; scribal, 29; stonemasons and, 156, 164, 167; tailors and, 87
Arab ancestry, claims of, 79, 92, 93, 176
Arabic language, 23, 28, 32, 158, 192n2
Architectural Survey of India (ASI), 168
architecture, Muslim religious, 17, 148; ceramic tilework, 166–67; constructed at behest of landlords, 156; contextualization of, 153–57; courtly patronage of, 155; *imāmbāṛās* (Shia commemoration sites), 149–50, 152, 153, 157, 160, 165, 169; Indo-Saracenic style, 163; Mahbub Ganj bazaar, 161–62, red sandstone and, 165, 166, 167. *See also* mosques; shrines; tombs
archives, 5, 9–11, 25, 51, 177

111–12; "Indianization" of railway labor, 130; locomotive steam engines, 125, 131, 134, 137, 145, 148; rise of boilermaking, 130–33; spaces for artisan Islam in, 138
Raina, Dhruv, 47
Raman, Bhavani, 26
Ramnath, Aparajith, 134
Rampur, princely state of, 14, 25, 28, 136, 152, 153, 154; Hamid Manzil, 163; history of, 155; Ḥusanī Press, 32–33; Jama Masjid complex, 165–66; Jashn-i Baynaẕīr (Unparalleled Festival), 162; public works department of, 156; Raza Library, 1, 163; technical hierarchies reorganized in, 162, 163
Rao, Nikhil, 101
risālahs (treatises), 9, 10
Risālah-yi banī Quṣṣá [Treatise of the children of Qussa] (Qureshī Naqshbandī, 1925), 93, 94
Risālah-yi fan-i talmīʿ [Treatise on the art of plating] (Ali and Khan, 1870), 52–53, 54
Risālah-yi Idrīsiyah [The treatise of Idris] (Khwaja Muhammad, 1909), 73–75, 76, 77, 80, 93, 96; Allahabad context of, 88; alternative narratives of Muslim past and, 178; community identity asserted for marginalized Muslims, 95; intended audience of, 94; Muslim pasts of tailors and, 89–90; piety and gender in, 90–91; as response to colonial representation of tailors, 77; tailors' intrinsic piety disseminated through, 87; technological change and artisan creativity in, 91–92
Risālah-yi jild sāzī [Treatise on bookbinding] (Hussain), 34–35
Risālah-yi roīdād-i jalsah-yi ʿām anjuman-i muṣlaḥ-i qaum-i āhangarān (Report of the events of the general meeting of the AMQA), 145
Robb, Megan, 25
Robinson, Francis, 144
Rohilkhand, 155
Roy, Tirthankar, 10, 174, 184n52

Saharanpur, city of, 98, 101; North-Western Railways workshops in, 102; woodworkers in, 102, *103*, 104, 105
Saraiki language, 12, 154
sarmāyahdār (capitalist/possessor of wealth), 1, 171,
Sarshar, Muhammad Nizam, 149
Sarshar, Riyasat ʿAli, 149–51, 156, 158–60, 165, 167, 173, 178
Sayyids, 79
science, 47, 69, 175, 191n71; colonial claims on scientific authority, 7; hierarchy of authority over, 134–35; "Islamic" models of education and, 142
scribes (*kātibs*), 13, 21, 151, 172–73; broadening of scribal classes, 28–30; educational lineages and, 43, 44; elite Muslim and colonial acceptance religious traditions of, 25; manuscript workshops of, 26; pay earned by, 33; scribal knowledge as Muslim knowledge, 30–32; secretarial (munshis), 26; strikes by, 39; transition to print economy and, 27; unions and, 23, 42, 43
sewing, 73–76, 78; educational administrators and, 81; feminization of, 16; girls' schools and making of ideal seamstress, 82–84; sewing machines, 80, 81–82, 91, 92; Shabihunnisa's school for girls, 84–86. See also *darzīs* (tailors); tailors/tailoring
Shabihunnisa, 74, 83–84, 85, 90
Shaida, Jawaharlal, 55, 56, 57
shārīf. See *ashrāf* [pl. of *shārīf*]
Sheikhs, 79, 80
Shibli Nuʿmani, Allamah, 142–43
shrines, 93, 114, 149; patrons of, 153; plasters used on domes of, 163; repair of, 152, 155, 168; *sajjāda nashīn* (shrine custodian), 168; shared between Hindus and Muslims, 88; Sufi, 51, 88, 100, 107, 115
Sialkot, city and district of, 49, 51, 68; artisan flexibility and electroplating manuals in, 67–68; carpentry in, 104; electroplating in, 63; Kashmiri Mohalla in, 65, 66, manual plating and decorative metalwork in, 63–64; surgical tools workshops in, 48, 65; woodworkers in, 105
Siddiqi, 161
Sikhs, 5, 34, 140; carpenters, 105; in metalworking trades, 50; princely state leaders, 154; Punjabi capitalists, 65; Punjab weaponsmiths and, 64
Singh, Bahadur, 106
Singh, Bhagat, 42
Singh, Charu, 8
Singh, Ranjit, 64
Singha, Radhika, 146
Sinha, Nitin, 147
Sirhindi, Ahmad, 117
Soviet Union, 147
Spence, W., 49, 63, 65
Sri Lanka, 80

Founded in 1893,
UNIVERSITY OF CALIFORNIA PRESS
publishes bold, progressive books and journals on topics in the arts, humanities, social sciences, and natural sciences—with a focus on social justice issues—that inspire thought and action among readers worldwide.

The UC PRESS FOUNDATION
raises funds to uphold the press's vital role as an independent, nonprofit publisher, and receives philanthropic support from a wide range of individuals and institutions—and from committed readers like you. To learn more, visit ucpress.edu/supportus.

Milton Keynes UK
Ingram Content Group UK Ltd.
UKHW022002291024
450273UK00007B/80

9 780520 398573